D0710572

The Nation's Image

The Nation's Image
French Grand Opera as Politics and Politicized Art

JANE F. FULCHER

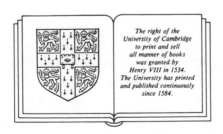

The right of the
University of Cambridge
to print and sell
all manner of books
was granted by
Henry VIII in 1534.
The University has printed
and published continuously
since 1584.

CAMBRIDGE UNIVERSITY PRESS
Cambridge
London   New York   New Rochelle
Melbourne   Sydney

Published by the Press Syndicate of the University of Cambridge
The Pitt Building, Trumpington Street, Cambridge CB2 IRP
32 East 57th Street, New York, NY 10022, USA
10 Stamford Road, Oakleigh, Melbourne 3166, Australia

© Cambridge University Press 1987

First published 1987

Printed in the United States of America

Library of Congress Cataloging-in-Publication Data
Fulcher, Jane F.
The nation's image.
Bibliography: p.
1. Opera – France.   2. Music and Society.   I. Title.
ML1727.F84   1987   782.1'0944   86-14694

British Library Cataloguing in Publication Data
Fulcher, Jane F.
The nation's image : French grand opera
as politics and politicized art.
1. Opera – Political aspects – France
2. Opera – France – History – 19th century
I. Title
782.1'0944   ML1727

ISBN 0 521 32774 1

CONTENTS

v

FIGURES

vi

Figures

ACKNOWLEDGMENTS

I WISH to thank the National Endowment for the Humanities, which awarded me a summer stipend that made the initial archival research for this book possible. I am also grateful to Syracuse and Indiana universities for providing me with funds for subsequent summer research in Paris, as well as for the illustrations and microfilming of the additional documents I needed. A fellowship from The American Council of Learned Societies made it possible for me to spend a full year in Paris, during which time I completed my research and drafted this book.

I am particularly grateful to my colleagues and friends in Paris who helped me so generously in all the stages of this book's development, and especially to Roger Chartier and Jacques Revel, who were always ready to talk with me about my ideas and material, to aid my research, and to provide me with a forum in which to present it in their seminars at the Ecole des Hautes Etudes en Sciences Sociales. Donna Evleth was of invaluable help in the Archives Nationales, and fellow musicologists Elizabeth Bartlet and Peter Bloom graciously helped me find the sources I needed in the various Parisian collections. I am also grateful to Françoise Parent-Lardeur and Odile Krakovitch for their advice concerning sources, as well as to American colleagues Nathan Therien and Marvin Carlson, who generously gave of their own materials.

Many other colleagues over the past five years have also played an essential role in the development of this book through their encouragement and unwaning belief in the importance of such a study. And so I am indebted to them as well, and in particular to Carl Schorske, Peter Gay, Robert Wohl, Saul Friedländer, and

Robert Isherwood. And I wish to express my special thanks to William Weber and Richard Leppert for their close and critical reading of the manuscript in its various stages. Their suggestions were essential to its growth.

INTRODUCTION

THE SUBJECT MATTER of this book is not narrowly an institution or the repertoire it produced: It is rather a set of interacting theatrical, political, and aesthetic phenomena. My study, then, is a cultural history and in a line of tradition that seeks the reasons for and consequences of such junctures or intersection of different sectors of culture.[1]

French grand opera, I maintain, is a genre that we must approach from this perspective if we are to grasp not only its historical significance but also its aesthetic force. For its nature as well as its meaning, or the signifying process of this body of works, was the product of a complex interchange between the artistic product and its institutional frame. The framework helped simultaneously to shape the character of the innovations possible as well as the audience's mode of construal and the character of the theatrical experience itself.

But in contending that the theater's function served on several levels to shape the genre (and thus denying the adequacy of a formalist approach) my argument is not entirely new. The established perspective is similarly one that insists on understanding social context and claims that the role that the theater played helped determine the experience and thus the utterance of this repertoire. For an utterance, to quote Bakhtin, derives from a common understanding of the situation and comprises "the simultaneity of what is actually said and what is assumed but not spoken." Here, however, the crucial point and the primary issue I wish to raise concerns "the larger body of discourse and social communication of which it was a part."[2] My study challenges existing interpretations of the kind of assumptions, understanding, and interaction that brought about both

I

the works and their meaning, and so in two senses, their historical significance.

My consistent argument, which runs both implicitly and explicitly throughout this book, is that our crucial miscontrual of the institutional frame has obscured our understanding of the art. Grand opera was a different, a far more complex kind of theater — in its several senses – than we ordinarily suppose, and we can see this only if we recognize the complexity of its function. As my title indicates, I believe this function to be most fundamentally a political one and that the theater was politicized both in the tactics applied to its management and in the experience within it. Throughout the period of grand opera's rise, its dominance, and its final decline – from roughly 1830 to 1870 – the theater was a subtly used tool of the state. Official intervention integrally affected the formation of the genre's artistic traits, the audience's construal of their significance, and concomitantly the gradual transformation they sustained in response. My argument here being so fundamentally iconoclastic in music history, it seems necessary by way of introduction to explain why I have challenged the existing view.

The clearest articulation of the now dominant interpretation of the genre appeared in 1948 in William Croston's *French Grand Opera: An Art and a Business*. Croston presents a sociological (and perhaps implicitly Marxist) explanation of both how the genre emerged as well as the nature of its specific values or traits. He begins, however, with the question of what occurred politically in 1830 in order to explain why the Opéra broke away from the tradition of state patronage in France.

Croston observes a decisive break with the past in 1831. The Opéra now becomes a business, catering to the newly ascendent bourgeois audience. Since a self-proclaimed "bourgeois king" had recently assumed the throne of France, cultural institutions now naturally turned to the needs and desires of this social class. And so it was as part of his program to buttress his new base of political support that Louis-Philippe encouraged the entry of bourgeois values into the Académie Royale de Musique.

Croston establishes this argument largely on the basis of the new director's contract or the "Cahier des charges" that designated him now a Directeur-Entrepreneur. Moreover, he cites

2

those clauses in the document that defined "grand" opera's attributes, for purposes of legal distinction between the theaters, as evidence of the common definition of its art. From here he links these traits, particularly the stress on size and lavish display, to the cultural character of the audience that the Opéra, in search of profit, now wished to attract.

Croston thus reaches a concomitant conclusion about the art that it produced: Calculated to titillate but not to threaten the beliefs of its audience, it was a compromise between tradition and innovation. More specifically, it was a popular romanticism, or one that superficially borrowed new techniques but balanced them with enough convention so as to remain acceptable to this social group. Grand opera, in sum, was an art "at once revolutionary and reassuring that extended one hand toward Romanticism and held fast to conventionality with the other." For it was a genre that was "engineered by men who were able to judge . . . to what extent that movement was acceptable to the theater public."[3]

From this point of view, the success of grand opera lay in its particular aptness for the audience it sought to address, an audience that responded more or less as its creators supposed. Their reaction to the works was passive: They derived a meaning that was not only unambiguous but rooted in their own values, which were simply reflected on the stage. Croston's interpretation is thus one that prominently stresses what was absent, or the fact that these works did not challenge or engage the contemporary audience in any real depth. This too has carried the further implication that they were devoid of authentic artistic force and that their long-lived dominance on the stage resulted from a sociologically explicable aberration of taste.

Such an interpretation, together with the condemnation of Wagner and others who echoed him, has encouraged the tendency to derogate the genre. For when seen from this perspective it embodies those features we routinely condemn, particularly in genres as elite as opera – above all, meretricious, sensational display. Such an attitude, in addition, has influenced our treatment of the genre in operatic histories and classroom surveys, encouraging us to present it as fortunately only a transient stylistic link. To quote one recent source, "much of what was truly grand in it was absorbed by the stronger and more durable personalities of Wagner and Verdi."[4] The "grandeur" intended here is most com-

3

monly defined in terms like the following: "forceful staging, sharp contrasts, stirring choral scenes, virtuoso pieces, and a large orchestra, in at least three acts."[5]

Grand opera, I maintain, as theater, was far more than this in nineteenth-century France; what we now see is merely the shell of a once powerful and provocative theatrical form. My argument to establish the fact that we have misunderstood the theater and its theatrical dynamic is based on several key points of contention, which can be summarized as follows. First, the idea of a break between patronage and private enterprise is one that is based on questionable evidence and debatable historical interpretation. Refuting the claim of administrative rupture is a multitude of archival documents that testify to the state's continuing substantial financing and substantive political intervention.[6]

Here, however, we necessarily face both a semantic and conceptual issue: How can we define the nature of such an institution and perceptions of it during these years? If it was not really a private enterprise, then was it still state-patronized or "official" art? Or was there, and indeed is there still, a more elusive intermediate realm? In this case, to understand the historical past we might well turn to the present and to the issue of the relation of the national theaters to the state in France. Of particular relevance here is that a prominent minister of culture has characterized the national theaters as distinct in being "organismes publiques" as opposed to "organismes privés." As such, they are endowed with what he has termed a "personalité morale"; they have a public resonance and are thus sustained by the state with which they are implicitly associated. It is not a question of overt political manipulation of the theater for propaganda but rather of "appropriation" of it for a more subtle political end.[7]

This intermediate realm is one, I propose, to which the Opéra belonged and in a particularly prominent way between 1830 and 1870. But to understand each government's goal in using opera in this manner we must look back to the French Revolution and its conception of legitimacy as expressed in art. It is here, I maintain, that we see the genesis of the Opéra's new role in political speech or the subtle new rhetoric that it was to communicate and to which Louis-Philippe returned. And here too we may observe the appearance of many of the phenomena that this book will trace, but particularly the emergence of the Opéra as a politically contestatory realm.

4

To understand the function that the Opéra begins to serve in the French Revolution we must turn to recent historical insights concerning its conception of political legitimacy. This, of course, will be of essential importance in understanding its politics of culture as well as the way in which the arts began to participate in the political culture.

As François Fûret has argued, with the French Revolution conceptions of power change; the locus of power is now the "people," and hence it resides in "public opinion."[8] To speak in the name of the people is thus to claim power in French society, for "the person who spoke successfully in the name of the nation was deemed to give voice to the general will."[9] But this immediately raised new questions concerning the exercise of power through culture, or the problem of political symbolism, of translating such claims into visual imagery or artistic discourse.

This is a problem to which a number of recent historians have devoted attention, and one that gave rise to another that has become the special province of historians of theater. It is they who have studied most extensively the issue of the gap that inevitably opened between such public revolutionary rhetoric in art and the actual political facts. For "public" culture, and the national theaters in particular, in order to remain true to such rhetoric had to represent public interests, embody public taste, and voice the common opinion. This became problematic as soon as the realities of power emerged, as they did very early in the French Revolution, immediately implicating the national stage. The state was forced here, for reasons of rhetoric, to try to respect an ideal of transparent public expression that clashed dramatically with the realities of the political world.

Historians of revolutionary theater have studied in depth the way in which the stage, as a result of this contradiction, now becomes a politically contestatory arena. As they have shown, despite its claim to be the voice of "opinion" this was not always the case, which compelled the audience to challenge it and at times to interact theatrically with the stage. Indeed, since the audience was now implicitly or theoretically "the Nation" or the political public, it could and often felt obliged to react to the message presented. And because of the theater's function such audience response was also a political act, similarly a statement of public opinion and consequently an act of political power. In effect, as a

5

locus of affirmation or revocation of the right to speak for the nation, the theater of the French Revolution played a central political role.[10]

The Opéra, however, was to become a particularly problematic and contestatory realm, partly because of its firmly established role in political representation. The Académie Royale de Musique in the late seventeenth and early eighteenth century had been the theater most closely associated with the personage and image of the king. His attendance at the Opéra was a political occasion to display himself to his subjects and to receive their homage both through prologues in the works and by the audience's applause.[11] But if the Opéra was used for a political message it is important to note that this message could change, and though the means were subtle it could still penetrate political awareness. Specifically, after the mid-eighteenth century the Opéra's repertoire turned away from "the legend of the Sun King" to "a new manner of operatic grandeur."[12] This shift in symbolic emphasis reflected a shift in political accent from a focus on the king himself to the abstract monarchical state. And such a transformation accordingly was accompanied by a change in administrative structure, from what has been termed traditional royal patronage to "an elaborate bureaucratic system." Further communicating the fact that the Opéra was no longer to be considered a court institution was that part of its administration was now entrusted to the city of Paris.[13]

But even if not uniform in nature, the Opéra's associations with monarchy still were strong, and so it is not surprising that the Opéra did not easily enter the Revolution's symbolic order. It waited until the Terror to follow the lead of the other national theaters there introducing a new repertoire with strong Republican connotations. On occasion it even belligerently offended Republican sensibilities, as in the case of Méhul's *Adrien,* which the Revolutionary leaders finally banned.[14]

All this made it particularly pressing to redefine the Opéra politically, to make it into an artistic forum for the expression of "*opinion publique.*" The Opéra was gradually purged and made a prime Republican symbol as well as a stop to be included on major civic ceremonial routes. The Assemblée Nationale voted the theater an annual subsidy, but it continued to be closely observed by authorities for its political content.[15]

The Opéra's repertoire made political statements now on several

6

levels, but the one of particular significance to us is the way it sought to embody public spirit and opinion. Like the other major theaters, it began frequently to use dramas of a popular nature, those that responded immediately to the events of the day and often seemed to confuse art with life. Like the boulevard theaters, in quest of greater *actualité,* or relating to current emotions and interests, it disregarded illogical stock settings and employed vividly realistic spectacle. Such "democratic" spectacle engaged the audience by blurring the boundaries between art and reality, often through powerful metaphors that carried explicit revolutionary connotations.[16] But beyond the language of spectacle, that of staging and décor played a similar role by often making explicit references to the political world beyond the stage. And sometimes the performers' costumes also helped draw overt connections between those classical subjects still employed and their current political significance.[17]

Yet other symbolic changes associated the Opéra even more closely with the public realm, and its repertoire, implicitly, with *opinion publique.* The new Opéra, with conscious symbolism, used the décor from the theater at Versailles, although, significantly, now rearranging the spacial disposition of the hall. There were no longer forestage boxes, meaning no presence of the aristocracy on the stage, but rather a now clear demarcation between the actors and the audience that attended.[18]

One important consequence is that now the actors, distinctly separated from the audience, were provocatively presenting the latter with public opinion in the people's name. This further encouraged the audience to accord its applause upon the basis of the political allusions it read, which sometimes created the problem for the authorities of controlling interpretation. And so the orchestra would here play a role, often instructed to reinforce the particular political allusions intended by playing specific political *chansons.* Indeed, one of the most violent episodes broke out toward the end of the Terror in reaction to the order that the orchestra play the Republican "Marseillaise" between acts. The royalists responded angrily by demanding the opposing "Reveil du Peuple," which often led to violent rioting and even closing of the hall.[19] But politics and art continued to merge when audience members threw political pamphlets or *chansons* on the stage and demanded that the performer, the embodiment of public opinion, read them.[20]

7

The Opéra was palpably a dangerous realm, one of contestation over the voice of the "people," and concomitantly officials saw it as potentially a realm of challenge to political authority. Not surprisingly they took special care to "control" the Opéra's public as part of an increased surveillance of the theaters and especially the national houses. This revolutionary experience implanted a nervous awareness of the Opéra's potential not only here but long after, including those regimes with which we are concerned. We can see such awareness manifest not only in Napoleon's stringent theatrical controls but, as is integral to my argument, in the Restoration's operatic policies as well.

The point of departure for my study is the Restoration for several reasons, but primarily because it is here that we see the return and transformation of revolutionary phenomena. For the Restoration ends by assigning the theater a political function or role that is not unlike what we have seen as characteristic of the French Revolution. Although no longer the vehicle of an explicit ideological propaganda, it serves once again as an image to associate the popular "spirit" with the regime. Through subtle controls, it continues to serve this "public" function throughout the next three regimes, and it is this, I shall argue, that is essential to our understanding of the development of the "grand" repertoire.

This quest for an "image" through the Opéra is one that affected the repertoire in several ways, shaping its definition, the audience's construal, and the way it was transformed in response. In every case, of course, these developments participate in each regime's political evolution, the tensions of which directly affect both theatrical utterance and operatic policies.

During this period the political public and thus the audience addressed perceptibly grows, and so we can trace an evolution of political concerns and theatrical tactics. The "image" and the repertoire is adapted as it addresses different groups who then apply different modes of construal and enter into operatic debates and controversies for their own specific political ends. What will interest me centrally, then, is how the image of the Opéra and the repertoire changed in a continuing process of subtle adaptation throughout these years; how this evolution relates to the changing political context; and how the works themselves reacted back on this context and helped to influence political perceptions. In all of these respects I shall emphasize the interplay of the phenomena

8

around these works – the creative, the political, the theatrical – and how they interacted historically.

To do so and to retell the story of the rise and decline of the genre, my study focuses on several works that are from this perspective particularly illuminating. In each case they are operas already well studied from the standard point of view, but it is my aim to show different sides of them and different aspects of their genesis and histories. The particular events on which I shall focus are those that I believe help reveal larger structures or those causal forces that historically intersected to determine the genre's "fate." They are also events that help us to see the way in which this repertoire indeed "made sense," that explain its theatrical and musical conventions and how they once cohered or "spoke." Moreover, these works and events reveal the diversity of experience that the genre comprehended and testify that at specific moments in its history it was a powerful and evocative kind of theater in France.

My first chapter centers on the seminal opera, Auber's *La Muette de Portici,* and the reemergence and transformation of those phenomena I have seen in revolutionary opera. Chapter Two then traces the results of this development in the context of the succeeding regime, or what the monarchy of Louis-Philippe did or did not learn from the Restoration. Here, in order to follow the emergence of the repertoire's basic traits within the real mechanism and concerns of the institution, I shall focus on *Robert le Diable* and *Les Huguenots.* Both are works the response to which helped to determine subsequent policy and hence works to which we can see political tactics applied in several ways. Chapter Three traces the theatrical meaning and symbolism of grand opera through the period of the Second Republic and its effort to broaden access to it. Here I shall center on a work whose history is bound up with this policy and its subsequent abrupt reversal: Meyerbeer and Scribe's opera, *Le Prophète.* My concluding chapter follows the increasing loss of credibility of the genre in the period of the Second Empire as its symbolism, its image, and thus its nature change.

Although in all of the chapters I am concerned with the audience's construal of these works, my study is not narrowly a "reception history" but, once more, a cultural history. For what interests me is how grand opera was implicated in a social and

9

cultural context – how it arose within these larger structures and in turn reacted back finally upon them. Grand opera in this sense is a challenge that forces us to see the cultural landscape anew, the way in which cultural functions and forms interacted in nineteenth-century France.

1

LA MUETTE DE PORTICI AND THE
NEW POLITICS OF OPERA

"*La Muette de Portici* a tout bouleversé"
EMILE VÉRON, 1829[1]

IT WOULD HARDLY be a novel proposition to claim that Auber's *La Muette de Portici* was a seminal work in the history of opera in nineteenth-century France. Our surveys often cite it as marking the origins of a new conception: of a new kind of libretto, a new concept of staging, if not yet a new musical style. As I have pointed out in the Introduction, this new conception and theatrical orientation is, according to the standard view, quite unambiguously commercial. From its perspective, the genesis of the work was inscribed in the institutional evolution of the Opéra toward a more popular, audience-oriented character and thus away from its royal function.

Within this framework the questions most often posed about the work have centered on explaining its historical impact despite the limited innovation in Auber's score. The most important recent literature has stressed the innovations in the text and theatrical technique that appealed to a middle-class audience and they thus dismiss a tenacious legend: that the work made a political statement, not superficially, but rather profoundly; as a symbol it helped incite revolution in 1830 in Belgium and France.[2]

The study that follows attempts, to the contrary, to establish that there is an element of truth in this so-called legend and that it is fundamental to our understanding of French grand opera. The motivation in staging the work was political, and in performance it derived its force from its integral theatrical utterance, which, as a result, was strongly politicized. With *La Muette* we can see the emergence of an awareness or set of perceptions that was subsequently to influence operatic policies and hence both the growth and construal of the genre. It is an opera, then, that was seminal not only in an artistic sense, or from the perspective of the kind of theater it was, but from the related perspective of political tactics.

Of essential importance here is a thorough understanding of the theater's political frame, or of the Opéra's function and associations both before and during the premiere of the work. As I hope to establish, it was an attempt to change these associations on the level of image that brought about the presentation of the daring opera and it was this that accounted for the distinctive, indeed peculiar, manner in which it was staged and thus for the complexity of its message and its subsequent, unexpected, political use.

The Opéra of the Bourbon Restoration, for contemporaries, was a curious, inconsistent institution: encouraged to produce a profit, it was still subject to the profligate whims of the state. As Balzac so pungently phrased it, the Opéra obeyed that notorious woman, so "capricious in her morals" but most "moral in her caprices," the king's private Liste civile.[3] And not only was the Opéra financed generously from the king's own personal funds, but with payments from the minor theaters as well as from the Fonds des théâtres.[4]

The Opéra, like the other royal theaters, and the royal school of music, came under the larger jurisdiction and surveillance of the Maison du roi. The other theaters of Paris, as well as those in the departments, however, came under a different bureaucracy and censorship structure, that of the département de l'Intérieur.[5] Governed first by the ministre de la Maison du roi, until 1824, it was thereafter under the control of the redoubtable directeur des Beaux-arts, Sosthène de la Rochefoucauld. The largest landowner in France, La Rochefoucauld wielded considerable power in the Opéra, whose nominal director was appointed by his father, the Duc de Doudeauville, the ministre de la Maison du roi.[6]

If complex in its structure, the Opéra's function and symbolic goals were clear: as the theater once again bound the most closely to the monarchy, its concern was with royal image. In this respect, it bore an illuminating relation to the Opéra of the earlier Bourbons, particularly in the later seventeenth and early eighteenth century. As then, it was a special kind of political instrument for the crown, a rhetorical means to proclaim the monarch's political achievements and glory.[7] But in this respect, however, there is an important difference to note between the Opéra in the Restoration and in the later years of the ancien régime.

12

La Muette de Portici *and the New Politics*

As we may recall from the Introduction, the Opéra underwent an evolution in its structure as well as its political meaning after the mid-eighteenth century. The emphasis shifted away from the personal power and cachet of the king to the more vague, diffuse sense of power associated with the abstract state. Significant, then, from this perspective, is that the Opéra of the Restoration represented a public and marked reversion toward an older symbolic conception. Certainly, it was no longer subject to the whims of the monarch, as it originally had been, being now a far more extensive and complex bureaucratic institution. But its function in public perception was clear: the Opéra was an exclusive domain, a realm of assembly, the social terrain of an elite royal court.

Its symbolic message is one, moreover, that can be particularly well illuminated by a comparison with the contemporaneous royal *fête,* to which it was linked by several common figures and with which it shared a *"décor."* As an official institution, the *fête* was charged, along with the Opéra, with reviving those aspects of the ancien régime with which the monarchy wished to reassociate itself, particularly after the Revolution and Empire. The ideology it was to communicate was ostensibly that of return to the past, to older political concepts and traditions that were to be made seductive and impressive once again. To win over "opinion," the monarchy reimposed lavish traditional ceremonies but with an imagery now that emphasized the most prestigious examples drawn from its historical past.

To achieve this goal, to implant such conceptions, the monarchy again depended on the services of the "menus plaisirs," as it had in the eighteenth century. The key figure here was the "architecte des menus plaisirs et dessinateur du cabinet de sa Majesté," who was assisted integrally by the services of the "premier peintre." Significantly, the latter was, from 1815 on, a major figure at the Opéra, its official painter, Cicéri. It is also important to note, in this context, that far more resources were available to Cicéri at the royal theater than in the more financially restricted *fêtes.*[8]

The Opéra was an institution whose purpose was similarly to seduce and impress, if not directly, by reaching a wide audience, by the aura that it gave the court. The repertoire and the style of the Opéra was intended to communicate the message of monarchical prestige, and through various means, using different but

13

complementary kinds of repertoire. One variety or genre, indeed that which many contemporaries perceived now as its staple, consisted of works with classical, mythological subjects dating back to the later years of the ancien régime. Certainly, at its core were the successful operas of those foreign composers of *tragédie lyrique,* now above all Piccini, Sacchini, and Gluck.[9]

But in this context, such a repertoire implied another message: approached as a learned, academic style, it was clearly the property of an exclusive elite. Consequently, censors for the Opéra were conservative men of letters, who evaluated the suitability of works submitted to them on the basis of strict academic correctness. For the Opéra, like the Comédie-Française, as the seat of elite, learned art, was also at the summit of the reestablished theatrical hierarchy in France.

But other genres as well continued to exist in the Opéra's repertoire, conveying different aspects of the larger political message intended. *Pièces de circonstances* remained, but now quite commonly in the form of works that attempted to draw connections between the monarchy of the present and those of the past. As late as 1830, for example, when the son of the duc de Berry received the title of "le comte de Chambord," the Opéra presented *François Ier à Chambord.* But another especially frequent genre, sometimes also serving the function of a *pièce de circonstance,* was the *opéra-féerie.* Often this genre, which served to enhance the magical associations of power, would fuse with remotely historical subjects, as in the case of *genre troubadour.*[10]

It was through all of these means that the Opéra was to radiate a conception of the Bourbon monarchy, but these interacted integrally with other aspects of the theater to determine its associations. The Opéra was the seat of power, just as it was the seat of monarchical prestige; unlike the *fête,* it was not for the humble to participate in but to view from afar. This aspect of the theater, as we shall see, was one that became particularly galling for the increasingly vociferous liberal critics of the conservative restored Bourbon throne.

As the symbolic seat of "privilege," its doors were obtrusively guarded by *hallebardiers* in order to keep an "unauthorized" audience from entering its august hall. Entry was literally a matter of privilege, based largely on a reestablished tradition of the awarding of free *billets de faveur* and *entrées de tolérance.* The former were routinely accorded the *gentilhommes de la chambre,* as well as free loges and additional free tickets to the *fonctionnaires de la Liste civile.* In addition, other major political functionaries were ordinarily dispensed free tickets, including high members of the *garde nationale* and the *police des Thuileries [sic]*.[11] Indeed, at the first three performances of a work, undoubtedly to insure the proper response and an impression of success, so important to the image of the royal theaters, the hall was almost filled by *billets gratuits.* But even beyond this, as contemporaries noted, it was simply established by tradition that no member of the *beau monde* ever needed to pay for a seat at the Opéra.[12]

It is not surprising, then, that the financial state of the Académie Royale, as in the late eighteenth century, was almost always approaching desperation. Moreover, the insistence on maintaining a repertoire that led consistently to financial loss made clear the Opéra's function as a locus of political representation. And so, significantly, it was, in the end, not a basically financial but rather a political concern that forced a redefinition of the Opéra's symbolic message and theatrical style.

By the mid-1820s, soon after the ascension of Charles X to the throne, the Opéra's exclusive nature and conservative artistic policies became increasingly problematic. The Restoration originally sought a compromise between the "principles of old bureaucratic monarchy, the surviving feudal aristocratic tradition, and the ideals of the Revolution." As Tocqueville incisively noted, the charter of the Restoration created aristocratic institutions in its political laws, but left a democratic principle in the civil laws that would eventually destroy the edifice.[13] Hence, in the course of the 1820s, this compromise became increasingly strained, resulting in the dichotomy and polarization of the two political extremes. Not surprisingly, the Opéra became the first symbolic target of a political opposition that was growing in strength. The situation, then, was somewhat analogous to the eighteenth century "querelle des bouffons" when, in the midst of political crisis, the traditionalism of the Opéra came under attack.[14] Now, the Académie Royale de Musique became the symbol of indefensible privilege, the bastion of an antiquated culture supporting the anachronistic regime.

In light of what we have seen of the symbolic message of the Opéra, the attacks upon it were highly resonant and instinct with political danger. This danger derived from a special force, from an otherwise ineffable communication of the fact that the regime was remote politically and culturally from the reality of modern France. The intransigence of the Opéra's officials in maintaining a repertoire of limited interest, or oblivious to public or national taste, thus became the expression of a political stance. It is perhaps more comprehensible in this light that the assassination of the duc de Berry took place at the Opéra (on February 13, 1820).

The reactionary character and political meaning of the Restoration's Opéra was certainly accentuated by revolutionary antecedents but also by two contemporary theatrical comparisons. First was the continuing awareness of political messages at the Comédie-Française and the increasingly open manifestations of political tensions there. Throughout the Restoration, the public of the Comédie-Française perceived it as a vehicle of the regime and thus a reflection of its political position. The theatrical culture of the Revolution persisted as the audience employed whistling, booing, and selective applause with political overtones, no repertoire remaining immune. But the theater was to become even more of a *rendez-vous des parties* with the entry of the heated romantic–classic debate in the national theater. It was an apparent gesture of political compromise that the theater's director began to turn from the classically inspired repertoire to a gradually attempted innovation.[15]

In this regard, the Comédie-Française appeared more progressive than the Opéra, helping further to define the political significance of its artistically intransigent stance. But this was exacerbated further by comparison with the contemporary boulevard theaters, where a new direction – and its political implications – was even more pronounced.

As if in a contentious dialogue, the boulevard theaters flourished throughout these years, catering to the contemporary public demand for a repertoire with action and topical resonance. Unlike the revolutionary period, when all theaters were expected to respond to the changing political directions of the state in order to remain immune from prosecution, the boulevard theaters now attempted to speak authentically in the name of the people, expressing dissenting opinion but circumventing censorship in a variety of ways. And so, in distinction to the national theaters as the expression of anachronistic goals, the boulevard theaters were said to embody, in opposition, the sentiments of "the new France."[16]

To grasp this phenomenon, we need first of all to understand the symbolic dimension of style, or the qualities assumed by the boulevard repertoire and its political implications. The vehicle of these theaters, beyond mere spectacle scenes, was the melodrama, which expressed, to contemporaries, a new aesthetic, moral, and political orientation. "Democratic" in both its message and means, as was incipient in revolutionary theater, it incarnated a new directness in style, being "clear and legible to everyone." Both visually as well as textually these melodramas now bore the stamp of reality, as engaging, living dramas employing realistic staging and décor.[17] As a result, visual reality was becoming a component of theatrical truth, a fact that now reflected poorly on the anachronisms of the royal stage. Thus the boulevard theaters now represented the taste, the interests, and perceptions of an increasingly broad social and political group in a double sense, in content and style.

But it was not just these factors that was to lead inevitably to crisis and change in the Opéra; it was a confluence of elements working together that forced the monarchy's hand. In addition to the boulevard theaters, a phenomenon that we have already observed now increasingly identified the Opéra's conservatism with political anachronism. By the 1820s the romantic movement was playing a prominent role in linking the values of reality and actuality to political legitimacy in France. This was a gradual process, the timing of which is important to understand, for it was primarily the later stage of it that integrally affected the Opéra's approach to style.

Indeed, at first, with the exception of a small group of "ultras," it was the supporters of the ancien régime who championed the romantic innovations in subject matter and style. But the situation began to change substantially upon the return of Stendhal to Paris in 1821, after his extended stay in Italy. In Milan, Stendhal had taken part, along with his revolutionary friends, in the battle in support of romanticism, which they saw as a battle against political tyranny. The decisive event, however, that triggered Stendhal's influential polemic was the visit of an English troop of actors to Paris in 1822. Their reception and, according to Stendhal, the misconstrual of the implications of the Shakespearean works they performed, prompted his incisive *Racine et Shakespeare* in 1823.[18]

As Stendhal here so trenchantly phrased it, "Romanticism is the art of presenting to people the works that, in the actual state of their beliefs, give them the greatest pleasure."[19] Now, in calling for an art that represented current propensities, romanticism contained an implicit political ideology, consonant with that of liberalism. Hence liberals came to realize that the principles of romantic art and their conception of political legitimacy were basically compatible also in France. Both were addressing what they perceived as the "real" constituency of the modern world, which the regime was politically obliged to address in the national theaters. Indeed, as Stendhal observed, in literature the new school was already triumphing, and as evidence he cited the novels of Walter Scott, which were more successful than any other works since 1814.[20]

It was in light of this rhetorical challenge that official uneasiness over the Opéra grew, the concern being less with receipts than with negative political perceptions and ridicule. The desire to popularize the Opéra grew from a concern with public perceptions of political legitimacy, based now, in an increasingly obvious manner, on cultural criteria. It was hence incumbent on the state to prove that its symbol, the Opéra, was not remote, not a fossilized institution alienated from modern France. And so the government faced a dilemma similar to that at the end of the ancien régime: how, subtly, to shift its symbolism and with it the repertoire of the Opéra. The problem was to recognize an audience with a broader artistic taste and in so doing to recognize a broader spectrum of the political constituency. Now officials saw no alternative, in their quest for an appropriate political message, to the kind of actuality associated with both the revolutionary and boulevard stage.[21]

The problem was how to implement this decision, to achieve this objective in a controllable way, or so as to make certain concessions while leaving the traditional symbolic structure of power intact. As typical for the Opéra now, its officials did not attempt to develop, consciously, a coherent ideology or plan, but informally sought out advice. In response, both government officials and private citizens with royalist sympathies began to address their suggestions for renovating the repertoire of the Opéra to its director.

The letters in the Opéra's archives stress the need for regeneration, implying here both a new spirit or attitude as well as new techniques. Recognizing the political danger now of conventional adherence to the *tragédie lyrique,* they urge the appointment of new personnel and artists more open to innovation. For example:

Une révolution complète dans le système de chant en usage actuellement à l'Opéra est indispensable, si l'on veut sortir ce superbe établissement de l'état de langeur et de decadence où il est tombé . . . En vain nos routiniers compositeurs et chanteurs se retranchent-ils par un prétendu esprit national qui leur fait repousser tout espèce d'innovation dans leur système de composition et de chant . . .[22]

[A complete revolution in the method of singing presently used at the Opéra is indispensible, if one wants to bring this superb establishment out of the state of languor and decadence into which it has fallen . . . In vain our routine composers and singers entrench themselves by a pretended national spirit that causes them to reject all kinds of innovation in their method of composition and singing.]

Given the stagnant repertoire, officials knew they had no choice but to encourage artistic innovation: the question now, however, was the precise form that it should take; given the desire to change only image, what should be the limit of such innovation? Should it be as thoroughgoing as some of the advisers suggested? Correctly perceiving that its changes would be construed symbolically, that is, politically, the Opéra proceeded toward innovation with the greatest possible caution. Officials at first were no more willing to experiment with radically new subjects or styles than they were to allow as yet untried artists on the first lyric stage.

The delicate problem of how to renew the Opéra's repertoire, within certain circumscribed limits, was one that three successive directors of the institution were forced to face. The first one, Habeneck, was followed in 1824 by Duplantys, who was in turn succeeded in 1827 by Lubbert.[23] Given the symbolism of the *mise en scène,* it is certainly not surprising that Habeneck turned his concern to it first and attempted a modernization. The spectacle at the Opéra was now to be competitive with that of the boulevard, and also to suggest the monarchy's splendor and the cachet of the royal house. The traditions of the repertoire were to be maintained, while the new staging was to communicate an acknowledgment of, and responsiveness to, the contemporary public's taste.

Apparently Habeneck's first response was to turn to a contemporary artist who had started on the popular stage but had later graduated to the official theater. The scenic designer Cicéri, had begun with his partner, Daguerre, in the boulevard theaters, and most notably at the Ambigue-Comique.[24] But, as we have seen, Cicéri went on to become *premier peintre* of the Menus plaisirs, designer for the Comédie-Française, and then a *peintre de l'Opéra*.

Naturally, Cicéri, known for his astounding illusionistic effects, began with caution at the stodgy Opéra, transforming the traditional *décor antique* only through the use of newer lighting effects. This was made possible by the installation of gas lighting on the Opéra's stage, a technical innovation by now already well established on the boulevard. But before long the Opéra was producing works designed to take maximum advantage of the lighting effects, among them a five-act *opéra-féerie* by Nicole and Benincori, *Aladin et la lampe merveille* (1822) (Figure 1). To update the traditional genre of the *féerie*, as his scenic plan reveals, Cicéri also employed a more realistic use of space, stimulated perhaps by the diorama.[25] The final result was undoubtedly intended to be one of royal enchantment, but one also now competitive with the blandishments of the boulevard theaters and hence ideal for the Académie Royale. So important was the spectacle, in fact, that the Opéra spent 200,260 francs on the work, the highest cost of any production in the first half of the nineteenth century.

But if the transformation of this genre provided a sort of provisional solution, the problem still remained of what to do with the traditional works. The Opéra, and indeed the monarchy, was not ready to abandon them, so closely were they bound up with monarchical tradition and the royal image in France. The challenge, again, was to present these works in a way that might rival the boulevard theaters, bringing arresting new effects and hence a politically safe *actualité;* the trick was to engage the audience safely, to involve it more immediately in these works, without, as in the Revolution, suggesting a politically dangerous reference or resonance.

20

Figure 1. Cicéri. Décor for *Aladin*. Bibliothèque de l'Opéra.

The only answer now seemed to be to aim for simple historical accuracy, first of all in the costumes, in emulation of the boulevard spectacles. But on the boulevard historical costumes helped create a greater sense of reality and thus to connect the reality of the present with that of the historical past. The Opéra, perhaps because of the political danger and its entrenched conventions, proceeded here in a half-hearted manner, employing an inconsistent, haphazard mélange. Because of its lack of a coherent historical sense, the theater soon became the butt of scathing jokes, as when Spontini's vestal virgins appeared in *coiffures à la chinoise*.[26] Audiences who frequented the boulevard theaters now expected accuracy in historical details, and were especially perturbed by anachronisms still forced upon them at the Opéra. The public quickly read this message in a politically symbolic sense, as a penetrating expression of the regime's increasingly pertinacious stance.

Clearly, the use of historical costuming for the old repertoire could not suffice, and gradually the Opéra realized that a more thorough innovation would have to begin. Officials finally rec-

21

ognized that the conventions of the old repertoire were so strong that, if the Opéra were to be regenerated, it would have to seek out new subjects. But subjects of an appropriate elevation, in accordance with the dignity of the grand royal stage, and commensurate with the scope of the older works, proved to be hard to find. For the new subjects would necessarily have to come from outside the traditional categories of the repertoire, preferably from artists familiar with the contemporary popular theatrical style.

One response was to turn to works that were popular in a traditional sense, historical in their setting but fanciful in content. Hence in 1823 the Opéra experimented with a subject drawn from popular literature, here from the corpus of the *Bibliothèque bleue,* a source to which it would later return.[27] In this case, the opera was a *drame historique,* in five acts, *Ogier le Danois,* a story that the purveyors of the *Bibliothèque* had drawn from traditional legend.

But the Opéra soon discovered that such subjects still could hardly compete with the topical and romantic subjects now on the boulevard stages and in the minor theaters. The Opéra-Comique had already begun to experiment with more romantic libretti, in works like Boieldieu's stunningly successful *La Dame Blanche* (1825), based on Walter Scott.[28] And smaller lyric theaters like the Odéon had begun to import and adapt the most successful recent foreign works to France. The French were hence coming to know provocative new operas like Weber's *Der Freischütz* (presented in 1824 as *Robin des Bois*), although, according to Berlioz, in "mutilated" versions by Castil-Blaze.[29]

With the public becoming increasingly demanding, the problem of the Opéra now was to locate subjects associated with neither enchantment nor an academic tradition but with the vibrancy and appeal of the boulevard theaters. This meant turning to either modern subjects, which would hardly seem appropriate to the grand Opéra, or to those historical subjects that had a vague emotional resonance for the present. Given the current situation, it was the latter course that appealed to Restoration officials, who hoped through this means to communicate an identity with the contemporary political spirit. They realized the implicit dangers, remembering the Revolution's Opéra well, but believed that through the right kind of attention the problems it engendered could be effectively forestalled. By presenting implicitly topical works through the right kind of *mise en scène,* the regime could co-opt revolutionary emotion or direct it in a safer way.

But the dilemma in which officials soon found themselves stemmed from the subject they were now forced to confront, one almost inherently inimical to safe presentation on the royal stage. There seemed, however, to be no choice but to engage in this inescapable contradiction, and so the Opéra consciously took a carefully calculated risk.

As contemporaries frequently noted, it was now on the boulevard in Paris that a bevy of works about notorious leaders of past revolts began to appear. Favorite among these were the stories of the leader of the first popular revolt in Naples and that of the legendary Swiss revolutionary leader, Guillaume Tell. Abetted by the language of spectacle, which officials could not easily censor, such works, to the alarm of the authorities, were stirring up febrile emotions and "patriotic aggression."[30] Certainly, these works interacted with a variety of other contemporary cultural forms in a larger network of meaning and cross-reference in contemporary Paris. "Patriotic aggression," or a sense of the identity of the nation, as opposed to the monarchy, was already being incited in popular singing societies or *goguettes.* Workers and artisans met in such contexts to sing or declaim *chansons* that, according to contemporaries, were "écoles puissantes d'enseignement patriotique."[31]

Also increasingly popular were the vivid *scènes historiques,* and particularly representations of past uprisings appearing now in the boulevard theaters. Moreover, interest in Italy and its past was further stimulated by the popularity of the novels of Alexander Manzoni, such as his *I promessi sposi.*[32] And finally, as historians of theater have noted, because of political tensions, attention was increasingly focusing on the socially restive sixteenth and seventeenth centuries, as opposed to the Middle Ages.[33]

All these tendencies, of course, created a dilemma for the Opéra, now forced somehow to relate to them but in the safest possible way: It was forced to turn to a kind of history that had long been banished from its stage, one far removed from the flattering implications instinct in historical *pièces de circonstance.* Now it seemed incumbent on the Opéra to represent historical events that were more ambiguous and even potentially dangerous in their political implications. It apparently had no choice, given the contemporary currents on the boulevard, but to represent the people in political revolt on the royal stage.

Officials, however, were cautious, well aware of the many channels through which such a work's constituent elements and content could be diffused (illustrations, *mises en scènes*, texts, and theatrical reviews). They also realized that specific numbers from such a work could well be abstracted and thus possibly be employed out of context as political weapons. In the 1820s the Préfet de police was particularly concerned about the often veiled, allegorical political criticism that was then proliferating in popular *chansons*. Authorities were increasingly aware of how key words in such a literary context, in either the theater or in *goguettes*, could trigger the expression of political passions; moreover, they were also cognizant of the fact that passages in the *style lyrique* or *style mystique* could be just as incendiary as those in the more precise *langage direct*. And particularly in light of generally increasing interest in the Fronde and its subtle tactics of political subversion, the caution concerning operatic texts and their uses was great.[34]

It is for this reason that *Le Siège de Corinthe* had several features that recommended it to a regime that saw it as a politically useful vehicle and apparently safe. It involved a sympathetic representation of revolutionary emotion but in the specific context of political domination by a distinctly foreign power.

The work, about the victory of the Turks over the Greeks in 1459, was a translation and adaptation, by Balocchi and Soumet, of Rossini's successful Italian opera, *Maometto II*. The most that worried officials here was that it included an element normally censored on the official stage: the literal representation of a religious ceremony. But in the case of the opera, officials decided to make an exception since, at this point, they saw safety in the fact that it took place in a tomb and was presented unobtrusively, without "pomp."

The other feature that recommended the opera was its composer, Gioacchino Rossini, who was currently at the height of his popularity and whom the Opéra had observed for some time. As letters in its archives reveal, it had long been in search of an artistic guide, an exciting new musical presence coming from outside a now politically troublesome tradition. Many advisers had expressed the opinion that Italy was the place to turn to, being a traditional leader in music and indeed in all the arts.[35] Since Rossini, who had been named director of the Théâtre-Italien in 1824, was clearly the most commanding figure on the operatic scene, he appeared to be a logical choice as the savior of the Académie Royale. Moreover, his style had the further advantage of being both liberal and royalist at once, or conveniently ambiguous as to its ideological implications in France. Initially, Rossini was associated with the aristocratic bastion, the Théâtre-Italien, and when attacked by liberal journalists the royalists had leaped to his defense. But through the efforts of writers like Stendhal, who were attempting to redefine "liberal culture," Rossini's engaging, appealing style seemed far closer to its political stance. His *Vie de Rossini,* like *Racine et Shakespeare,* was essentially a political pamphlet that took aim simultaneously at political and cultural "immobility." Rossini, for Stendhal, was a "modern" composer because his means of appeal were "calculés sur nos besoins actuels" [calculated on our actual needs], and hence his music was eminently romantic.[36] It was, then, in the midst of this complex political-cultural debate that Rossini entered the Opéra, an institution confident, finally, of a safe if perhaps moderate success.[37]

Le Siège de Corinthe premiered at the Opéra in October 1826, fulfilling expectations and encouraging even bolder artistic innovations. Ready for another opera that would co-opt the revolutionary spirit, the Opéra began to search conspicuously for another appropriate work. It was in this particular context that a text came to its attention, about the first popular revolt in Naples, by the successful playwright, Eugène Scribe.

Although several scholars have claimed or assumed that La Rochefoucauld initiated the commission of the work, this seems unlikely for a number of different reasons.[38] The documents that we do have suggest that, typically for the Opéra, the work was submitted as a script or sketch after which a contract eventually followed. Contemporaries claimed that it was upon leaving a performance at the Opéra-Comique, where a *comédie mêlée d'ariettes* using a mime had been performed, that Scribe, attending with Auber, conceived the dramatic idea of using a mute girl as a central figure in a grand opera.[39]

But whether it was Scribe or the Vicomte who first conceived

25

the basic idea, there are several reasons why the latter proceeded deliberately and with extreme caution. Scribe and Auber's opera was not the first setting of the story of the leader of the revolt in Naples in 1647, Tomasso Aniello, known as Masaniello. In 1766, a German, Kaiser, wrote *Masaniello Furioso,* and more recently, in 1825, Sir Henry Bishop, *Masaniello, the Fisherman of Naples.* But a more relevant precedent in France was a recent interpretation of the story at the Opéra-Comique, with a text by Lafontelle and Moreau, and music by Carafa.[40]

The text had already been presented at the Odéon theater as a play but became particularly controversial when set to music as an *opéra-comique.* The censors immediately accused the work of attempted political subversion, of trying to instigate revolution by openly encouraging a growing spirit of revolt. In fact, despite a period of relative flexibility in theatrical censorship, it took six different censors' reports for the work to be authorized. With the slightly more liberal laws of theatrical censorship in 1827, "patriotic" tableaux of national revolts, with depictions of the lower classes as a part of them, had multiplied.[41] But Masaniello caused special worry for several different reasons, as we can see from the following excerpt from one censor's later report:

Sur l'Opéra-Comique, la révolution de Naples était présentée dans toute sa crudité . . . le peuple souverain et surtout Masaniello parlaient trop d'insurrection, de liberté, de patrie . . . et la teinte de l'ouvrage était généralement triste et funèbre.[42]

[At the Opéra-Comique, the revolution of Naples was presented in all its crudity . . . the sovereign people and above all Masaniello spoke too much of insurrection, of liberty, of country . . . and the coloring of the work was generally sad and funereal.]

And:

Cet homme émeut la populace de Naples, et commit des cruautés qu'on ne peut souffrir que huit ou dix jours, après lesquelles finit son règne et sa vie par les mains de ses complices . . . Son rôle est fort ennobli dans l'Opéra-Comique.

[This man stirred up the populace of Naples, and committed cruelties that could not be suffered more than eight or ten days, after which his reign and his life were ended by the hands of his accomplices . . . His role is strongly ennobled in the Opéra-Comique.]

The censor then goes on to accuse the authors of falsifying history "pour encourager un certain air d'insurrection qui, chaque jour, l'affecte davantage" [to encourage a certain air of insurrection that, each day, affects more and more].

But what was so objectionable about the stylistic features of the work, together with its specific vocabulary and general tone? First, it is important to note that the idea of sedition is introduced immediately in the score, asserted already in the *couplets* which here serve as the traditional solo interpolations in the opening choral scene. Moreover, inflammatory words such as "quelle injustice" [what injustice], to which the authorities, as we have seen, were so sensitive, are set in powerful unison passages near the opening of the work. And words such as "le vain orgueil de la naissance" [the vain pride of birth], which would undoubtedly have been read with a political subtext, are set with extensive repetition, thus underlining them. But, in addition, the simplicity and directness of the rhythms also serve to intensify the force of the words, and thus it is no surprise that the censors came to consider the work tangible proof of the danger of representing revolution.[43]

To the dismay of the authorities, however, even censored the work was a smashing and enduring success, which immediately resulted in the dangerous process of excerpting numbers from it.[44] The separate pieces of the work were printed successively as soon as possible, and apparently without distinction as to content: as symbols, they were all important. So too, it seems, were the *quadrilles* and *contredanses* "sur les plus jolis motifs de l'opéra," arranged for popular consumption – for piano with the accompaniment of flute, violin, or flageolet "ad libitum." But just as these excerpts helped to evoke the theatrical experience or event, or to extend its meaning beyond the theater, supports or aids to define its meaning further also appeared. Most notable were books on the subject of the uprising sold by the *marchands de nouveautés,* such as *Masaniello, Histoire du soulèvement de Naples en*

1647, par M. C. F.★★★. Indeed, advertisements for such books make a point of stressing that they will undoubtedly be sought out by the numerous spectators of the continuing performances at the Opéra-Comique.[45]

And certainly the performances must have been forceful and the message particularly direct, given the nature of the costumes and settings that were employed. Not only did the costumes strongly emphasize class distinctions, the aristocrats being dressed with gaudy opulence and in bright colors in marked contrast to Masaniello; the opening set, a view of a "public place" in Naples, is framed starkly and symbolically with the palpable causes of the revolt, two small *Bureaux de taxe.*[46]

Masaniello, then, had proved itself to be an unavoidably politically troublesome work, which makes it particularly surprising that the Opéra would choose to produce one on the same subject. But we can see the reasons why officials believed that the grand opera should be presented, and indeed would be politically useful, by examining the process of review.

Normally, a work proposed for the Opéra would be examined by its official body, the *Jury littéraire et musical,* comprising five men of letters and five musicians. As we have noted, their main concern had to do with academic correctness, which now was to have serious implications for their perception of the suitability of Scribe's libretto. The questions they were all asked to address concerned both the content and style of the text, particularly the clarity and elegance of the poem, as well as the accuracy and finesse of the musical treatment of the prosody. Essentially, they still considered and approached opera as a *drame en musique* and hence judged it in terms of the content and merit of the literary text above all.[47] And the same was largely true in the next stage of the examination process: the submission of the text to the Comité de censure des pièces de théâtre. The censors in the Restoration, significantly, were also largely men of letters; some were academicians, and some even of a liberal political inclination.[48]

In the case of Scribe's text, the censors were clearly aware of the manner in which the plot could be read in the light of current political developments and growing tensions in France. They were open to topicality, but in an attenuated form; and they approved an appeal to patriotic emotions, but only in an abstract sense. Part of the appeal of Eugène Scribe's text was the manner in which it handled these specific, delicate problems in a sure and elegant way. From this perspective, Scribe's text appeared to correct the flaws in the *opéra-comique,* as the censors attempted to argue by proceeding systematically through the characters and plot.

Contrary to existing theses, it seems unlikely that Scribe's primary concern was a simple adaptation of the story to the technical exigencies of the operatic stage; nor was it simply to cater to the demands of a middle-class audience in search of an entertaining drama with the minimum of intellectual demands.[49] Undoubtedly Scribe, in composing the text, was aware of how officials would read it and hence exercised an auto-censorship, knowing just how far he could go.

To explain the approbation of the censors fully, we need to examine the text itself, and note particularly the way in which Scribe attempted to defuse the explosive story for performance at the Opéra. (For a plot summary, see the Appendix.) Of particular note is the way in which he transferred attention to the personal level and hence away from the ideological in order to represent revolt, if possible, safely. The individual motivation of the major characters clearly overshadows social or intellectual conflict and results in an ambiguity that was probably conscious on the part of Scribe. This especially concerns the way in which the character of Masaniello should be seen, which is far less clear in the opera than in the *opéra-comique.* But one implication of the text is that Masaniello is, in the end, a figure of "order" who is sacrificed to the rebels and without whom the people run immediately amuck.[50]

In every respect, the text of the opera seemed preferable to the *opéra-comique,* and it is sentiments such as the following that Scribe might have anticipated in planning it for the Opéra. According to the censors:

> On sortit un *Guillaume Tell* adapté par la Comédie Française. Celui-ci est compté non au nombre des brigands, mais des héros de révolution. Cependant, aux yeux de la raison et de l'impartialité, les héros de ce genre ne sont que des chefs des rebelles, rendus ou cannoisés par cet événément. Comme toutes les révoltes qu'on croit aujourd'hui légitimes en les appelant des insurrections ou des révolutions . . . on trouve . . . plusieurs passages qui rappellent les horreurs de 1789.[51]

29

And:

> On distingue au contraire dans l'Opéra la touche fine et
> délicate d'un peintre habile . . . Rien de plus ingénieux que
> l'ordonnance de ses tableaux, rien de plus (?) que sa con-
> struction . . . La contestation (?) de l'autorité légitime, le
> tumulte populaire, . . . tout se perd et s'oublie ou plutôt se
> confond dans l'intérêt (?) inspiré par un seul personnage.
> C'est une femme . . . C'est à elle que s'attachent tous les
> coeurs . . . L'invention n'est pas nouvelle . . . c'est d'avoir
> détourné l'attention d'un sujet un peu trop grave par lui-
> même en usant aussi habilement d'un artifice . . . Il faut
> aussi savoir gré à l'auteur d'avoir adouci le caractère du far-
> ouche Masaniello, et de lui avoir préfiguré à lui-même sa
> chute au moment où les flots populaires l'ont poussé au
> pouvoir.[52]

And finally:

> . . . il n'est pas question d'imôts ou de révolte à l'occasion de
> recouvrence de contributions publiques . . . La sédition na-
> politaine qui se lie à cette intrigue n'est point excitée par la
> violence et les exécutions des percepteurs d'impôt. Le peuple
> de Naples . . . ne se soulève que contre cette domination
> étrangère. Il n'y a dans cette combinaison rien qui sorte du
> cercle ordinaire des moyens dramatiques.[53]

> [One has just brought out a *Guillaume Tell* adapted by the
> Comédie-Française. This one is counted not among the brig-
> ands but the heroes of revolution. Yet, in the eyes of reason
> and impartiality, the heroes of this type are nothing but the
> leaders of rebels, restored or canonized by the event. As all
> the revolts that one believes legitimate today in calling them
> insurrections or revolutions, one finds many passages that
> recall the horrors of 1789.]

And:

> [On the contrary, one distinguishes in the opera the fine and
> delicate touch of a skillful painter . . . Nothing is more inge-

nius than the arrangement of the tableaux . . . The contestation of legitimate authority, the popular tumult, . . . all is forgotten or blended into the interest inspired by a single personage. It is a woman . . . It is to her that all hearts are attached . . . The invention isn't new . . . it's having diverted the attention from a subject that is a little too grave in itself by using an artifice so cleverly . . . One should be grateful to the author for having softened the character of the fierce Masaniello, and to have him prefigure his own fall at the moment when the popular tides pushed him to power.]

And finally:

[. . . it is not a question of taxes or revolt on the occasion of the collecting of public contributions . . . The Neapolitan sedition that is tied to this plot is not excited by violence and the enforcement of the collectors of taxes. The people of Naples only rise up against this foreign domination. There is nothing in this combination that goes beyond the ordinary circle of dramatic means.]

As we might expect, given their backgrounds, the censors' approach was clearly an intellectual one: they reasoned carefully and deductively about the possible implications of every aspect. Above all, for them, the revolt is not presented as a legitimate revolution and Masaniello's eventual fall is prefigured from the very beginning. In addition, the refinement of the theatrical treatment as well as the general lightness of tone and focus on Fenella all promised to make it a very good risk. And there was nothing in the text that they read that would seem to make it a pretext for riot – nothing to inflame the revolutionary spirit, only the means to subvert it subtly. Moreover, it contained no implied references to the present situation in France, for the revolt Scribe depicted was one triggered by foreign as opposed to domestic oppression.

Hence the only alterations that the censors decided to ask in the text were the omission of certain phrases that, in themselves, might have an inflammatory effect. To be excised were: "il faut armer le peuple" [it is necessary to arm the people], "le peuple est maître" [the people are master], especially as repeated four times, "votre reine est à vos genoux" [your queen is at your knees], and "vengeur de nos droits" [avenger of our rights].[54] All of these phrases clearly might have encouraged reference to the political present, especially in the context of a performance at the Académie Royale de Musique.

The line between allowable and unallowable representation on the royal stage of the Opéra now, as we can see, was fine. For the regime did want to communicate a conciliatory attitude, or toleration of public opinion, but only in an abstract sense. For even in the ancien régime certain works in opposition to royal views had been tolerated in the theater in the interest of *opinion publique*.[55]

Stylistically, the music as well as the text had everything to recommend it for this end: neither was crude, too direct, and hence threateningly *populaire*.[56] Auber's style was far from the bare and simple manner of Carafa's *Masaniello,* which relied liberally on compelling, often military rhythms and much literal repetition. Auber included the popular, but in a refined and selective manner, particularly in the *ariettes* and barcarolles, which the censors saw as delicate and gay. Indeed, the censors were undoubtedly relieved further by the fact that the passages dealing with subversion were framed by the lilting barcarolle. In addition, those choruses that could make the strongest impression in the hall dealt only with vague collective emotions that seemed unlikely to incite a strong response. And, appropriately, the more Italianate, virtuosic style Auber reserved for the elite and noble characters, Alphonse and Elvire. Auber's eclecticism, here intended to introduce the appropriate breadth to this kind of libretto, as we shall see, was to have considerable stylistic implications later in France, and so too would his emphasis on the chorus, whose style is far more homogeneous and which thus overshadows the solos in scope and musical weight.

But since the censors clearly believed that the opera's message would largely inhere in the text, their only concern with both style and *mise en scène* is that they be appropriately grand. Now their belief was clearly that spectacle could defuse dangerous content, and that a more modern spectacle was essential to the image of the Académie Royale. Indeed, a Comité de mise en scène had just been established in 1827, in order to ensure that the necessary attention was devoted to this essential aspect.[57] But apparently the concern of the committee here was less with the semiotic dimension than with an attention to certain historical details and competitive theatrical effects.

Certainly this was the emphasis of the scenic artists involved in the work, who lavished all their imaginative resources and experience on the opera. Cicéri again was responsible for the sets, and Duponchel, originally a painter trained in Guérin's studio who then turned architect, designed the costumes. Solomé was a *régisseur* and apparently also the *metteur en scène,* responsible for the acting and the movement of the characters on the stage.

To achieve dramatic force, this team freely mingled theatrical genres, drawing intuitively on the symbols and techniques so effective in the boulevard theaters. This, too, undoubtedly seemed logical given the heterogeneous nature of the score and the mandate to outdo the effect of the boulevard theaters on the royal stage. And perhaps they believed, as the censors did in the case of the written text, that the mixture of genres would cancel out the dangerous associations or effects of each style. But all seemed to be aware of the need to create a new kind of realism on the royal stage: not that of the traditional illusionistic *féerie* but rather that of the boulevard stage. As we have seen in the case of *Masaniello,* this was less an archeological than a social realism, or a blunt and stark projection of the socially or politically significant.[58]

Cicéri aimed, above all, for greater reality in the physical setting, particularly in the treatment of theatrical space, into which he introduced more illusion while retaining classical simplicity (Figure 2). As in *Masaniello*'s first set, the space is firmly three-dimensional, although here overtly inflammatory objects are assiduously suppressed. The setting, however, like those of the boulevard, was designed in such a way that the characters could actually move about the stage and the architecture in a realistic manner.

And this is precisely what they did, as indicated in Solomé's *mise en scène:* from the very first act, the movement, particularly that of the crowd, was new to the Opéra. Instead of being lined up in symmetrical bodies, according to convention, the chorus (or the Neapolitan mob) dispersed itself freely, as if it were a real crowd. And not only did the crowd stand openly in confrontation with the lords, pages, and guards, but by the end of the work confronted them violently in a realistic, vivid mélange. And certainly the use of a mute figure, a purely mime role, was concurrently an increasingly popular spectacle on the boulevard. Indeed,

33

Figure 2. *La Muette de Portici*. Décor by Cicéri, 1828. Bibliothèque de l'Opéra.

in early February 1828, a *La Muette* was being presented at the Gaité and one at the Odéon, as well as Scribe's inspiration, *Les Deux Mots,* at the Opéra-Comique.

At the Opéra, the costumes similarly aimed for a vividness of effect, as well as for visual clarity in the definition of the characters, as in melodrama. But here the definition was apparently less social, as in *Masaniello,* than it was political, although again here carefully ambiguous in its specific connotations. This is especially true of the costume designed for the ill-fated Masaniello, which Duponchel might well have modeled on a long tradition of popular representations (Figure 3). Not only was he dressed realistically as a barefoot Neapolitan fisherman, his costume projected a political identity with its specific associations, now, in France. The colors chosen, as often in the Revolution, were those of the revolutionary *tricolore;* and in addition, Masaniello clearly sported a Republican Phrygian cap.[59] There are several different ways to construe the rationale of this choice: perhaps the intent was to

Figure 3. Adolphe Nourrit as Masaniello, 1828. Bibliothèque de l'Opéra.

make Masaniello a manipulated enthusiast of the Republican Left. But in either case, Duponchel, in the tradition of revolutionary theater, again, was attempting to clarify the text's ambiguity, one rooted in the political prudence of Scribe. And cleverly, perhaps, given the censorship laws as to what could be said, Duponchel was skirting them through visual representation instead. (This was by no means a new technique in the Restoration; in 1814 the famous actress, Mademoiselle Mars, had appeared on the stage in *Tartuffe* with a bouquet of violets pinned to her dress, a clear symbol of *ralliement* for partisans of the Empire.) Here, perhaps, such a gesture was intended to flatter "*l'opinion publique*," particularly given the patriotic significance of the tricolored flag. Moreover, if Masaniello was to be associated with the forces of order, this was a further means to associate such order with true patriotism.[60]

35

But perhaps the most vivid borrowing from the contemporary theaters of the boulevard was the spectacular grand finale, the eruption of Vesuvius on the stage. A popular spectacle during the Revolution, perhaps for its political connotations (of eruption after compression), it was now making a reappearance on the boulevard. But even more significantly, in the fourth act of the controversial *Masaniello* a volcano had already erupted on stage, and though less grandly, with similar connotations. The Opéra, which obviously wished to outdo the effects of the other theaters, even sent Cicéri to Italy to study the techniques that were used at La Scala.[61] Again, perhaps, it believed that a revolutionary spectacle would be safe enough, or lose its semiotic significance, if it were executed in a lavish manner.

The Opéra, however, was wrong, for on February 29, 1828, at the work's premiere, the audience's construal and response took it by surprise. The theatrical phenomenon that was grand opera here seized the authorities unprepared, for two specific reasons that we must examine in detail. First, the semiotic aspects of this complex theatrical product did not work in a coherent harmony but rather in an ambiguous, sometimes dissonant counterpoint. Second, these interacted with the physical and temporal unfolding of the spectacle, which included the dynamic in the hall as well as that which occurred outside it.

Moreover, the audience's perception was simultaneously aesthetic and political and hence the two were inextricably fused in the meaning that they derived. For the opera was inscribed in a network of references – of images, texts, and even *chansons* – all of which interacted with the ambiguity of the political message in this institutional frame. It was not the music alone that created the meaning and hence the effect of the work, and neither was it simply the text, as the authorities had naively supposed: It was rather a complex conjuncture that we can best understand by turning to the contemporary Parisian press and the wealth of information that it provides. Indeed, it is the press that helps us explain not only the event but also the political myth that formed around *La Muette de Portici*.[62]

The clamorous Parisian press seized upon the opera for several reasons: in fact, every major political journal discussed it, and often at length and on the front page. But the press not only analyzed the message of the work in minute detail, it attempted to analyze its political significance and indeed to use it as a political weapon.

This was made possible, of course, by a curious political conjuncture, one that affected censorship of the press and of the stage in different ways. In an attempt to ease the political tensions that were growing more taut by early 1828, a new group of ministers was named on January 5. The key appointment here was that of the vicomte de Martignac to replace Villèle as minister of the interior, a man whose stubbornness and defiance were virulently hated by the liberals. Martignac, as his replacement, sought to promote a spirit of moderation and liberalism, and to satisfy the quest for liberty and progress that the recent elections strongly indicated. But he was forced to tred a narrow path between a stubborn king and still angry liberals ready to carry on a "posthumous" battle against Villèle, motivated by a strong sense of vengeance. The ministry, then, was caught between liberals and ultras, and forced to contend with an aging monarch still hostile to reform who saw it only as a temporary and pragmatic compromise.[63]

This tenuous position greatly influenced the contemporary policies of censorship, not only as they affected the theater, but also, significantly, the press. Under Villèle, particularly during the political troubles in 1827, censorship of the press became increasingly strict, to the indignation of the liberals. But policies gradually became less harsh under Martignac, who finally did away with the hated *délit de "tendence"* [breach of "tendency"]. However, significantly, while press censorship loosened in 1828, that of the theater did not follow suit, creating an explosive situation.[64]

And so the press was eager to pounce and to exploit the situation, especially to exploit the regime's inconsistencies, within the allowable limits. The opera was seemingly a perfect occasion to make an incisive political point and yet to make it obliquely, with impunity, under the current laws. The press of the Left was particularly engaged, for shortly after the elections it accused the government of having countenanced the bloody battle on the rue Saint-Denis.[65] And in addition, journals of the Right that had supported the regime began now to desert it and similarly to attack it in a variety of subtle ways. Such journals, especially,

37

were to use the opera in a particularly clever manner, employing the growing *esprit frondeur* that the regime now feared.

This goal determined the details chosen as well as the ways in which they were discussed, for all had political meaning and were intended to have a political effect. The first significant detail concerned the events that framed the performance and that clearly, in all the reviews, helped to provide the political subtext. First, it is important to be aware of the rumors that preceded the opera, making the public particularly attuned to its political meaning or message. The *Gazette de France,* up to this point progovernment but now also turning against the regime, noted the rumor that the work was another *Masaniello,* but with a different title.[66] In addition, it mentions another detail that was an important aspect of the political frame: that the performance was attended by the duc et duchesse d'Orléans, accompanied by their family. Signficantly, the king did not attend, but his more liberal protégé did – the future Louis-Philippe – who, for the moment, had no choice but to play such a conciliatory role. Although we now have few details about who comprised the rest of the audience, there is little reason to believe that it was an atypical audience for Restoration premieres. But now the elite political public it included was one that was clearly divided against the regime, simultaneously from both the Left and the Right.

Moreover, the excluded audience was similarly present here in force, well aware of the work's significance and anxious to be present for the event. According to the *Journal des Débats,* an open adversary of the government, the crush outside the hall was almost as violent as the events on the stage:

> La foule se pressait devant la porte avec tant de force et d'agitation que l'on marchait sur les corps des assaillans et que plusieurs ont été lancé dans l'intérieur en passant sur les épaules de bons gendarmes qui s'efforçaient en vain de ramener le calme sur cette mer agitée.[67]

> [The crowd pressed before the door with such force and agitation that one walked on the bodies of the attackers and that several were hurled inside, passing over the shoulders of the good policemen who tried in vain to restore calm to this agitated sea.]

And as it cleverly notes, the success of Fenella's description of the disorders in the city and the fury of the rebels was thus particularly meaningful and vivid for the audience: "Les spectateurs étaient d'autant mieux disposés, à comprendre cette symphonie, qu'ils venaient eux-mêmes de prendre part à un combat terrible pour entrer dans la salle" [The spectators were all the more disposed to understanding this "symphony," having themselves just taken part in a terrible battle to enter the hall].

And it was just this stress on the interplay between the reality presented on the stage and that of the events surrounding it that provided the criteria of evaluation. The press criticized and judged the work on the basis of what it considered to be both historical and social reality – or rather all but the official press. The *Nouveau Journal de Paris,* a generally progovernment paper, now turning against the regime, criticized the work for depicting the motivation for the revolt in an historically inaccurate manner, associating it, as the title indicated, with Fenella.[68] And, further, it hints at the role of the government and its goals in staging the work, by noting "une volonté étrangère à celle de l'administration était venue inspirer du mouvement à ce grand corps" [a will foreign to that of the administration had come to inspire movement in this great body].

The *Journal des débats* (hostile to the government) also criticized the stress on Fenella, emphasizing less the historical inaccuracy than the dramatic incongruity of her role. And here it goes on to raise the key issue of what an opera, dramatically and theatrically, is to be, or the level of verisimilitude it should contain. Already, the issue of the kind of spectacle or the theatrical genre that French grand opera ought henceforth to be here explicitly enters the political-aesthetic debate. According to the *Journal,* and, as we shall see, in contradiction to the official paper, "un opéra n'est pas fait pour les divertissemens [*sic*], c'est au contraire . . ."[69] It goes on to note the charm but the lack of verisimilitude in the market-place scene, in comparison with the bald facts of contemporary social reality.

Le Globe, also in opposition as a clearly liberal journal, begins as well by noting how obviously historical facts are changed in the work; but yet it praises certain details that are indeed naturalistic, revealing "le portrait vivant de l'époque," especially the realistic crowd scenes. And significantly, it notes the considerable task that

39

the composer had to face in translating the ambiguous text into forceful and compelling musical terms. The composer is most successful, it claims, not in the arias but in the crowd scenes, or those sections that are integral to the action as opposed to those that lie outside it. The *Gazette de France* had already made the same point several days before, but also expressed the opinion that the work was indeed seditious – another *Masaniello* – for this very reason.[70]

The issue of why it expressed this perception brings us back to the so-called myth of the work: that even before the riotous performance in Belgium, its seditious power was established in Paris. Nineteenth-century accounts, such as the popular *Album de l'Opéra,* imply that the audience refused to accept, and in fact protested, the work's tragic end.[71] Such an event is not reported in any of the contemporary papers, although, in *La Quotidienne,* something else revealing is. The journal begins by taking issue with the opera's portrait of Masaniello, one it finds flattering to power, since it presents him as sacrificed: "Mais ce que les historiens n'avait pas prévu, c'est que ce dictateur de vingt-quatre heures trouverait encore des flatteurs deux siècles après . . . [since he is presented as] un prodige de grandeur d'âme, un héros de générosité."[72] [But that which historians didn't foresee is that this twenty-four-hour dictator would still find flatterers two centuries later (since he is presented as) a wonder of grandeur of spirit, a hero of generosity]. But it then goes on to report that the curtain was hardly lowered before "toutes les voix de parterre ont démandé le nom des auteurs" [all the voices of the parterre demanded the names of the authors]. Yet this traditional sign of approbation was apparently not responded to immediately, according to the *Nouveau Journal de Paris,* which noted the force and duration of the request. Evidently the reaction at the end of the work was not what the authorities expected, for it seemed to indicate not the success of the tragedy but rather solidarity with the people on stage.

In the end, evidently, the depiction of the people was the work's most gripping aspect: the people depicted as grand and heroic, through most of the work, on the first royal stage. As we have seen, the blocking of the crowd scenes presented them as an active and self-assured group, now themselves in a position to inspire fear and awe in the authorities. Moreover, their choral scenes, by far the most musically powerful parts of the work, similarly projected a sense of dignity and pride that clashed openly with what occurred at the end.

And here we must turn to the *mise en scène* in order to understand this disjuncture and the perception that it was unnaturally imposed by the authorities on the work:

Borella, montant la scène et regardant vers le côté droit – "Masaniello, grand Dieu! Il a triomphé, le destin se prononce." Ici la moitié des choristes et tout le peuple traversent le théâtre en fuyant, en regardant derrière eux comme des personnes épouvantées; ils sont suivis des soldats qui, les armes croisées, les poursuivent avec rapidité . . . Alphonse, suivi de six chefs, rentre de la droite; aussitôt la moitié des choristes qui n'ont point traversé paraissent au côté droit, se mettent à genoux; ceux de gauche en font autant; tous ont l'air de demander grace. Alphonse fait un signe, on se lève et l'on écoute son récit . . . "Masaniello n'est plus; ils ne savent que fuir" . . . [Fenella] monte l'escalier du fond. Arrivée au sommet, elle se précipite dans les laves . . .

Après le choeur final, tout le monde s'agite avec le plus grand effroi. Un homme arrive en haut de l'escalier; du haut de la terrasse, le bruit d'une détonation s'écoule et l'engloutit lui et trois enfants, (dont il tenait) deux à la main, un sur son dos . . .

Le peuple remplit tout le théâtre; des mères portent leurs enfants; des hommes soutiennent leurs femmes; les un tombent à terre, d'autres se soutiennent aux colonnades.

Ceux qui viennent par la terrasse expirent sur les marches . . . Des bruits souterrains continuent . . . Presque au moment où l'on baisse la toile, on fait tomber du cintre, depuis le Vésuve jusqu'au marches, des pierres de toute grosseur qui sont censées sortir du cratère.[73]

[Borella, entering the stage and looking to the right – "Masaniello, good God! He has triumphed, destiny is pronounced." Here half the chorus and all the people flee across the theater, while looking behind themselves like terrified people; they are followed by soldiers who, their weapons crossed, chase them quickly . . . Alphonse, followed by six officers, reenters from the right; immediately the half of the chorus that hasn't yet crossed the stage appears on the right, and get down on their knees; those on the left do the same; all seem to be asking for grace. Alphonse makes a sign, they get up and listen to his narration . . . "Masaniello is no more; they didn't know what to do but to flee" . . . [Fenella] climbs the stairway at the back. Arriving at the top, she hurls herself into the lava . . .

After the final chorus, eveyone is shaken by the greatest fright. A man arrives at the top of the staircase; from the top of the terrace the sound of a detonation is heard and engulfs him and three children, two held by his hands, and one on his back . . .

The people fill the entire theater; mothers carry their children; the men support their wives; some fall to the ground, others support themselves on the colonnades.

Those who come by the terrace expire on the steps . . . The underground noises continue . . . Almost at the moment when the curtain is lowered, rocks of all sizes are made to fall from the arch, from Vesuvius up to the steps.]

In a sense, the audience reacted to this incongruity like an audience during the French Revolution, responding to what they experienced on the basis of a political subtext. Indeed, revolutionary audiences had frequently imposed their interpretations in the official theaters, sometimes deriving a message consciously contrary to that which the government tried to imply.[74] And perhaps the audience now, in addition, was making another reference, an intertextual one, to another recent opera about crushed revolt. In *Le Siège de Corinthe* the Greeks were defeated, but the clear implication nevertheless was that morally they had won, finally burning their city now held by the Turks.

We learn of the government's response and attitude in the official *Moniteur Universel,* which reported on the opera at unusual length on March 2, 1828. It opens by noting the munificence of the government toward the Opéra dc Paris, contrary to the criticisms leveled at it on the part of "quelques frondeurs." To prove the contrary, it stresses the gradual evolution of which *La Muette de*

Portici is a part, implying that innovation had not been suddenly forced by circumstance but had indeed been continual.

Yet surprisingly it goes on to compare the opera with the *opéra-comique Masaniello,* and indeed to praise the latter over *La Muette,* in an effort to distance itself from the opera. For it claims that in *Masaniello* the insurrection and its motives were more successfully exposed than in the ambiguous libretto, which was clearly no longer an asset in official eyes. Not surprising is that the journal goes on to praise the role of the mute girl in the work and the artistry of its succession of tableaux, used effectively by the musician, choreographer, and decorator. For as it goes on to remark, "N'est-ce pas tout ce qu'on peut démander à l'Opéra quand on désire un auquel ce nom soit véritablement applicable?" [Is not this all one can ask of the Opéra when one wishes something to which this name can be truly applicable?] An opera is a spectacle of fantasy here: it is not a realistic drama; despite its references to the real work, it is not to be read as such. The review finally ends with a statement somewhat curious for a work considered generally, from an historical perspective, to have been a triumph: "Nous suiverons avec intérêt ses progrès dans l'opinion publique, et quand elle aura subi de nouvelles épreuves, nous entretiendrons de nouveau nos lectures" [We will follow its progress in public opinion with interest, and after it has undergone new tests, we will converse with our readers again].

The work, for the government, was not a triumph, or not the kind that it intended – not a success of subtle propaganda in support of the legitimacy of the regime. As we have seen, for officials it was now even more dangerous than *Masaniello* because of its very ambiguity and thus the ways that it could be used.

It was not only in performance, however, that the state was unable to control the work that it had originally been compelled to present in the interests of political image. We must recall, again, that an opera was considered a multiple source of danger, existing as a score, a libretto, illustrations, and a printed *mise en scène,* all of which could be used to evoke the meaning of the theatrical performance. Because of the events at the Académie Royale, according to contemporaries, the *mise en scène* immediately became a source of great interest, the equivalent of a modern best-seller.[75] For through it, those who were not present at the performance could nevertheless gain a sense of what was said in

43

the royal theater, or come closer to the theatrical utterance. And the *mise en scène,* we must remember, included not only description of the stage effects but also of the music, as well as explanations or interpretations of motivations and feelings.

But individual numbers from the opera lived on outside the theater as well, which is probably responsible for the myth that it could be heard all over Paris. For as in the theater, the public perceived that it could remove certain elements from their immediate context in such a manner so as to reverse their originally intended message. Apparently the fears of officials initially over individual numbers were well justified, although their theories as to what was safe were completely wrong. According to the press reports, in the theater the most popular numbers were not the solo airs but rather the stirring choral scenes, particularly the two barcarolles and Masaniello's "Refrain en choeur," "Amour sacré de la patrie." Significantly, both barcarolles deal with cleverly disguised subversion, beginning with the benign words, "Amis, la matinée est belle" [Friends, the morning is beautiful], but then continues "conduisez votre barque avec prudence; sur le rivage assemblez-vous . . . pêcheur, parle bas . . ." [steer your boat with prudence; assemble by the river bank . . . fisherman, speak softly].

It is important to note that *Masaniello* also contained a barcarolle, but in the form of a solo air sung by Masaniello himself. It too contained seditious lines; however, its theatrical effect appeared to be somewhat less seditious than Auber and Scribe's potent conflation. Indeed, here the framing of an incendiary text by a light and flowing rhythm had an effect precisely opposite the one officials had thought. The powerful contrast increased the resonant sense of subtle sedition, and immediately, for that reason, became symbolically charged. The chorus, then, embodied not the people in the sense that it would later in the operas of Verdi, but rather the contemporary spirit of subversion, or the ever growing *esprit frondeur* now magnified by numerous journals.

And because of the special symbolism of the choral barcarolles, it was not, as in *Masaniello,* the solo numbers that were immediately abstracted. Although other numbers from the opera lent themselves much more readily to such treatment in a thematic sense, apparently the first works to be transcribed were the barcarolles. Telling evidence may be found in Berbiguier's Fantaisie pour la flute avec accompagnement de piano composée sur des motifs favoris de *La Muette de Portici,* printed in Leipzig by H. A. Probst, in 1828. The favorite motives were largely those drawn from the seditous barcarolles as well as from one of the *cavatines* with equally potent words. The "Cavatine du Sommeil" would have been more appropriate material for such an instrumental *fantaisie,* with far more prominent and tuneful melodic material that would have seemingly been popular. But given the symbolism of the opera as determined by the theatrical event, the excerpts here symbolically evoked the text with which they were originally associated. The *cavatine* chosen is sung by Elvire, in the theater, to the resonant words "Ne repoussez pas votre souverain qui vous demande asile et tremble devant vous" [Don't thrust aside your sovereign who asks refuge of you and trembles before you]. Clearly, in a culture in which the tune of a *chanson* could evoke its subversive text, the same could certainly be true of operatic excerpts as well.

That the work was unstable or uncontrollable in meaning, that it could easily be radicalized both inside and outside the theater obviously caused the authorities great concern. Not only did they confront the subtly politicized reviews, the proliferation of popular arrangements and of the *mise en scène,* but also the many requests of provincial theaters to perform the work. Everywhere the regime now seemed to face the dilemma of its own success, or rather the fact that the opera had turned out to be the wrong kind of theatrical success. It had no choice but to allow one hundred performances within the next year at the Opéra, all of which drew great crowds (although the Opéra remained in debt). And the Maison du roi, similarly, had no choice but to praise the Opéra, if not for the political, at least for the technical effectiveness of the work.[76]

But *La Muette* was the kind of success that the regime could not now afford, and hence it led, in the end, to a much more sophisticated and scrupulous operatic surveillance. In June 1828 it established a new committee to oversee the Opéra's *mise en scène,* undoubtedly in a more semiotically conscious manner.[77] And by 1829, with the breakdown of Martignac's coalition of constitutional liberals and moderate royalists, further restrictions were imposed in the form of a new submission and authorization process for texts. No longer could decisions be made by either the

Opéra or the censors alone; all works to be performed were to be delivered to the minister of the interior before submission to the theatrical commission.[78] Presumably, officials there would spot dangers that might be overlooked by the academic censors, who were apparently unable to judge all the elements and dynamics of the theatrical experience.

A new set of operatic proclivities, then, began to arise from *La Muette,* as well as a new set of themes in discussions and commentaries on grand opera. It was clear now that not just different interpretations of grand works were possible, as in the Revolution, but indeed different, unexpected political messages as well. For these reasons, the power of grand opera, for the regime and for its opponents, was henceforth to become practically synonymous with *La Muette de Portici.* And hence it is not surprising that its history soon waxed into legend, extending beyond the limits of France by 1830 and enduring long after. Nor is it surprising that, as we shall see, when revived in Paris it was always approached with the most extreme care with respect to political timing and to the *mise en scène.*

La Muette de Portici helped establish a manner of reading and interpreting grand opera, both from the perspective of content and style and on the basis of a political subtext. And so it led directly to a far more discerning *"politique de l'Opéra,"* as a vivid reminder of the complex ways that the political could be imbricated with the art. It brought an awareness of the way in which this fusion could both affect artistic and political perception and alert the audience to contradictions between cultural rhetoric and political fact. The opera, then, if it heralded a new departure, this departure was the tendency to use the Opéra both to claim political legitimacy as well as to contest this claim.

The opera stands at the origins not only of technical innovations in staging and content; it articulates the rise of conceptions and policies to which they were causally bound. *La Muette de Portici* is the opera that ushers in a new operatic politics both in terms of official rhetoric and subsequent political exchange through the works. For this reason, it is not surprising that political and operatic terms could fuse around it, as they did at a *fête* for the king of Naples on May 3, 1830. The future Louis-Philippe, present, as we may recall, at *La Muette*'s premiere, and acutely aware of its tensions, remarked, "Nous dansons sur un volcan."[79]

2

THE POLITICS OF GRAND OPERA'S RISE AND DECLINE

"L'Opéra entrera en régie intéressée et le Directeur ne sera plus soumis qu'à la surveillance de la Commission chargée de faire exécuter le Cahier des charges dans l'intérêt de l'art et du gouvernement."[1]

[The Opéra will enter into a partnership and the Director will only be subject to the surveillance of the commission charged with seeing that the contract is executed in the interests of art and of the government.]

ROBERT LE DIABLE and *Les Huguenots* have long been the cynosures of attention in established accounts of the rise or the development and efflorescence of French grand opera. As I have noted earlier, within the perspective that considers its dynamic inscribed within a commercial evolution, these become the key works in which to trace how the new conventions emerged: They mark successive stages in the articulation of a theatrical art that was consciously and effectively designed to appeal specifically to the French bourgeoisie. In consequence, these two operas have come to be considered perhaps the most lucid illustrations of such institutional goals and by extension of a sensationalized theatrical art.

I maintain that they are indeed apt illustrations, but of something substantially different – of the theater's new political function and the impact this had on its art. Both operas were bound up in the attempt to define an operatic genre appropriate to the Opéra now as a public institution, still serving a politically representative function. And so the appropriate background against which to understand the goals that the institution and art were to serve is that of the politically symbolic problems the new regime faced. For *Robert le Diable* and *Les Huguenots*, like *La Muette de Portici*, were works whose evolution and meaning were inextricably tried to the problem of "image." All three were presented with a view to this specific political function, but all three instead eluded it and made the Opéra a contestatory realm. In *Robert le Diable* we see the search for an image, in *Les Huguenots* an attempt to protect it, and in both cases an aesthetic-political commentary that centered on image versus fact. Both works led to artistic change through a transformation in operatic policies on the basis of perceptions of their success as a political image diffused through art.

It was not long after its heady triumph in the revolution of July 1830 that the regime of Louis-Philippe faced a series of exigent political decisions. Not least among these was the nettlesome problem of political symbolization, or of how to define a political identity that could be conveyed legibly through symbolic means. Since a certain ambiguity of identity had abetted the regime's precipitous triumph, it now faced the delicate problem of maintaining the very diverse sources of its support.

Aware that the contradictions of Bourbon policies had been exacerbated by its cultural symbols, the new regime sought carefully to define itself conclusively against them. It was aware that its new symbols would have to establish a link with the people of France but also confirm its political credibility and legitimacy in a different sense. For it had to seek an image that would balance its claims to a new liberal future, based on a new social support, with its roots and precedents in the national past. Its cultural challenge, then, was partly to establish an image appropriately befitting the dignity of a monarch of France but one now in touch with social reality.

While traditional histories of grand opera have stressed the innovative aspects of the new regime and its desire to appear both socially as well as politically progressive, a trend of revisionist history over the past twenty years has emphasized the opposite aspect, focusing on the key issue of the so-called myth of a bourgeois revolution. It has raised the question as to whether the perceptions of contemporaries such as Tocqueville and Marx accord with the actual social facts that we have at our disposal today.[2] Did the bourgeoisie, in fact, obtain political power at this point in French history? And indeed, to whom or what, historically, does this designation properly apply? These are all, as we shall see, of relevance to the problem of defining what the state actually wished to accomplish, in time, in institutions like the Opéra.

A number of historians over the past two decades have explicitly argued that the French bourgeoisie did not "make, fight, or profit from the Revolution." The new chamber elected in 1831, moreover, which according to general terminology might be called bourgeois, did not represent what we could properly call "business interests." Several studies have thus questioned the dictum, so fundamental to the present historiography of grand opera, that "the rule of the middle class equals the rule of the bourgeoisie, and the rule of the bourgeoisie equals the rule of businessmen." Indeed, they have rather established the substantial dominance of landed wealth, thus revealing to the contrary a strong social continuity with the Restoration.[3] And after the 1830 revolution not only was there no real "purge" of the higher state offices, but the social composition of the office holders was, in fact, not new.

The resulting alliance was one between the aristocracy and the great bourgeois dynasties, and it produced in the end a socially conservative and yet a seemingly politically liberal regime. Soon after 1830, then, artisans and workers, intellectuals and peasants, were to find themselves extruded from political power in France.[4] The monarchy was in fact a compromise between democracy and legitimacy, one that rejected the principles of legitimate monarchy but also the democracy of the French Revolution.[5]

But at first it appeared a compromise between several different political factions, each with its own *chimère,* its individual conception of the social and political future.[6] And so, in attempting to secure his hold on power, the monarch used symbols, being fully aware of both the potential political benefits and risks they could bring. Too precise a definition would be dangerous, and yet he needed an image, one that would not involve ideology but would communicate responsiveness and cultural vitality.

Louis-Philippe was well aware that symbols were conceptual forces, and that they would be taken seriously as indices to the vision and spirit of an otherwise amorphous regime. And he desired that his regime resuscitate a sense of grandeur and glory that was now presumed dead and hence felt the necessity of finding an alternative to the Restoration's unheroic *mise en scène.* The new one was to impart a sense of both a political and a cultural revolution, although the precise implications of these revolutions could be construed in different ways. For some, the fall of Charles X meant a renewal of the revolutionary tradition; for others, it was only an incident in the process of the restoration of the monarchy in France.[7]

But the regime also faced more specific requirements in its choice of political symbols: It had firmly to establish the principles that distinguished it conclusively from royalism. And since it hailed the revolution as a "patriotic reprisal" in the "people's name," the public expected the symbolism it chose to evoke a sense of the nation. For several reasons, the regime was thus obliged to seek legitimacy in public emotion, or in the people's "will," the ostensible principle from which the revolution had sprung.[8]

The immediate problem was the kind of cultural material the regime was to use to convey this message, or of where it would find the most resonant expressions of the popular will. One answer was to turn immediately to the visual representations that had sprung up almost immediately in the popular arts and crafts. In addition, revolutionary sentiment seemed to express itself almost spontaneously in song, in a flood of political *chansons* unleashed by the ideological and emotional tide. Already, in the theaters as well as in the streets, popular *chansons* such as "La Parisienne" (quickly dubbed the hymn of the July Revolution) could be continually heard.[9]

It was to identify with this wave of sentiment that one of Louis-Philippe's first politically symbolic acts was to publicly lead the singing of the revolutionary "Marseillaise."[10] He immediately sensed the necessity of accommodating the virulent revolutionary sentiment and hence of assuming the appropriate gestures as well as the stance of a "*roi citoyen.*" But it is important to note that governing was following the necessities of circumstance for Louis-Philippe; his political guide was not doctrine but the quest for order, which sometimes meant going against his own preferences. Louis-Philippe, in fact, was far from being a bourgeois citizen-king: he was rather thoroughly aristocratic in his orientation and his tastes.[11] His first reactions, then, were clearly intuitive and pragmatic and thus far less problematic for the immediate future than the next major challenge he faced. This was to redefine institutions of culture with a view to the future, and in a way that would simultaneously seem consonant with his political identity and his immediate goals.

In the realm of elite culture, the primary problem was to define both an institutional structure as well as a goal for the art to be produced that was symbolically different from the preceding Bourbons. In structure as well as in ideology the challenge was to achieve a special kind of balance that would conciliate conflicting expectations and the regime's own diverse political claims. The political power of the monarch being based, in theory, on a popular consensus, it was certainly incumbent on traditional institutions of culture somehow to acknowledge this fact. They also were expected to seek legitimacy in the public will, in its emotions, tastes, and interests, in telling contrast with the preceding regime. The people were to be the only source of political sovereignty now, and hence all institutions were to take this as their point of orientation and be guided by popular feeling and interest.[12] This fact has led to the frequent claim that such recognition constituted a deferral to public taste, in effect a simple recognition of the supremacy of the new bourgeois public.[13] Yet did this complex regime, while seeking to beguile a new electorate, ignore other aspects of its identity and support and keep them out of the realm of culture?

To penetrate the new cultural policy we must also remain aware of the compromise required by the political ideology it professed. The regime, after all, was *Orléaniste*, which in its time connoted far more than simple identity of interest with the increasing predominance of the bourgeois class.

Like the revolution itself, Orléanism stood for more than the bourgeoisie and their values, and it was the Orléanist perspective that guided the reform of state institutions of culture. As recent scholars have observed, the bourgeoisie was not all of Orléanism, and the Orléanist bourgeoisie was only in part a business bourgeoisie. There was an Orléanist aristocracy, which prominently included the nobility of the Empire; there was an aristocracy of birth, and, significantly, an aristocracy of talent as well. Orléanism, if anything, was "not simply the egotistic defense of its own interests by a commercial or financial bourgeoisie . . . it was government by the elites."[14] This factor should alert us to certain significant aspects of the structure and nature of both leadership and surveillance in Orléanist institutions of culture. It should alert us also to the existence of a gap between the public rhetoric of the new regime and the institutional reality beneath it – one of special importance here for it was to affect the Opéra.

The rhetoric of the victorious Orléanists, the basis for the once commonly accepted interpretation of the 1830 revolution, was perhaps most clearly articulated by François Guizot. According to him, this was the moment of the rule of the *"classes moyennes,"* as opposed to both the *"classes populaires"* and the *"classe aristocratique."* But historians have recently emphasized the context in which Guizot employed such rhetoric; they have pointed out that here it was more a statement of principles than a description of reality. The idea of middle class rule was, in fact, still extremely vague and often employed for polemical purposes by both journalists and politicians.[15]

The new regime did recognize a danger in simple deferral to popular taste, both in national, public symbols and in institutions of culture. Having observed the cultural politics of the later 1820s, it perceived the possibility of unintended radical construal of political symbols.[16] In addition, it also recognized the importance of upholding artistic quality, for the Legitimist press continually reminded the public of the prosperity of the visual arts under the Bourbons. Recognizing that the failure to foster great art was a significant reflection on the regime, it lost no time in making dire predictions for the future unless leadership was immediately assumed.[17] One response to these challenges was an attempt on the part of the crown to identify with France's great and established tradition of excellence in the arts. This identity could be communicated visually through the construction of new museums or through the symbolic reorganization of those that already existed. It was, in part, through his museum at Versailles that the monarch attempted to identify himself closely with the outstanding epochs of the nation's art.

Such facts have led to the observation that official culture in nineteenth-century Europe "mirrored the tenacious perseverance of preindustrial civil and political societies": that "in form, content, and style, the artifacts of high culture continued to be anchored in conventions that relayed and celebrated traditions supportive of the old order."[18] It is important to note that in the specific case of Louis-Philippe, such traditions played a strong legitimizing function, helping to balance the regime's identity, to relate it to France's past and future.

But in both popular and elite art, the regime at first recognized the need simultaneously to express and control more radical ideological aspirations. The question was where these ideals could be publicly but also safely expressed, and in the visual arts, at least, it showed great sagacity in this regard. It was in the placid, monumental context of great public buildings that Louis-Philippe attempted to inscribe the visual attributes of the revolutionary tradition in France. Public buildings could communicate identity with this tradition in a safely iconic manner, balancing the inflammatory with the monumental and hence with the stable. Here, then, we see another example of the Orléanist trait of "accommodation to what exists," in this case to tradition and new aspirations at once.[19]

However, the monarch's decisions were sometimes more difficult and often incorrect, and in specific cases they involved contradictions that were to become increasingly problematic. It is significant that the history that the July Monarchy originally mobilized as ideology against its enemies was also to be turned against its own eventual conservatism. Such was the case of the column erected at the Place de la Bastille, a *"double hommage"* to 1830 and, explicitly, to 1789. And at the Arc de Triomphe, on which Rude exalted the *élan national* of 1792, again, the reference turned out to be far more to the Revolution than to the constitutional monarchy. Of course, at the beginning of the regime it was difficult to honor the recent revolution without exalting the French Revolution and the Republic at the same time. But the monarchy was to pay a price for the bold claims made through such symbolic means, not only here but prominently in the Opéra as well.[20]

It is in light of these observations that we must now attempt to see the specific problems that the Opéra presented in 1830, the regime's responses and its subsequent dilemma. Again, the issue was not only repertoire but also institutional structure, which carried its own symbolic message in the context of the preceding regime. And once more the structure that communicated the right political message was not always the structure that would best insure the development of the right kind of political content.

Having been embroiled in the political tensions that brought about the fall of the previous regime, the Opéra was a particularly delicate and public issue now. Officials were acutely aware that the public would read their decisions about the Opéra in view of the message that it had communicated immediately before. The structure would also have to avoid the pitfalls of the Restoration, which was obviously unable to effectively oversee its own repertoire. For reasons of symbolism, of the organization of surveillance, as well as general practicality, they knew, first of all, that it could not continue to belong to the king's Liste civile.

Officials were aware, however, not only of the dangers of the Opéra; they recognized its unique potential if the right structure could be defined. It could, if effective, establish ties to public emotions and tastes, encourage current interests and enthusiasms, and thus underscore the responsiveness of the new regime. But at the same time, this structure would have to insure the production of a dignified image, one appropriate to the royal house and the great artistic tradition of France. Moreover, it would have to make sure that the repertoire engaged only the right kinds of political emotions, hence avoiding another embarrassing *La Muette de Portici*. But ironically, for symbolic reasons, *La Muette* had to be one of the first works performed after the revolution of 1830; not only was it hailed as being "an authentic picture of the barricades," but to emphasize its patriotic significance and topical resonance, Nourrit sang "La Parisienne" on stage.[21]

The structure that the regime defined was one that addressed all these troublesome issues, one that involved substantial innovation, but in which certain traditional elements remained. The new Opéra, like the original Académie Royale de Musique, was a *privilège* – a concession or trust, a protected theater that was accorded a national status. Like Lully's original institution, it was both commercial and official at once: It was expected to be a paying institution while still remaining responsible to the crown. A telling expression of this public, political identity is the fact that the curtain at the Opéra throughout the period of Louis-Philippe was a depiction of the granting of the initial *privilège:* it clearly showed Louis XIV handing the keys of the Opéra to its original founders, before Lully, the team of Perrin and Cambert.[22]

But the official *privilège* communicated a new kind of political message now, particularly in light of the direct control by the state in the preceding regime. To understand this message we must carefully examine the Opéra's statutes, or the Cahier des charges, and the reality of how it both symbolized and furthered specific political interests.

The new Cahier was not intended to model the Opéra on a liberal vision of culture by making it into a bourgeois business enterprise in a simple sense. It was rather intended to apply the Orléanist principle of conflict of interests, as constituting the fabric of political life, for the common good, to the Opéra. The new Opéra's motor was indeed this conflict – one between the desire to please public taste, to respond to its interests and enthusiasms, and the exigencies of political prudence. The Cahier set up a tension between a director with the status of "*entrepreneur*" and an official commission, representative of the state, designed to protect its interests. In this sense, the contradictions of the state's political plans for the Opéra were institutionalized or inscribed in its structure, a fact that was to be decisive for the development of the repertoire.

These innovations seemed daring to many, particularly in view of all that was now at stake, including the acknowledged danger of opera after *La Muette de Portici*. In fact, the very idea of transforming the Opéra from a *régie directe* to an *entreprise particulière* aroused much immediate opposition. But proponents not only believed in the symbolic usefulness of the new structure, they were convinced that it could more effectively thwart trouble than a *régie directe*.[23]

In terms of political symbolism, the Opéra was no longer "le royaume de droit divin, élévé à la Maison du roi" [the realm of divine right, erected from the Maison du roi] as in the Restoration: it was not to be subject to the caprices or vagaries of the royal court, a fact that officials now observed had undermined all the director's constructive efforts.[24] For both symbolic and practical reasons, different interests would be represented, and from this process of compromise would issue a safe and effective art. As so often stated by contemporaries, the goal was to avoid the "arbitrary"; everything was to be thought out now and planned with a view to the probable consequences. To the extent that it was run on the model of a bourgeois business, then, it was less for purely financial reasons than for ideological and political ones.

The primary changes involved concerned the place of the Opéra in the bureaucratic structure, and concomitantly, its means of funding and its manner of surveillance. Again, for symbolic and financial reasons, the Opéra was removed from the Liste civile and now placed under the general auspices of the Ministry of the Interior. And conveniently, this had the practical effect of relieving the Opéra of the legal obligations to pay the considerable pension that the former regime had promised Rossini.[25] As we shall see, it was no longer clear, despite the success of *Guillaume Tell,* that Rossini could create the appropriate image for the new Opéra. And despite the political content of *Guillaume Tell,* Rossini's associations were still quite strongly with the preceding regime; also the Opéra now wanted a fresh stylistic departure. Just as important was the fact that the Opéra would no longer be administered separately from the other Parisian theaters, but would be subject to the same criteria. Again, this was not only for symbolic but also for practical reasons: if it was to relate artistically to the boulevard theaters, then it should be placed under the same controls.[26]

The financial implications of this change of structure are often overstated, for the expense of the Opéra under the new system was not substantially less. Certainly, under the Restoration the Opéra's expenses had grown prohibitive, its expenditures finally reaching the sum of 1,670,000 francs per year. This had necessitated a raise in the subvention from 600,000 to 800,000 francs, and then in 1830 to approximately 950,000 francs.[27] Under the new regime, the budget of the Opéra began at the slightly higher sum of 1,700,000 francs, with a subvention of 800,000 francs; this amount was gradually to be reduced as the Opéra prospered financially, the first and second years to 760,000 francs, and then to 710,000 francs for the next three. The Opéra did lose the traditional payments made to it by the minor theaters, but as we shall see, this loss was to be compensated by a stricter policy regarding free entries.[28] However, as will soon become evident, the Opéra was to profit financially for only a very short time. For reasons connected with its political function, it was within several years to fail.

The new director, Emile Véron, was clearly optimistic about the opportunity to make the Opéra into a profitable institution. As his initial rhetoric reveals, he was apparently unable, at first, to see the real rationale behind the new structure or to understand the forces with which he would contend. In fact, he resorted to

56

considerable machinations to obtain the *privilège* for himself, wresting it from the incumbent, Lubbert, who had hoped to try the new arrangement. Véron, however, had several advantages: important friends in the world of the arts and letters, proven entrepreneurial and marketing skills, and considerable financial backing.

The son of a *marchand papetier* (stationer), Véron had begun his career in medicine, soon achieveing financial success by discovering the market potential for someone else's invention. Véron purchased the rights to a promising *pâte pectorale* (chest paste), proceeding to promote it commercially by introducing pioneering techniques of modern publicity. Soon he was involved in journalism, becoming a collaborator on *La Quotidienne,* and then founding the *Revue de Paris,* which published the young French romantic authors.[29]

Véron was already a wealthy man by the 1830 revolution, but significantly, he did not substantially risk his own funds in the Opéra. He relied, rather, on the aid of one of the wealthiest financiers of the day, the Marquis de Las Marismas (originally a Spaniard named Aguado). Indeed, when Véron was seeking the post, he used this support to his advantage, letting it be known that he had the backing not only of the marquis, who had already proved useful to the government, but also potentially of the Rothschilds. Indeed, Aguado's title was the result of the considerable financial aid with which he had supplied the French state, a practice that he was now continuing, in another form, through the Opéra. The marquis lent Véron a large portion of his *cautionnement,* or security, supplying 200,000 francs to Véron's 50,000, at the low interest of five percent.[30]

The Opéra awarded Véron a contract for a period of six years, which he began on March 1, 1831. He was, however, to undergo what was ostensibly a period of trial, running the Opéra for the government until June, and thereafter as entrepreneur. So insecure were officials about the potential results of this change, especially in a period of mounting political tensions, that they moved with the most extreme caution. Little of this, apparently, did Véron perceive, or that a provision in his Cahier des charges, seemingly a routine formality, would so integrally affect his interests.

This was the institution of a Commission de Surveillance to oversee the Opéra, but specifically charged with making sure of

57

the enforcement of the Cahier des charges. This body was, in effect, to oversee every movement of the new director, acting as agents of the state and hence protectors of its financial and political interests. As will become evident shortly, the freedom of the director was, in fact, strictly limited despite the implications of his title as Directeur-Entrepreneur.

Created by an *arrêté* of February 28, 1831, the members of this body were appointed by the comte de Montalivet, the minister of the interior.[31] Perhaps reflecting a division of power or responsibility for the Opéra, it was the king who appointed the director, as opposed to the minister of the interior. Again, the commission was carefully chosen for both symbolic and pragmatic reasons, as we can see by examining the major figures in the original body.

The first commission comprised five members, all of whom were drawn from the various elites that now characterized the Orléanist regime. All were identified in the decree by their official, political function, or in terms of their status as representatives of different governmental agencies: "M. le Duc de Choiseul, Pair de France, Président; Edmond Blanc, avocat aux conseils du Roi et à la Cour de Cassation, membre de la commission chargée par nous d'examiner l'état actuel des théâtres; Armand Bertin, rédacteur du *Journal des Débats;* D'Hennerville, Inspecteur du mobilier de la Liste civile; Royer Collard, Chef de la division des Beaux-arts."[32]

In examining the careers of these individuals, there is an important point in common to note: in the Restoration all had faithfully served what was then the opposition. Its president, Antoine-Gabriel de Choiseul, duke and peer of France, had served in several administrations, extending back to the ancien régime. Born in 1760, he began his political career in the midst of the turbulent meetings of the parliament, in 1787. During the Revolution he had tried, unsuccessfully, to lead a group of counterrevolutionaries into France, but was caught, imprisoned, and escaped. He later returned to France, but was deported under Napoleon, only to return to the Chamber of Peers during the Restoration. He soon became a popular political figure, commanding public confidence in the period of growing tension during the final years of the regime; in fact, he found himself named, along with Lafayette and the Maréchal Gérard, to the new provisional government. Soon thereafter he became an *aide de camp* to the new king, Louis-Philippe, as well as the Gouverneur du Louvre, while continuing his role in the Chamber of Peers.[33]

Hippolyte Royer-Collard was another member of the commission who was obviously being rewarded for his stand in the late Restoration. The son of a noted doctor, he himself went into medicine, being named, upon his father's death, the personal doctor to Charles X. He began, in addition, to publish not only on medical matters, but also on politics and literature, making a great deal of friends in the more progressive world of the arts and letters. When these friends achieved positions of political power in 1830, they promoted Royer-Collard, who became "Le Chef de Division au Ministère de l'Instruction Publique."[34]

The pattern of reward continues with other members of the commission, but another pattern also emerges: that of prominence in literature or the press. The secretary of the commission, Edmond Cavé, had become a well-known literary figure in France during the final years of the Restoration. Shortly before the revolution, he published a series of dramatic proverbs with a clearly political intent, entitled *Soirées de Neuilly*. The work was timely, highly successful, and gained Cavé considerable renown, as did his position as editor of the liberal journal, *Le Globe*. Again, his friends took care of him after the revolution of 1830, and he became the director of the *Beaux-arts* and the theaters in the Ministry of the Interior. Moreover, as such, Cavé was known to have exercised the function of "une sorte de haute censure sur les pièces qui pourrait blesser le gouvernement du roi Louis-Philippe."[35] It is significant that through a figure like Cavé, censorship entered through the back door so to speak, as we shall see when examining the Commission of Surveillance's reports.

The premise of these appointments was undoubtedly that all the individuals chosen would identify with the government's interests and would protect them against the director. Not seeing this, little did Véron suspect, at the beginning of his administration, how contestatory their relationship would be and how much power the commission would have. Although technically the commission was charged with the task of overseeing the enforcement of the Cahier, in fact this involved a great deal of legal interpretation of the document itself. Little was explicitly spelled out, and so the issue of what was acceptable and what constituted an infraction was one that the commission, in reality, had to define.

As in the Cahiers of his predecessors in preceding administrations, the director was limited to the production of operas and ballets of a certain genre; and as in the Restoration, as well as the Napoleonic period, the genre here was designated by the ambiguous appellation, *grand opéra*. Although the term had been applied in the latter years of the ancien régime, its ostensible meaning became explicit under Napoleon's theatrical hierarchy. The *grands théâtres* were, above all, distinguished by the nature of their subject matter: "les sujets ont été puisés dans la mythologie ou dans l'histoire, et dont les principaux personnages sont des rois ou des héros"[36] [the subjects are drawn from mythology or history; principal subjects are kings or heroes]. As we may recall, the question of content, while still fairly clear under Napoleon, had become increasingly problematic in the Bourbon Restoration. We shall soon see that the problem of what can be considered grand in a more contemporary style continued to plague the commission throughout the reign of Louis-Philippe. After *La Muette,* it could no longer be associated with the *féerie,* or the magical aspects of the monarchy, nor with classical or academic models.

However, certain connotations of grandeur, or of the *grands théâtres,* continued to endure and to remain a fundamental part of their definition. Grandeur was traditionally defined by qualities of luxury and spectacle, which in the Cahier des charges now translated into certain specifications: costumes and decors were to be entirely new in the production of new works, and nothing too worn or shoddy was to be allowed on this royal stage. But now, in the light of the Restoration's experience, another clause entered the Cahier des charges, one mandating scrupulous accuracy in all historical designs and details.[37] The "first" royal stage was still, after all, a projection of royal image, which had to be protected against the possibility of attacks on its credibility. Officials had learned the lesson well that anachronism would not be acceptable, making their concern with authentic detail, at times, almost an obsession.

The commission, then, was charged with the awesome task of upholding grandeur, but having no clear conception, beyond the forces employed, of what this really implied. A grand opera was clearly in five acts, employing a certain number of performers and sets, but what this meant qualitatively proved to be another question indeed. Such ambiguity, however, did not prevent the Commission of Surveillance from exercising its power immediately and in every conceivable way.

A later commission, in retrospect, defined the way in which the first commission initially exercised its power, and the specific mechanisms that they used:

> L'ancienne commission adressait au Ministre des rapports fréquents; à la fin de chaque mois, pour expliquer les certificats concluants au paiement de la subvention; à la fin de l'année, sur l'ensemble de la direction . . . Tous ses rapports embrassant ordinairement deux ordres de faits; d'une part, les questions et les circonstances intéressant l'art, la pompe et la dignité de l'Opéra, la tendance de la direction et ses efforts, la situation de l'entreprise, etc., et d'autre part, l'exécution des obligations imposées au Directeur-Entrepreneur, relativement au personnel, au matérial, au nombre d'ouvrages nouveaux à représenter etc.[38]

> [The old commission addressed frequent reports to the minister; at the end of each month, to explain the certificates for the payment of the subvention; at the end of each year on the ensemble of the direction . . . All these reports ordinarily em braced three things; on the one hand, the questions and circumstances concerning the art, the pomp and the dignity of the Opéra, the tendencies of the direction and its efforts, the situation of the enterprise, etc., and on the other hand, the execution of the obligations imposed on the Directeur-Entrepreneur, relating to the personnel, to the material, to the number of new works to be performed etc.]

The commission, then, supplied both monthly reports and yearly evaluations concerning the director and technical, financial, logistic, as well as purely artistic matters. In effect, the commission intervened in practically every aspect of the institution's functioning, making it impossible for the director to proceed without its authorization.

No expenditures could be made for the building, no committees reorganized, no artists given raises, hired, dismissed, or retired without their mediation.[39] Véron, moreover, was obliged to make all his requests and complaints through them, and they, in turn, offered their advice to the minister or other relevant authority. Véron had constantly to seek their approval from relatively minor to major details regarding each of the productions that the Opéra undertook.

Véron, however, apparently assumed that there was a great deal more flexibility in the statutes of his Cahier des charges than did the officious commission. Frequently he wished to request exceptions to some of its explicit rules, particularly to the stipulation that old costumes not be allowed for new productions.[40] But often, too, Véron attempted to bypass or defy the commission, only to meet with harsh retribution in the form of immediate and expensive fines.[41] From the start, Emil Véron was on a collision course with the commission, and slowly the tensions would increase to the point of forcing Véron, in effect, to resign.

The commission's intervention in artistic matters took many and varied forms, extending from the most minor details to substantive decisions of policy. Although there was still a nominal *Jury littéraire et musicale,* the commission heard readings of all libretti and had a major voice in such decisions. It oversaw negotiations with all composers for the Opéra, sometimes summoning those whom it considered experts in order better to inform themselves.[42] It attended dress rehearsals to verify whether a premier should indeed take place, and then, immediately after the premiere, prepared a detailed report on its effect.

Here, of course, it is essential to grasp the kinds of criteria the commissioners used, the standards of value they applied, the guiding concepts from which they worked. For they not only applied their developing understanding of what grandeur in the state theaters now comprised but also their sense of what was to happen theatrically around the repertoire, or of the kind of spectacle it was to be. The commission gauged its decisions upon an understanding or a sense of the theater, of what it was to accomplish in relation to the other theaters, and of the ambience they considered appropriate. They also had a conception of the implicit audience for the theater: the new political public, to whom all state institutions were now addressed. They had, then, a certain conception of the kind of image that the theater was to project, and hence of the kind of political message that the Opéra, as an organ of politics, was to emit. It was this that informed its decisions, that imbued it with a sense of the cadre it desired, and which in some cases (and perhaps misleading to all) converged with Véron's interests.

For example, it was now a matter of national symbolism, as well as of financial interest, that the former *entrées de tolérances* and *entrées de faveurs* be curtailed. Now, as opposed to the Restoration, only a small number of the highest state officials, as well as selected journalists, were granted free entry to the Opéra. Significantly, as a matter of symbolism, in the public record the king himself was not set apart for special treatment in this regard. Listed under "R," for "Roi des Français," in the Opéra's subscription file is Louis-Philippe, who took the first three *loges d'avant-scène* at 18,300 francs for the year.[43]

Interests also converged in matters of audience behavior or comportment: again, Véron's concerns were practical and that of the commission symbolic and political. Both were intent on defining a new kind of ambience for the Opéra, and hence on dissociating it as clearly as possible from "the exclusive habits" of the court. In 1831, for example, the commission ruled that the official *corps diplomatiques* would no longer be able to interrupt the performance by entering its loges during the *entr'actes*. For the audience given priority now was theoretically the entire electorate of France: the Opéra was their domain, their property, and no longer that of the court.

Véron's statements concerning the audience, however, are often misleading, for as usual he failed to see, at first, just how he was being used. His simplistic slogans, so often cited, have led to much misunderstanding, especially his famous claim that the Opéra heralded "l'événement de la bourgeoisie." As we have seen, such claims among politicians like Guizot were more the reflection of a program or goal than a social fact. And the same was true with reference to the Opéra, which here played an important role in promoting the mood of economic expansion and capitalism integral to the image of a bourgeois monarchy.[44]

Certainly the bourgeoisie was included in the audience that officials hoped to reach, but it was an even broader spectrum of French society that they had in mind. For there was no desire to alienate the various Orléanist elites, including the new aristocracy of talent as well as those of money and birth. Significantly, the other half of Véron's statement, so often omitted today, concerns the importance of "le public élite qui payait ses stalles et ses loges"

63

[the elite public that pays for its stalls and loges]. Also generally omitted but equally important is Véron's other statement that "Il faut que le succès et les recettes de l'Opéra soient un démenti donné aux émeutes"[45] [the success and the receipts of the Opéra should discourage riots].

Where Véron was successful in realizing his specific aims, it was in those cases where his interests coincided, for different reasons, with those of the commission. As we shall see, the question of who determined which values or policies triumphed is a complex and difficult one, and involves perceiving the compromise reached. It was only in a partial sense that the Directeur-Entrepreneur shaped the character and the art of the Académie Royale de Musique. For the Opéra was not an institution of patronage, and neither was it a business enterprise: it was rather a subtle complex amalgam peculiar to nineteenth-century France. And it was from this amalgam that the new conception of grand opera emerged, through a gradual and painful process in the early years of the new regime.

The first work in which we can see this process and the specific, often subtle manner in which such surveillance worked is the case of Véron's first large new production, Meyerbeer's *Robert le Diable*. By tracing the interplay of director and commission in this opera, we can see how a new aesthetic goal emerged, as well as its relation to a political goal; or how it was that both director and commission, together with the artists, "engineered" the success of a work and then evaluated its "effect." But it is important to remember that the genesis of the opera as well as the evaluation of it was inscribed in the process of defining a new kind of grandeur that would be appropriate to the theater now. *Robert le Diable* turned out to be the test case through which the commission arrived at its initial criteria for defining an operatic success "in the government's interest."

Many histories of *Robert le Diable* have emphasized that the opera began as an *opéra-comique* in the later years of the Restoration and was then transformed into a *grand opéra*. But few have noted or stressed the fact that for the "new" Académie Royale du Musique the work was an inherited obligation, one imposed on it for both legal and ethical reasons. Despite its obvious desire to begin afresh with a completely new work, the commission agreed with the Ministre de Commerce et des Travaux Publics that a commitment

64

had already been made.[46] Hence the opera presented a delicate problem, being a work neither director nor commission chose, yet the one through which Véron was to prove himself and the commission in their ability to guide the theater. More specifically, through it they had to establish that the Opéra was no longer the *vieille machine* that it was accused of being in the previous decade, that it had a new artistic vision.

As previously noted, Meyerbeer had initially conceived *Robert le Diable* for performance at the Opéra-Comique under its director, Pixérécourt, the noted writer of melodramas.[47] The composer had arrived in Paris in January 1825 to oversee the production of his *Il Crociato in Egitto* at the Théâtre-Italien. Upon its success, the Odéon produced his *Marguerite d'Anjou* the following year, which, like his previous opera, was based on a melodrama by Pixérécourt. Fortunately for Meyerbeer, his younger brother had become friends with Casimir and Germain Delavigne and the latter had arranged to collaborate with Scribe on a libretto for the composer. Apparently the idea had come to Scribe after the success of *Le Comte Ory*, which he perceived as being in a similar vein to the story of Robert. Scribe thus proposed the idea of such a work, one with a *décor médiéval*, to Meyerbeer early in 1827. Although Meyerbeer distrusted Scribe because of his "caractère incertain et changeant," he maintained cordial relations with the writer and saw that it was in his interests to agree.[48]

Scribe produced a text in three acts; considered appropriate to the Opéra-Comique, it was read in the spring of 1829 and accorded a unanimous vote for performance.[49] The censors who examined the work noted its affinities with *Der Freischütz* and thus considered it, like the Weber opera, to be devoid of danger. Although there were questionable passages, good won over evil in the end, and hence only a small reference to "un seigneur chevalier" was suppressed. Meyerbeer, moreover, was someone long known to the Opéra, his name having appeared in the reports of the Maison du roi as early as 1821. At that point he was referred to as "a German composer of great merit, who, while not imitating Rossini too much, seeks originality too much."[50] But by the late 1820s, as we have seen, this very quality was at a premium at the Opéra as well as at the Opéra-Comique.

Meyerbeer himself, however, was not content with a performance at the Opéra-Comique, sensing the possibility now of in-

65

terest at the Opéra; and knowing further that La Rochefoucauld was disposed kindly to him after his success at the "Italiens," and was seeking the subject for a ballet, he decided to approach the vicomte. Indeed, as early as 1823, Meyerbeer, in a letter to his friend Levasseur, stated his desire to work for the Opéra because of all that it offered him creatively, "les moyens immenses qu'offre l'Opéra français à un artiste qui désire écrire de la musique véritablement dramatique"[51] [the immense means that the French Opéra offers an artist who wants to write truly dramatic music].

Undoubtedly, in the wake of the tumultuous *La Muette de Portici,* La Rochefoucauld was looking for a safer work, yet one with an historical atmosphere requiring lavish spectacle. After reading the scenario, the vicomte determined that it could be made suitable to the Académie Royale and promptly ordered the necessary revisions to make the work into a *grand opéra.* Hence, in the autumn of 1829 the libretto passed from the Opéra-Comique to the Opéra, although in March 1830 La Rochefoucauld was still pressing Scribe to finish the revisions. To make the work into an historical *féerie* suitable to the Opéra, Scribe deemphasized those minor characters who were familiar types from *opéra-comique,* such as Raimbaut. But given the tense mood of operatic officials in this period, as we have observed, this was not an easy task, even for someone as dramatically adroit as Scribe. Upon receiving the text, Meyerbeer immediately set to work, and was able to deliver his score to Lubbert in May 1830, just three months before the revolution.

The political events, the change in administration, and subsequent deliberations over the Opéra's fate delayed the planned premiere of the work for eighteen months. The new administration, including the director and the Commission of Surveillance, had mixed feelings about the work and their obligation to put it into production. But if there were elements of anxiety, there were those of assurance as well, particularly the fact that Scribe and Meyerbeer were known artistic commodities.[52] And in light of *La Muette,* performed boldly at the start of the new regime, *Robert* represented a safe reversion to a different kind of theatrical genre.

Now it would have been highly inappropriate to summon up memories of *La Muette,* for already the Opéra was confronting the inherent dilemma that issued from the distance between its image and fact. Eighteen thirty-one was a highly tense period for the new regime, for restive groups were beginning to express disenchantment with its apparent lack of direction. And they undoubtedly found the political *fêtes,* such as that of July 29, 1831, commemorating the revolution (complete with music by Hérold and words by Hugo) to be particularly ironic now. For already even liberals were beginning to criticize the regime's lack of moral commitment, its general lack of principle or system, and its flaccid vacillation in foreign policy.[53] Violence, including conspiracies, riots, and rebellions, was intense and frequent, and as contemporaries noted, the cultural chasm between groups was beginning to grow. As republican radicalism increased and utopian movements grew in force, youth and workers frequently joined together with a menacing boldness.[54]

Theatrical censorship, if temporarily suspended in its older form in the interests of political image, nevertheless reappeared on other levels. Artistic centralization increased, as implemented by the renewed requirement that all works to be performed in the provinces be evaluated through a first trial performance in Paris. Already in 1831, the minister of the interior was pushing for the reintroduction of preventive censorship in France.[55]

The commission was thus as nervous for political reasons as Véron was for financial ones, and both realized the necessity of making the proper kind of first impression. This explains why Véron, having invested a borrowed security payment, in turn required that Meyerbeer pay the Opéra an indemnity of 40,000 francs. In fact, so concerned was Véron with remaining financially solvent for the first large production under his regime that he even required the composer to assume, personally, the costs of renting the organ he requested. The reality, then, was far different from the myth that Meyerbeer had manipulated the Opéra, or that he had been able to take substantial advantage of his personal wealth.[56] Any manipulation by Meyerbeer, as we shall shortly see, was indeed necessitated by the bureaucratic and political maneuverings of the Opéra.

Moreover, the reality was that the first lavish production of *Robert le Diable* was made possible only by a direct and considerable investment of government funds. The commission realized what was at stake in terms of political image, and hence played a crucial role in insuring that the opera would be mounted in an

67

appropriate way. Although highly distrustful of Véron, the commission did come to his aid in this matter, arguing to their superiors that the extraordinary expenditures required ought to be assumed by the government. But, typically, they made this decision not only on the basis of Véron's opinion but after having attended a reading of the libretto to ascertain if additional funds were really called for. They confirmed that the sum requested, of 70,000 francs for the work's production beyond the 30,000 for the restoration of the hall, was a necessary, not exaggerated figure. But here again, Meyerbeer was forced to play a personal role, having learned that Lubbert, whom he distrusted, had created complications during his tenure. The former director had given an estimate to the Commissaire de la Liste Civile for the *mise en scène* of the work at the greatly inflated price of 120,000 francs. And so Meyerbeer scrambled to parry this blow by going personally to the commission, both to lobby for an adequate production and to secure an appropriate date for the premiere.[57]

But the commission, of course, having helped to provide the necessary funds, had finally to rely on the artists involved to realize their ambitious artistic aims. As other historians have remarked, *Robert* first brought together the major creative figure and the "chief architects" of the new version of grand opera in France.[58] *Robert* involved the henceforth frequent collaboration of four major figures: Scribe and Delavigne on the libretto, Meyerbeer on the music, and Duponchel and Cicéri on the *mise en scène*. As we shall see, that aspect of the work that was to succeed and survive in France was the result of a felicitous, indeed remarkable coordination of theatrical conceptions and aims.

In order to examine this collaboration and the nature of the theatrical conception involved, we must begin by considering the curious, hybrid nature of the libretto that Scribe finally produced. As we have seen, Scribe proposed the idea to Meyerbeer originally because of its similarity to the successful *Comte Ory* and the opportunity it presented for a popular *décor médiéval*. Moreover, this particular story had already achieved prolonged popularity, being one of the stories most frequently reedited in the *Bibliothèque bleue,* which it had entered in 1645. And it had achieved renewed popularity more recently in several versions that appeared in the popular boulevard theaters in the early nineteenth century.[59]

Scribe not only sensed how the work could be made to appeal to current tastes and to the needs of the Opéra in the later years of the Restoration. He also realized how the nature of the story would have to be changed in order to meet the needs of the Académie Royale under the new regime. Originally the story must have appealed very much in the same manner as *Ogier le Danois,* as an historical fantasy combining magical elements with historical details, as in the *genre troubadour.* But now Scribe and Germain Delavigne were to recast the story in such a way that it would continue to suggest the *féerique* element while borrowing the traits of a well-made *mélodrame.*

In addition, however, both Duponchel and Meyerbeer made suggestions concerning details and the *divertissements,* and the former especially sensed the way in which the work could be made politically topical. As we have observed, in the Restoration it was forbidden to represent religious ceremonies on stage, thus *Robert,* with its oblique references to religion, provided a conciliatory substitute. But under the new regime, at least in the beginning, the situation substantially changed due to the wave of anti-clericalism that it at first seemed to unleash. And so Duponchel astutely attempted to exploit the new situation by adding the spectacular as well as scandalous "Ballet of the Debauched Nuns" in a prominent place.[60] As we can see from a synopsis of the libretto (see Appendix), the story is a curious generic blend that resulted from the concerns of two regimes and their interaction with the imaginations of the artists selected.

Although it does not and did not appear to be dangerous in the contemporary context, the commission nevertheless worried about the work's appropriateness and safety. Well aware of the care and expense being lavished on the *mise en scène,* and remembering what had happened in the staging of *La Muette,* they insisted on attending a dress rehearsal. But in their subsequent report to the Ministre du Commerce et des Travaux Publics, they felt comfortable in reassuring him that the presentation would involve no risk. Their primary argument had to do with the nature of the literary genre involved and the fact that the general effect, including the details, did not seem seditious. The work could hardly create the kind of dangerous dynamic of *La Muette,* which the commission communicated carefully to the minister in the required report five days before the performance:

69

1° *Robert le Diable* est un ouvrage qui rentre dans un des genres exploités jusqu'à ce jour sur la scène de l'Opéra.

2° Qu'elle n'y a rien vu ni dans l'esprit général de l'ouvrage, ni dans les détails, qui puisse en rendre la représentation dangereuse.

Pour plus de garantie, comme la mise en scène peut présenter des tableaux qu'une simple lecture du poème ne laisse pas apercevoir, la Commission a décidé qu'elle assisterait en corps à une répétition générale.[61]

[*Robert le Diable* is a work that returns to one of the genres exploited up until the present day on the stage of the Opéra. (The commission) saw nothing in it, in the general spirit of the work, or in the details, that can make the performance dangerous.

For more of a guarantee, since the *mise en scène* can present tableaux that a simple reading of the poem cannot allow to be perceived, the commission decided that it would attend a dress rehearsal as a group.]

Their reassurance lay in the text's similarity to an established genre, although there were subtle but significant innovations in the text as well as in the *mise en scène*. The latter was one that aimed at and achieved the peculiar blend of the real and the imaginary that was to become increasingly characteristic of the Académie Royale de Musique. The novel elements perhaps seemed less threatening in view of the décors by Cicéri, whose style in works of this genre was known since the later years of the Restoration.[62] But more definitively new was Duponchel's famous cloister scene that increased the element of visual realism, thus attempting to engage the audience through recognition, although not in a political or threatening sense. For the scene was no mere creation of fantasy nor a traditional, conventional *décor roman;* rather, it was a model of a specific, identifiable cloister still existing at Arles[63] (Figure 4). Moreover, with the striking new effect of moonlight on the Opéra's stage, Duponchel achieved a degree of reality and splendor unmatched even on the boulevard.

But an even stronger kind of association with royal display seemed to be invited by the costumes, all of unprecedented splendor, rich in materials and lavish in detail. Especially brilliant was

Figure 4. Opéra, interior, Salle Le Peletier, n.d. Bibliothèque de l'Opéra.

the armor, made of iron, steel, and gold, and the sumptuous coats of mail created a particularly impressive effect.[64] Here the artists, perhaps intuitively, sensed the effect of representing arms on the royal stage in this splendid and ceremonial manner and the peculiar conflation of experience that would result. For this stage, above all others, was still the realm of royal representation, particularly now with everyone curious to see what had become of the Académie Royale.

Through such displays, although used ostensibly in a dramatic, fictional context, the monarchy was still displaying itself, representing its image and grandeur. And if, in Lully's day, the ballet had served to reinforce the connection between the spectacle unfolding on the stage and the monarchy ostensibly supporting it, it was now such spectacle scenes that served a similar function, playing at once an essential dramatic as well as a politically symbolic role. The audience indeed expected pomp because of its political associations, regardless of the particular dramatic context of the production involved. And in light of the concern with the real, it is significant to note here that not all the costumes were medieval or in the historical style of the drama; some, like that of Alice,

71

were in the style of the Restoration. This clearly had the effect of increasing the work's *actualité* and encouraging references to the present, within the Académie's political frame.

It is in the framework of this peculiar fusion apparently sought in the *mise en scène,* its blend of the real and the actual, the fictive and the entertaining, that we should examine the role as well as the concomitant force and coherence of the musical dimension. It is in this framework too that we can see the larger conjuncture – stylistic, theatrical, and political – into which Meyerbeer's innovations and ideas fit. Meyerbeer, indeed, had an important role in determining the larger theatrical conception, having consulted with Cicéri and Delavigne on the décors, and in fact was responsible for changing elements of the story and the place of the action to Sicily.[65]

Musically, *Robert,* of course, still retains many elements of Meyerbeer's earlier Italian style, particularly in its vocal writing and in the fully developed aria forms. And it also retains certain features stemming from its original conception as an *opéra-comique,* especially in the declamation and aria types selected for the minor figures.[66] The major characters, by contrast, as in *La Muette de Portici,* especially Robert and Isabelle, are given a more virtuosic, Italianate style. Hence one of the most striking elements, as in *La Muette,* is stylistic eclecticism, later to become an even more refined and integral element of Meyerbeer's style.

Here one can clearly see his familiarity with the German romantic operas of his former friend, Carl Maria von Weber, in addition to Italian opera (Rossini and Bellini), *opéra-comique,* and the French grand tradition (Spontini). In *Robert,* the styles still largely vary according to the appropriateness of the particular scene, as opposed to the individual dramatic moment (as in his later works). But it still achieves dramatic breadth, as in *La Muette,* as well as vividness in content, helping to clarify the drama. In addition, the orchestra now serves to insure unity, continuity, and clarity of content, in keeping with the demands and nature of Scribe's melodramatic text. From this perspective, Meyerbeer, a scrupulous student of French culture, was here attempting to update the French tradition of close adherence to the nature and pace of the dramatic text. Here it is melodrama, which required a new legibility of style, a visual projection of the content, in addition to a continuous dramatic pace. In *Robert,* Meyerbeer responds to the new emphasis on visual qualities in melodrama, focusing on them and finding their aural concomitants, just as he highlights the tightly focused action. Clearly he was not a composer of dramatic psychology but of action, who immediately sensed the affinity of his talents with the new kind of text. Indeed, the basis of his aesthetic, a sense of the way that music is to translate and project the text, to make it even more theatrically compelling, is already present in *Robert le Diable.*

At this stage his quest for legibility is especially evident in the orchestral writing, to which Meyerbeer brings the rich resources of the German orchestral tradition. Certainly, there is an evident influence here of Weber and the new techniques of local color that he introduced in *Der Freischütz.* But Meyerbeer attempts to do even more in his descriptive use of the orchestra: He attempts to engrave physical and, by association, spiritual traits of his characters on the listener's mind. For Bertram, he chooses a particular color, a combination of ophicleide, trombone, and bassoon – somber colors that project his essence onto an orchestral plane.[67] In a sense, Meyerbeer was thus exploring the contribution of sound to the network of references or associations already established between image and word in melodrama, thus creating a new degree of coherence in theatrical language. And in doing so, he also moves beyond older conceptions of musical representation toward a new kind of literalness, one that is not intellectual but rather almost physical. Berlioz was especially appreciative of this skill, and particularly the way in which Meyerbeer was able to find sonorous equivalents for spatial effects on the stage, such as in the third act, with the bands that accompany the demons and the solo trumpet that is played under the stage.[68]

But the orchestra serves and projects the drama here in another sense: it becomes a "common denominator," the center of the action, connecting individual parts and scrupulously following the action on stage. Already Meyerbeer shows himself to be a master of transitions, particularly in his ability to keep the movement going even when working with striking contrasts. The orchestra provides a new range of commentary, underlining, helping to characterize, and at times developing its own ideas. But Meyerbeer always models the incidents of his symphonic drama closely and almost visually on the incidents of the drama itself.[69] His rich

73

use of motives in the orchestra as well as his particular choice of timbre is almost invariably linked to a specific action or gesture on stage, as a musical analogue. His orchestra, as contemporaries often observed, always comments on the action, "cédant à l'intelligence de la scène par le coloris, par le rappel ou le pressentiment de certaines phrases typiques."[70] The orchestra keeps the action continuous and helps to modulate the movement from one large musical-dramatic structure to the next, structures which are in turn based on units of décor. But Meyerbeer was soon to find other means beyond those we see in *Robert* to link the music to the scenic action, to dramatic units, and to decorative tableaux.[71]

Meyerbeer was well aware of the novel departures in his score, not only in the orchestral coloring, but in its relation to the theatrical genre. And it is for this reason that he was particularly concerned that the opera be presented, as promised, before those of a number of rival composers. Among these works were Hérold's *Zampa,* which Meyerbeer saw as similar in coloring, causing him to lobby Scribe to delay his work on Hérold's libretto. For what Meyerbeer, and indeed his collaborators as well as the Opéra, sought was, to use his words, "les effets d'un genre qui n'a jamais été porté à la scéne"[72] [the effects of a genre that has never been presented on the stage]. The new Opéra was to have a new look and a new genre associated with it – both rhetorical means to project a new image for the monarchy of Louis-Philippe.

To judge from the public response, they succeeded in presenting an opera perceived as new, although, as we shall see, the real question was whether it was appropriate to the Académie Royale. The commission was to learn much from reactions, both positive as well as negative, that determined their sense of the work's success and thus what should be encouraged and what suppressed.

The goal of the team at work on *Robert* was to achieve new vividness and theatrical coherence, a new kind of theatrical legibility and pomp appropriate to the new clientele. By all accounts, they succeeded admirably in achieving this particular goal, in presenting a work that combined actuality with scenic grandeur and a new directness and force. Public curiosity before the premiere was matched only by the generally enthusiastic response, judging both from the contemporary press as well as from the work's receipts.[73]

Critical praise of the opera in the press concentrated on its integral impact, on the new kind of theatrical coherence, often referred to as its "prodigious" effect.[74] If, as Duponchel commented, "Rossini est mort pour la composition scénique" [Rossini died for scenic composition], Meyerbeer, to contemporaries, seemed to have arisen, with genius, to this challenge. And if Auber had been praised for "une vive intelligence des effets dramatiques, et plein d'énergie et d'action" [a lively intelligence for dramatic effects, and full of energy and action], this appeared to be even more true of Meyerbeer.[75] Contemporaries saw neither his music nor the work in general in terms of compromise, or of a deft conflation of innovation and tradition, but rather as substantively new.

We find perhaps no better statement of the theatrical attractiveness and perceived novelty of Meyerbeer's style in *Robert* than in the writings of Berlioz's friend and supporter, Joseph d'Ortigue. D'Ortigue, above all, praised the legibility of Meyerbeer's new style, or his "expository technique," which the critic found to be one of unprecedented richness and vigor. He stressed the propinquity of Meyerbeer's dramaturgy to the contemporary romantic drama, both being free of convention, responding to dramatic situations with forms that were always varied and new. Because of this close relation to the character of romantic drama, Emile Deschamps was to claim that it was Meyerbeer, not Berlioz, who was to music what Delacroix was to painting and Hugo to literature.[76]

Far more controversial, however, was whether or not the opera was grand, and hence whether it was truly worthy of presentation at the Académie Royale. For those who supported the production, it was grand in an external, physical sense, "un ensemble d'effets plus beau, plus majestueux, plus séduisant que tout ce qu'on avait vu depuis fort longtemps à l'Opéra"[77] [an ensemble of effects more beautiful, more majestic, more seductive than anything anyone has seen at the Opéra for a long time]. But for the work's critics, precisely what it lacked was grandeur in a dramatic sense: grandeur in terms of content, which seemed antithetical to the libretto's genre.

Robert le Diable was an essentially modern work in a theatrical sense, but this was clearly not enough for the Académie Royale de Musique. The accomplishments of the artists here, as so many

75

times in the future, were to be assessed in terms of the institution's image-making goals.

At the premiere there was no question as to the work's official frame, for it was attended by members of the royal family (although not the king, for the work was still a risk). Present were two of Louis-Philippe's sons, the duc d'Orléans, or the "Prince Royale," and Charles d'Orléans, the duc de Nemours.[78] Almost all the reviews acknowledged this and then considered the work within the context of the theater's nature or its public, national function and its ties to the political leadership.

The liberal *Revue des deux mondes* declared that "le poème est absurd et indigne d'être présenté même à l'Opéra." The *Courrier des Théâtres* expressed its special indignation at the undignified ballets, and above all the scandalous success of the "Danse orgiac des nonnes." Such spectacles, common in the boulevard theaters, were totally inappropriate to the Opéra, which lowered itself and hence demeaned a tradition in presenting such a work on its stage. And it could hardly be overlooked that the work immediately became the subject for a number of popular parodies, beginning one month after the premiere and continuing the following year. In addition, selections from the opera were being used in a most undignified way – by December, quadrilles drawn from it were being performed at the Tivoli d'Hiver and the notorious bawdy "bal Musard." The latter consciously borrowed the most scandalous sections of the work, creating provocative *quadrilles infernaux* and *galops tartaréens.*[79]

For all these reasons, *Robert le Diable,* for its critics, was unworthy of the dignity of the Opéra, and moreover failed to create the kind of experience appropriate to the theater. A clear implication was that, because of the fear of unleashing the passions associated with *La Muette,* the work totally abjured the element of broad and wide social reference or of elevation in subject. Certainly, attacking the resulting opera and focusing on its lack of elevation and dignity was one way of indirectly or obliquely attacking the monarchy, again in an incipient *esprit frondeur.* Another means was to do precisely what officials obviously wanted to avoid in staging the work: to read it consistently in the light of political *actualité.* Perhaps here as in *La Muette,* Duponchel played a contributory role by suggesting current references in some, if not all, of the costumes.

Not surprisingly, then, several reviews attempted, in a manner we have seen in the revolution and Restoration, to provide a political subtext for the work. For example:

La situation est pleine d'intérêt. Dès qu'elle est reconnue et que l'esprit en fait à l'ordre social une juste application, le développement de l'action prend un attrait nouveau, la raison s'y attache, et ce qui apparaissait d'abord comme une esquisse frivole et insignifiante devient un drame plein de grandeur et qui s'empare à la fois de toutes ces facultés . . . Comme Robert, la France a deux natures ennemies, deux penchants contraires, deux conseillés adversés. Voilà une lutte grande et terrible, un puissant intérêt.[80]

[The situation is full of interest. As soon as it is recognized that the spirit is applicable to the social order, the development of the action takes on a new attraction, it makes sense, and what appeared first as a frivolous and insignificant sketch becomes a drama full of grandeur that seizes at once all the faculties . . . Like Robert, France has two opposite natures, two contrary penchants, two opposing counselors. Here is a great and terrible struggle, a powerful interest.]

Ironically, it was such a reading that seemed to give the work both the depth and resonance that would qualify it as grand, or as appropriate to performance at the Académie Royale. Others saw a political subtext in very much the same terms, among them Heinrich Heine, an incisive observer of the French stage, who made it even more trenchant:

N'en déplaiser aux enthousiastes de Meyerbeer, je pense que beaucoup de gens se sont pas seulement attirés par le charme de la musique, mais bien par le sens politique du livret. Robert le Diable, fils d'un démon aussi dépravé que Philippe Egalité et d'une princesse aussi pieuse que la fille de Penthievre, est poussé au mal, à la Révolution, par l'esprit de son père; et par celui de sa mère, au bien, c'est-à-dire vers l'Ancien Régime. Ces deux natures innées se combattent dans son âme; il flotte entre les deux principes: il est juste milieu.[81]

77

[Not to displease the enthusiasts of Meyerbeer, I think that many people are not only attracted by the charm of the music, but by the political sense of the libretto. Robert le Diable, the son of a demon as depraved as Philippe Egalité (the father of Louis-Philippe) and a princess as pious as the daughter of Penthievre, is pushed to evil, to the Revolution, by the spirit of his father; and by that of his mother, to good, that is to say toward the ancien régime. These two innate natures combat each other in his soul; he floats between two principles: he is juste milieu.]

The official response to such tactics was dual – one immediate and one more deliberate. First, the work was redefined and reclaimed by performance at Fontainebleau. This might be seen as an effort to define the genre more conclusively as an official *féerie,* in the manner of the Restoration, and thus reduce the regime's embarrassment. Second, *Robert,* like *La Muette,* was proclaimed only partially to be a success: it was successful financially and publicly but not politically, not as an image. Not only the public but also the regime evaluated it in its official frame, in terms of its political function as theater, and here it had clearly failed. As a result, it was not a prototype but only a step toward a new kind of theater, one held back by a literary genre that was now apparently conclusively dead. More sophisticated than *La Muette* in one sense, it was still regressive in another, and hence again the question of grandeur and its definition at the Académie Royale reappeared.

The direction indicated now was back to history, but to history with a topical resonance, for such a reading seemed so endemic to the Opéra that it appeared preferable to approach it consciously. If watched carefully, which the commission was henceforth to do with rigor, such a model, they believed, could create a new and modern kind of grandeur. Perhaps Emile Véron, indeed uncharacteristically, put it best when he summed up the resulting conception of what a grand opera was to be. A grand work was one that would "mettre en jeu" "the grand passions of the human heart," which Véron explicitly identified with "powerful historical interests."[82] This undoubtedly meant topicality, at least by reference, which would bring engagement and hence a complex blend of responses, but those that skirted narrow ideological conflict.

The laws of grand opera were thus emerging in the light of pragmatic experience, laws associated integrally with the theater's function, its official image or rhetoric. Henceforth, the artists associated with the theater had a mandate to help articulate the new genre that was indicated in the wake of *Robert,* and the commission to oversee it. It was clear that *Robert* was unsuccessful in the political function originally assigned it, and so in the future it was to be used to play a very different kind of political role. If *La Muette* was deployed now only to help stir up revolutionary sentiment, *Robert* was performed for the opposite reason: its role was to distract and to calm.[83]

Robert, then, remained in the repertoire as one of the Opéra's most reliable, popular works, but the institution began an ostensible policy of seeking out historical subjects. Officials still believed that if handled correctly such operas could indeed straddle the contradictions of the Opéra's liberal image and the emerging political reality of the regime.

As in the Restoration, the Opéra henceforth began its search for a new kind of operatic subject that would respond to its current political needs. And, again, in turning to history the Opéra was once more in competition with the popular theaters, which had sustained this interest since the Restoration.[84] We can surmise the Opéra's effectiveness in communicating its new dramatic priorities by surveying the file of libretti submitted by hopeful authors for the Opéra. The subjects are overwhelmingly historical, and indeed the Opéra was often explicit in its letters of rejection when anachronistic or inappropriate subjects now were proposed.[85]

For the moment, the government seemed more concerned with the potentially seditious implications of romantic dramas such as Hugo's *Le Roi s'amuse* than with specifically historical subjects. If the image of the king in Hugo's drama was a troublesome point, however, it was to become far more so in the historical libretti being sought by the Opéra. But the regime was still relatively tolerant, in general, for historical subjects in opera and especially those that would titillate or "faire vibrer le public."[86]

Véron participated actively in the quest for the ideal subject, and soon concluded a contract with Meyerbeer for a second work, which was to be *Les Huguenots.*[87] Little could he foresee what a

79

political problem it would prove to be since it seemed to serve precisely the kind of function that the regime so strongly desired.

But in the interim, before the new work was ready, the Opéra faced several problems, including the cholera epidemic of 1832, which left it deserted for seven months and with only 500 francs in receipts.[88] But fortunately, another historical work was ready for production in 1833, Auber and Scribe's *Gustave III ou le bal masqué,* and it was given with great success. It far overshadowed a number of lesser works that were also tried: *La Tentation,* by Cavé, Duponchel, and Halévy, and *Le Serment,* by Scribe, Auber, and Cicéri.

Because of these relative failures, the Opéra and its audience now looked forward to the next large-scale historical production, Halévy and Scribe's *La Juive.* But while the new work relieved anxiety in one sense, it created it in another, for again in the shadow of political tensions, the Opéra was clearly worried about audience response. The political tactic of projecting a liberal image through the Opéra was already becoming a problem in light of recent political reality. Officials increasingly feared that the Opéra's performances could become pretexts for thinly veiled political demonstrations, as in *La Muette de Portici.* In the current conditions, its political reference, even the mere presentation of authority on the stage, could be more a political liability than it could potentially be an asset.

If the Opéra was implicated in the increasing ridicule of the monarchy's image in *Robert le Diable,* its response of moving in the opposite direction proved to be just as futile. For the problem was not only to assume a new form, even more serious, in *La Juive,* but to become more vexing in the succeeding and long-awaited *Les Huguenots.* Nowhere, indeed, can we see more clearly the political meaning, the theatrical frame, and the use of grand opera's conventions not only by the monarchy but by its opponents.

The premiere of *La Juive* was to occur at a time of increasing opposition to Louis-Philippe. In 1834 and 1835 a series of riots broke out in Paris. And in 1835 the violence focused on Louis-Philippe himself, when a member of the opposition made an attempt on the monarch's life. It was becoming clear that the intention of the king, the so-called *roi des barricades,* was in fact politically pragmatic: that although he had posed as a "king of the people," his plan all along had been eventually to extend his authority, to "s'afranchir de la tutelle populaire" [to free himself from the popular tutelage]. The monarchy, then, in the eyes of many, had been, in its origins, a political lie, winning the necessary support by making promises that it did not intend to keep. As historians have observed, political liberties were subject to the vicissitudes of events, and so it is not surprising that harsh forms of censorship reappeared.[89]

The attempt on Louis-Philippe's life was made in July 1835, and by the following September preventive censorship was reestablished not only in drama but also in a wide range of visual images, including drawings, emblems, engravings, and caricatures.[90] The great concern in theater now was whether a specific work could possibly be construed as a threat to social order or as a manifestation of a contestatory spirit. According to the law of September 9, 1835, it was now officially a crime to "exciter les citoyens à s'armer contre l'autorité royale"[91] [to excite the citizens to arm themselves against royal authority].

Responses to this policy were several, but they occurred first among dramatic authors and most notably in the Société des Auteurs Dramatiques. The significant exception to their objections, however, was that of their president, Eugène Scribe, who argued pragmatically that a clear policy of censorship was better than merely arbitrary intervention. But the prudent Scribe, perceived as a spokesman for the government in counselling his colleagues not to resist the law, finally ended by resigning his presidency over the issue.[92]

Tactics of resistance to these laws appeared in a several modes of cultural expression, and first, as we might expect, in the theaters, thus renewing a long tradition. Performances again were frequently interrupted by demonstrations originating in the parterre, ones that often demanded an expression of solidarity on the part of performers. But manifestation of sentiment against the regime was also appearing in other forms, in a subtle but especially potent manner that attacked the current concern with image. For now was the period when the revolutionary symbols originally invoked by the new regime began to be used against it, as was to be increasingly the case.[93]

It was in this context that *La Juive* aroused no small concern at the Opéra, still worried about its stage as a realm of political representation. For at a moment when the dignity of the regime was coming increasingly into question, the dignity of the Opéra and its representation of monarchy was once more a central issue. Although the work seemed to meet the needs of the Opéra at this point, or its quest to present an attractive image, there were still evident risks involved. The fear was clearly that audience reaction to the image of authority on the royal stage would be intended and perceived as an indirect reaction to the monarchy supporting the stage. From the experience of *La Muette,* the Opéra knew to expect exploitation of this convergence, and that negative reactions to presentations could serve a politically seditious end. At a time when the regime feared derision, then, nowhere was the official concern in theater greater than with the public, politicized stage of the Opéra.

With *La Juive,* the commission's concern, as in *Robert,* was the effect, but also now with the presentation of religious ceremony on the stage. The special concern with religion here is one that should be seen in a wider context, that of the regime's now politically conciliatory attitude toward the church. Along with its increasingly authoritarian character and turn from its earlier revolutionary stance, the older anticlericalism, so evident in *Robert le Diable,* disappeared as well. For the Catholics were clearly benefiting from the increasing social disquiet. The fear of political and social disorder was creating a rapprochement with the church. Just as the issue of clericalism became a point of contention between royalists and liberals in the Restoration, it was again a similar point of division. And again as in the Restoration, the magnificence of royal pomp now was to be joined imposingly with the solemnity of religious ceremony.[94]

Hence in *La Juive* as in *Robert,* the criterion of political image determined those aspects of the production that received the greatest expenditure, a lavishness again made possible by the state. Here the outstanding feature of the production was the effect of luxury it sought to create, motivated, as we have seen, far less by dramatic than by political reasons. The costumes were entirely new, designed by the talented Paul Lormier, who engaged in considerable historical research before preparing his detailed designs[95] (Figure 5). But significantly, Lormier's quest for accuracy was again focused on the armor, on which the Opéra spent 30,000 of the 150,000 francs of the production costs. Already,

Figure 5. Costume for the Emperor Sigismund, *La Juive,* 1836. Bibliothèque de l'Opéra.

perhaps, Lormier was aware that, given the public resonance of the genre, illustrations of the costume designs would be seen by those who either planned to or could not attend.

But the Opéra went even further, again in an attempt to outdo the very popular military spectacles attracting attention on the boulevard. Once more, Duponchel had just the right instinct for meeting this demand, for he arranged to borrow the horses of the Cirque-Olympique for the emperor's grand procession.[96] In addition, the Opéra's decorators outdid themselves in the five colossal, and again painstakingly detailed, historical sets that they designed for the work. Indeed, it was the success of the opera's scenic element that was to lead to an even bolder step by the now somewhat over-confident institution in *Les Huguenots.*

But although the work was as lavish as *Robert,* the dignified representation of religious ceremony was here a central issue, studied carefully by the commission. They scrutinized the libretto, and were especially concerned with one element of *actualité* that might be seen in the text. In 1835, much to the consternation of the political opposition, the budget of the church was aug-

83

mented by 700,000 francs, and cardinals were given a supplementary salary.[97] Evidently, the representation of a cardinal on the Opéra's stage, here so prominent dramatically, immediately caused concern that it would provide a pretext for a demonstration. (See synopsis in the Appendix.)

Although there are evident similarities between *La Juive* and Scribe's previous opera libretti, now, in the light of specific political concerns, certain traits, and particularly the focus on the personal element, were no longer considered assets. The commission, after reading the libretto with less than critical approbation, decided that it could determine the effect only by attending a dress rehearsal, as recounted in the following letter to the minister of the interior:

A la lecture qui avait été faite de cet Opéra, la Commission n'avait trouvé rien qui fût très digne et très convenable, et s'était décidée de juger par elle-même de l'effet que pourrait produire sur les spectateurs les scènes . . . les 1er, 3e, et 5e actes dans lesquels les cérémonies religieuses devaient avoir lieu avec une sorte de solemnité . . . tout ce qui se passe est tellement pris aux sérieux qu'il y aura impossibilté pour les esprits les plus mal intentionés de rien tourner en dérision.[98]

[From the reading of this opera, the commission didn't find anything that was very dignified or suitable, and so decided to judge the effect that it could produce on the spectators of the scenes itself . . . the 1st, 3rd, and 5th acts in which the religious ceremonies were to take place with a sort of solemnity . . . all that takes place is taken so seriously that it would be impossible for the most ill-intentioned to turn anything into derision.]

In this case, their concern was less one of demeaning religion itself than of creating a situation for ridicule of authority, using the opera as a pretext. The intrigue concerned them only in the context of political image, of presenting a spectacle of dignity and elevation that transcended the limits of the written word. For the Opéra was, above all, in their minds, a cultural frame for authority, and because its spectacles had dual meaning, lying both inside and outside the work.

But the Opéra was also a subject of commentary for the increasingly hostile press, which saw its opportunity here to make a subtle political innuendo. Indeed, the spirit and tactics of the seventeenth-century *frondeurs* were not only becoming a subject of interest, they were increasingly to provide a model. The details the press chose to discuss of the opera were by no means politically innocent: it knew, certainly, that the motives of the government were not, and neither were the interpretations of the audience. Hence, like the *mazarinades* of the seventeenth century, also responses to tactics of power, the reviews of the opera expressed themselves in a manner that similarly had to be decoded.[99]

The press incisively noted the inordinate emphasis on spectacle in *La Juive,* pointing out that "leurs fêtes et leurs pompes triomphales étincèlent, brillent, résonnent, éclatent sans interruption, pendant cinq heures"[100] [their celebrations and triumphant pomp sparkle, shine, resound, burst without interruption for five hours]. But the focus was less on this, which the government evidently desired, than on that aspect least emphasized in the work – its specific historical background. Undoubtedly, given the current political situation with regard to the Catholic church, *Le Constitutionnel* (strongly anticlerical since the Restoration) focused on the historical significance of the Council of Constance. Not surprisingly, it stressed that "Les richesses et les prodigalités des prélats y témoignent de leurs moeurs cupides et corrumpues, lèpre de l'église" [The riches and prodigality of the prelates here was witness of their greedy and corrupt morals, a leprosy of the church]. And concomitantly, and again topically, it stresses the church's hypocrisy: "les saintes hymncs et les saintes prières mêlées aux ruses et aux jeux d'esprit des docteurs et des clercs"[101] [the saintly hymns and prayers mixed with the ruses and witticisms of the doctors and clerics].

But again in the end, and despite all the sniping, the commission still felt obliged to pronounce the work a success, although in spite of, not because of Véron. It would have preferred a work with greater dramatic substance, which it was soon to get, yet for the moment it was relatively satisfied with the effect. But understandably it was in this moment of increasing concern over staging and the Opéra's image that the simmering tensions between Véron and the commission reached the boiling point. Their complaints about his direction had been accumulating steadily, and

85

particularly complaints about his indifference to the Opéra's dignity or to that of the artists themselves.

The commission had frequently overruled his decisions and imposed stiff fines as well. It forced Véron, for example, to delete certain episodes from his *bals masqués,* given for the benefit of the Opéra.[102] It attempted frequently to fine Véron, and sometimes its decisions were upheld, while on other occasions they were seen as unreasonable and overruled by the minister himself. The commission's charges most frequently concerned Véron's attempts to cut his costs by employing old costumes or scenery, thus sacrificing the Opéra's brilliance and image.[103]

Their concerns were both artistic and political; as we have seen, for them the two were inextricably bound. A poor showing or lack of grandeur in staging or text was a political reflection. Hence the commission foresaw disaster if Véron were allowed to remain in his post, claiming that, because of his greed, the theater was surely headed for decadence. Finally, it blatantly refused to accept "la responsabilités d'événéments qui doivent amener la décadence du théâtre à cette epoch et n'avoir qu'une salle sans acteurs. La vanité et l'intérêt de M. Véron sont d'accord pour ce résultat" [the responsibility for events that must lead to the decadence of the theater and to having a hall without performers. The vanity and interests of M. Véron are in agreement with this result]. Foreseeing the imminent departure of the Opéra's great tenor, Adolphe Nourrit, they finally suggested that Véron be discharged and the commission itself temporarily administer the Opéra.[104]

In the end, the commission succeeded in removing the greedy entrepreneur, but accomplished this indirectly, through authorized, legally acceptable means. They undoubtedly advised that Véron be attacked in the area that would hurt him most: certainly not that of reputation or pride, but rather in the pocketbook. To please the commission and the assembly, the Ministre du Commerce et des Travaux Publics, Adolphe Thiers, decided to modify Véron's Cahier des charges. This meant reducing his subvention prematurely, in the third year of his regime, from 710,000 to 670,000 francs. Knowing that Véron would thus see his financial interests substantially diminished, he stipulated that the director could have the option of resigning his position early. Véron duly took his cue while he was financially still ahead, and resigned his post on September 1, 1835.[105]

86

Véron acquiesced undoubtedly, however, because of his alternative plan, by which he would continue to be involved in the Opéra but only in a financial sense. He was also evidently offered a role in the choice of his successor, and in fact his second choice, Edmond Duponchel, was selected. Véron henceforth entered into an association with the new director and with his original first choice for the post, Loewe-Weimar.[106]

Duponchel, unlike Véron, was an artist, originally a painter, who began his career in the atelier of Guérin, as we have seen. He went on to take courses in architecture at the prestigious Ecole des Beaux-arts, and then to become a designer and *metteur en scène* for the Opéra. There were important changes in the conditions of Duponchel's appointment, owing either to his background and personality or to the commission's experience with Véron. He was to labor under even greater restraints in the form of a new, more restrictive Cahier des charges as well as a newly composed commission, one even more zealous than before. Again contrary to the established view, and perhaps now even more so, the entrepreneur was only partly responsible for the Opéra's artistic direction.

The commission was newly constituted on August 31, 1835, although it reatained several of the members of the previous commission. Significantly, given the state's concern with the image presented by the Opéra, only one of its members was not a politician or a government bureaucrat. The duc de Choiseul remained its president; now, de Kératy, a deputy, was vice-president; the other members were the baron de Lascours, pair de France; Edmond Blanc, deputé; Pedre La Caze (to become a deputy); Armand Bertin; and d'Hennerville, Inspecteur du mobilier de la Liste civile.[107]

Duponchel's Cahier des charges, which the commission was again to enforce, included the provision for even higher fines in case of any infraction: "Chaque contravention aux dispositions du présent arrêté pourra entraîner, contre l'Entrepreneur, une amende de 1.000 fr. à 10.000 fr."[108] If Véron was plagued by his commission, especially with respect to fines, Duponchel was to be even more so, for he constantly attempted to use old costumes and sets. The commission reacted immediately, in accordance with the Cahier, and proceeded to levy a series of extremely stiff penalties against him.[109]

87

Another provision in Duponchel's Cahier reflects this commission's specific concerns, here with maintaining order and propriety of deportment in the hall. Because of the fear of violence during theatrical performances, it now specified the increased presence of police inside the hall: "Pendant les spectacles, ils se placeront sur le théâtre, soit dans les coulisses, soit en tout autre endroit où leur présence sera jugé nécessarie par le Directeur ou Inspecteur en Chef"[110] [During the performances they will be placed in the theater in the wings or in any other place where their presence will be judged necessary by the director or Inspector-in-Chief]. More than ever, officials worried about the monarchy's image as represented on stage, and of the possibility of metaphorical attacks upon it within the hall. As they knew, if the public perceived the Opéra as conveying a political message, then political debate could very well be conducted through reactions to what was happening on its stage.

These concerns increased in the context of the growing political extremism that accompanied the apparent defeat of dangerous Republican and Bonapartist factions.[111] The regime was ineluctably shifting from its earlier uncertainty into what contemporaries perceived as a period of rigidity and reaction. Public sentiment seemed increasingly to be that the regime had reneged on its promises, or betrayed its original political identity by neglecting to implement the necessary reforms. By 1835 it thus faced not only a pervasive disillusionment, but the explicit discontent of workers and the alienation of intellectuals.[112]

Because of these developments, the regime now worried increasingly about its earlier radical imagery, as evidenced by its removal of Delacroix's *Liberty Leading the People* from public display.[113] But in the Opéra, the situation was delicate, for it was a public and widely publicized stage, and hence the regime could only go so far in contradicting its political rhetoric. In light of the recent resurgence of the popular symbolism of 1830, now turned against the regime, it did put off revivals of the symbolic *La Muette de Portici*. It had no choice but simply to alter the liberal claims it had made through the operatic stage, and where necessary to impose a censorship that it believed would protect the monarchy's image.

But especially troubling was that audiences now seized every possible opportunity to express their discontent with its produc-

88

tions through open, physical violence. By 1836 the singing of patriotic *chansons,* ostensibly as a sign of political protest, once again became a frequent phenomenon in all the theaters. And now, last-minute substitutions of artists would frequently trigger an audience revolt, often of such intensity as to require armed police to put it down.[114] For the audience read these substitutions as reflective of authority, and hence officials interpreted such insurrections in a distinctly political sense. Now always wary of seditious décors or costumes, they nevertheless seemed unable to foresee what was likely to provoke disorder.[115]

Naturally, censorship became preoccupied with public order in the theaters, and with the use of theater as a means to express *l'opinion publique.* Moreover, because of the political significance of the subventioned theaters, they were now being watched the most closely of all and were frequently singled out for censorship. Certainly, there was a strong fear of pieces that would evoke the idea of "the people," particularly in light of the still vivid message of *La Muette.* But the great concern now, as before with *La Juive,* was the protection of the image of the monarch and the royal family. The king and the Orléans family were now to be shielded by political censorship from not only injurious allusions but any lack of respect.

And in light of the resurgence of Bonapartism, an additional concern of the censors was the protection of the once-hated Bourbons, since they were cousins of the present royal family. Thus dynastic royalty was a tender issue, as was the sacred character of the royal function, preoccupations already present in *La Juive.* It was, however, not easy to protect a monarch who now presumed to rule by *droit divin,* even though he had actually been enthroned by a *révolution populaire.*[116]

And so, more than ever, officials were attentive to every aspect of the Opéra's management, extending to the most minute details of the productions on its stage. Nowhere do we see this more directly expressed, even more clearly than in *La Juive,* than with the long-awaited opera of Meyerbeer and Scribe, *Les Huguenots.* As we shall see, in a sense it repeated the phenomenon of *La Muette,* similarly leading to artistic success and yet embarrassment to the regime.

As we have noted, in the wake of *Robert* the Opéra's management had determined that the future lay in historical libretti that would "mettre en jeu les grandes passions." Véron had soon after concluded a contract with Meyerbeer and Eugène Scribe for an opera not only on an historical subject but one from the nation's own past. Even after *Robert,* it still seemed appropriate to stage a drama that was, by implication, anticlerical, given the political circumstances; for after the revolts of the Legitimists in 1831 and 1832, the regime experienced a renewed fear of a clerical restoration.[117]

The new opera was to have been a vehicle for Meyerbeer, who signed a contract with Véron including several carefully specific stipulations. Meyerbeer had to agree that if the score were not delivered by a certain date he would have to pay a penalty of 30,000 francs. Six months before the score was due, Meyerbeer's wife became extremely ill, causing the composer to return to her (in Germany), thus delaying the work. Knowing Véron's character, particularly after his experience with *Robert,* Meyerbeer immediately sent Véron the sum of 30,000 francs. Instead of generously returning it, in view of the circumstances, Véron retained the sum, which apparently greatly angered the proud Meyerbeer. Although he was wealthy, it was evidently the principle at stake that mattered, and the composer hence refused to have the work produced at all under Véron's administration.[118]

Upon assuming the directorship, Duponchel, however, avidly sought the work, pursuing Meyerbeer to Berlin and promptly returning the controversial sum. Meyerbeer thus agreed to have the work put into production at last, and it was scheduled to appear in Paris in 1836. But now, however, the work was less than ideal in terms of its subject matter. In 1832, as we have seen, it related aptly to the political climate. Moreover, the links between Protestantism and political liberalism were then very strong, on both an ideological and personal level, in figures like Guizot. And so, for several reasons, at the start of the regime, anticlericalism (as anti-Catholicism) was, if not encouraged, at least officially condoned. But after 1832, once "the popular explosion of anticlericalism" that had initially occurred became more temperate, the authorities consciously sought to dampen it. This, of course, now made *Les Huguenots* hardly ideal for the regime's current political purposes, and thus extremely problematic.[119] And yet it met an artistic need, and if successful, it could still defuse revolutionary tensions and result in a prestigious success that would be associated with the regime.

In terms of the production of *Les Huguenots,* the major problem hence became precisely how to shape the political significance of Scribe's inherently ambiguous libretto. As in his previous libretti for the Opéra, Scribe attempted to concentrate attention on the love story between the characters, thus directing attention away from controversial aspects of the plot. Through such means historical interests and lofty sentiments could be "mis en jeu" and narrow partisan ideals or the conflict of ideological extremes might be avoided, as the state wished. (See Appendix.)

But there were, of course, certain clear political implications in the libretto, given the present political context and the institutional frame of the work. Royalty is presented attractively in the person of Queen Marguerite, who, along with the king, wishes to resolve the factional strife. The nobles, on the other hand, are presented as contentious and immature, as are the personifications of the Huguenot and Catholic forces. But evidently the stress is not on the political dimension of their conflict and violence; rather, it focuses on religious belief, again as in *La Juive.*

Several scholars have observed that the text seems to be based, if loosely, upon Merimée's popular and suggestive *Chronique du temps du Charles IX.* Indeed, the contemporary press proposed that the libretto was, in effect, an intelligent, effective arrangement of Merimée's provocative work. Mérimée's chronicle, like the libretto, juxtaposes an amorous intrigue with the larger political events that brought about the St. Bartholomew's Day Massacre. A review of the large and small events of 1572, it is a series of very different and carefully documented historical scenes.[120] But Scribe's libretto, while obviously drawing on some of the same techniques, does so for very different reasons and within a different generic context. And one should note, as well, that Meyerbeer did have a certain role in the final form of the libretto that he set. The composer had the text modified by his former Italian collaborator in 1834 for specifically musical and dramatic reasons. He wanted to add more female voices and to have the character of Marcel refashioned so as to serve his own personal dramatic intent more effectively.[121]

Although modern scholars have offered interpretations of the message of *Les Huguenots,* it is still important to be aware of the essential resulting ambiguity of the text. Despite the fact that the libretto does not present a completely unattractive picture of roy-

91

alty, and does not directly attribute guilt to it, other stylistic factors in both music and *mise en scène* helped to qualify this message.

If officials had learned a lesson about the message of the *mise en scène* from *La Muette de Portici,* they had forgotten the danger of leaving such decisions to the artists themselves. The artistic impulse was again to lead to what was considered a politically dangerous and hence undesirable, indeed unacceptable, result.

As before, the commission insisted on an accurate and lavish *mise en scène,* still undoubtedly believing that splendor would offset the risky subject. In fact, as was often the case, the first version produced by the Opéra was found wanting in this respect and so rejected by the commission.[122]

In its modified version, the production was one of almost unprecedented magnificence, widely considered to be even more sumptuous than that of *La Juive.* Particularly striking, as in the case of *Robert le Diable,* was the depiction of a specific locale in all its concrete detail and hence readily identifiable to all. Again, the goal was to engage the contemporary public in the work, to bring a sense of *actualité,* of the continuity of present and past. But apparently little did the Opéra suspect that, given a subject from the history of France and especially its political history, this technique would reinforce the political frame. For here the depiction was a royal residence of particular historical resonance, the Château de Chenonceaux, presented as dramatically bathed in shadows (Figure 6). If historical drama makes a "greater pretense at engaging with reality" than other forms of drama, then such a setting further increased this inherent tendency.[123] But this was to become a source of real tension when it came to defining the point of the work, since its references to the real or to the political world seemed to be particularly acute.

Once more, the force of the work, its sense of *actualité,* its utterance, resulted from the close interaction of text, staging, and of course, the musical style. Again Meyerbeer unerringly sensed the role that his music was to play, the way it could make the text more legible in conjunction with the stage effects. This extended not only to the definition of the dramatic by the musical boundaries, or to an adaptation of the music to the visual emphasis. Here, as in *Robert,* he attempted to project and magnify certain aspects

Figure 6. Décor, *Les Huguenots*, 1836. *Album de l'Opéra*, Bibliothèque de l'Opéra.

of the style and content of the literary text itself through his treatment of different musical genres.

But in *Les Huguenots* Meyerbeer carried specific tendencies even further, seeking greater flexibility and legibility not only in the orchestra but in the arias and choruses. He realized that here, despite certain melodramatic aspects of the text, being cast as a chronicle its movement was of greater weight and hence required a slower place. Yet he still sought legibility or clarity, "imitation" of the text and the staging, and further, he sought to foster the kind of engagement with the real world implied by both. The question he faced then was how to balance the different layers of the text and *mise en scène,* the references to the historical and contemporary, in terms of musical style.

In response, he employed a technique that carried his eclecticism even further to what has been called a "mosaicist approach," an eclectic juxtaposing of styles within the scene and one particularly suited to the chronicle character of the text. The choice of style emanated from the dramatic function of the individual number. In general, these functions can basically be divided into two major categories: In many of the choral numbers (those not devoted to the culmination of the action) he attempted to capture the characteristic element, or local color, whereas in the solo numbers he commonly resorted to popular aria types.[124]

But always, Meyerbeer groups his individual numbers into larger units, stressing their dramatic continuity, and even more so than in *Robert*. In the tradition of *opéra-comique,* he calculated the popular numbers to fit the specific speed of the dramatic movement and weight that the particular situation required. The popular arias, moreover, provided the valued quality of *actualité,* which interacted in a provocative manner with the suggestiveness of the historical scenes. And in keeping with the French tradition, they provided moments of either relief or of rhetorical emphasis to the otherwise fluid drama. In addition, they invited a kind of identification between the audience and the characters, further conflating present and past.

In this sense, then, Meyerbeer was projecting the very duality of the *mise en scène,* the presentation of present and past, onto the level of musical style. Both freely mingled the responses of the present with the resonance of the historical past, creating a contemporary, and in this context, an inherently politicized experience.

There was then a dramatic rationale consistently at work in Meyerbeer's eclectic procedures, governing his approach not only to formal units but to his choices of musical style; and this rationale explains the obvious shift in emphasis toward the choral numbers, given the function they were here to play dramatically.

Further evidence of this rationale and its coherence can be found in the audience reactions, their comments centering on the careful plan informing the deployment of styles: "Tous les genres y sont représentés, non pas isolés, individualisés, jetés pêle-mêle, mais intimement unis, je dirais presque disciplinés, en marchant vers un but commun"[125] [All the genres are represented here, not isolated, individualized, thrown in *pêle-mêle,* but intimately united, I would almost say disciplined, heading toward a common goal]. It was for this reason that Meyerbeer's French contemporaries, grasping the dramatic context of his style, did not see him as a calculating or derivative composer in a disparaging sense. His intent was to convey the drama's content and to project its dramatic complexity, seeing it as much a task for the composer as for the *metteur en scène.* Meyerbeer did understand the limits of musical expression allowable in the genre – the ne-

94

cessity of the composer limiting himself to a largely clarifying role. The strength and coherence of his style resides in just this awareness of the exigencies of the kind of engaging, visually oriented melodramatic texts he set.

Further proof of a general acknowledgment of this can be found in other comments on Meyerbeer, especially those of Berlioz, who was inherently alienated from the genre. Meyerbeer's skill in this genre was unquestionable to contemporaries; far more at issue was the values of the dramatic model itself. Berlioz, because of his attitude, was both "impressed and repelled" by Meyerbeer's "snakelike flexibility," and yet he did still admire *Les Huguenots*. For him, as he expressed it in a letter to his sister in 1836, *Les Huguenots* was no less than an "encyclopédie musicale."[126] He recognized immediately that it was "more severe, nobler, more grandiose" than *Robert le Diable,* that it was "a vast canvas richly embroidered," outstanding in "its sweep and control of detail." Even Wagner, who turned from Meyerbeer soon after his first stay in Paris, still continued long after to admire Act IV (perhaps the most continuous) of *Les Huguenots*. In 1840 he asked: "Whence did the composer draw the power of developing, and through all its astonishing length, a continuous augmentation of effect which never wearies and which, after a tumultuous burst of the wildest passions, finally attains its uttermost height, the ideal ecstasy of fanaticism."[127]

For the work's admirers, it was less a fiction than a veritable "history of France," one fashioned according to a contemporary conception of historical truth. For the new historical school, led by Michelet, had already begun to present history and art as a compelling, suggestive, and hence almost inextricable blend. Stressing social and political developments while attempting to convey a sense of everyday life, it employed novelistic devices, freely incorporating epic, dramatic, and lyric techniques.[128] It was in this context that many contemporaries especially appreciated Meyerbeer's skill in both historical suggestiveness as well as his simultaneous appeal to modern needs:

> Le génie consiste surtout à bien comprendre son époque, à rendre un compte exacte des idées, des sentiments, des passions auxquels on veut agir. L'oeuvre de Meyerbeer semble répondre à des besoins instinctivement sentis et dont le

public cherche vaguement, même au sein de plaisirs, la satisfaction.[129]

[His genius consists above all in understanding his epoch well, in producing exactly the ideas, sentiments, passions on which one wants to act. The work of Meyerbeer seems to respond to instinctively felt needs whose fulfillment the public searches for vaguely, even in its pleasures.]

Meyerbeer's public here had a strong sense of the kind of theater the composer was after, taking the genre seriously as history, and understanding its utterance in light of the present. And it was because of its artistic force that the genre had a political effect; the political element, conversely, was a central part of its theatrical appeal.

Meyerbeer, as well as Scribe and the opera's *metteur en scène,* grasped precisely the kind of experience now desired at the Académie Royale. But from the perspective of political authority, they grasped it now a bit too well, for it was the work's very seriousness as history and drama that led to contestation and finally embarrassment. The conflict was over the ending, the final determinant of the message of the work, the portion that clarified its political message, the interpretation that it proposed. For again, as in *La Muette,* Scribe's care to avoid the controversial in the text was undermined, in the end, by the artistic efforts of the *metteur en scène.*[130] The latter, perhaps perceiving the need to project a clearer idea of the causes and consequences of the event, and for artistic reasons, took certain historical liberties.[131] But now, probably because of the lessons learned from *La Muette,* the authorities viewed the presentation in advance, and ordered the ending changed before the premiere. Little did the regime suspect the furious controversy this would provoke in the press and the flood of politicized commentary that would issue from the affair, far surpassing that of *La Juive.*

In the initial choice for the ending, an important influence might well have been specific precedents in the dramatic treatment of the story in the revolutionary period. Chénier's *Charles IX,* a play that was banned under Louis XVI, depicted the king as responsible personally, in the end, for the bloody massacre. Hence the monarchy perceived the work as a not so subtle means on the part of an ambitious dramatist to stimulate revolutionary opposition to the crown. But significantly, Chénier's drama implicated two other figures as well, for it showed the duc de Guise and Catherine de Médicis as influencing the king to give the order.[132] And indeed Merimée's chronicle indirectly implies Catherine de Médicis's guilt by putting her words into the mouths of the Huguenots' bloody assassins.

In the *mise en scène* for the opera, perhaps for reasons of dramatic pathos as well as for historical clarification, or perhaps as an act of contentious revisionism, a kind of pantomime was to end the work. Originally, Catherine de Médicis was to have been carried on the stage sitting inside her litter, surveying with horror the destruction that her forces had wrought. The effect would have been, in fact, to reverse the implications of the whole work; far from presenting an ideal picture of royalty it would have done just the opposite. Obviously, this was not acceptable to the authorities, for from their perspective it conveyed the idea that the mother of a king of France was responsible for the massacre itself. Again, this related to the predominant concern of censorship, that of protecting not only the king but indeed French dynastic royalty.

The new censorship laws were meant to communicate that the monarchy of Louis-Philippe was henceforth absolutely indisputable in its legitimacy. No longer was the personal authority of the king to be contested, and the dynasty behind him was similarly to be "hors de discussion." Although a monarchy born of a revolution, its fear of opposition and disorder now impelled it to proclaim the monarch immortal and inviolable.[133]

As we have seen, the concern of censorship in the theater was to control not just the written word, but the whole living effect of the stage as well. But the theatrical message normally so difficult to monitor on the stage was an especially acute problem in opera with its complex profusion of signs. Knowing well the response to images, especially on the part of the illiterate or semiliterate, and the possibility of removing theatrical elements from their context to use them politically, officials were scrupulously cautious. Again, décor, costumes, gesture, all became objects of scrutiny as elements that potentially could enter the realm of political dialogue. This was particularly true of the censors now, who, as opposed to those of the Restoration, were chosen consciously as

97

representatives of the regime's position. They were now routinely suspicious, and most of all of theater directors in whom they were always wary of the presence of the insidious *esprit frondeur*.[134]

But, of course, the decision of the censors on the opera by no means went unchallenged: immediately the press began to speculate, centering on just what the regime feared most at the moment, its essential hypocrisy. If the *esprit frondeur* had been developing here since the time of *La Muette* and was evident in reviews of *Robert* and *La Juive*, it was now particularly mature. Given the current press laws, such an indirect means of political expression became increasingly important and led to an even greater refinement of this particular technique.

One useful ploy was, as we have seen in *La Juive*, to focus on just those historical issues that the libretto attempted deftly to skirt. As background to the political commentary now emerging around the work, a number of journals even ran articles on the implications of the term Huguenot.[135] But more specific and malicious articles, such as that in *La Quotidienne*, centered immediately on the most vulnerable point – inconsistency and the ridiculous result. Through this mode, as through the contemporary vehicle of caricature, critics of the regime could emphasize its essential political hypocrisy:

Les sentiments religieux et monarchiques de M. Thiers, ces sentiments que tout le monde lui connaît, lui ont fait un devoir de prendre en main la défense de la mémoire de Catherine de Médicis . . . M. Thiers a trouvé de si bonnes raisons pour justifier les massacres de Septembre, n'a pas voulu que le titre de Saint-Barthélémy fût donné à l'opéra nouveau . . . L'associé de Simon Deutz s'est ému à l'idée de voir outrager la reputation de la mère du roi de France . . . Mais la censure a laissé dans l'ouvrage de M. Scribe assez d'attaques contre la royauté et la religion pour prouver . . . que M. Thiers est toujours l'ami le plus dévoué des révolutions.[136]

[The religious and monarchical sentiments of M. Thiers, those sentiments that the whole world knows, imposed on him the duty of taking in hand the defense of the memory of Catherine de Medici . . . M. Thiers [who] found such good reasons for justifying the massacres of September, didn't want the title of Saint Bartholomew to be given to the new opera . . . The associate of Simon Deutz was roused by the idea of seeing the reputation of the mother of a king of France insulted . . . But the censorship has left enough attacks against royalty and religion in the work of M. Scribe to prove . . . that M. Thiers is still the most devoted friend of revolutions.]

Adolphe Thiers, an historian, had become minister of the interior on February 22, 1836. The political conjuncture is significant here, for *Les Huguenots* was to premiere just seven days later, on February 29. Thiers's reputation, from the beginning, was one of political inconsistency, of being a master of oratory but also of a tactic of détente that generally pleased no one.[137] The reference to Simon Deutz is significant, for he was, in fact, a Legitimist agent who offered to betray his protectress, the duchesse de Berry, to Thiers in 1832.[138] Hence now that a rapprochement with the church was occurring, there was an incisive irony in these remarks, which threw the regime's vacillations and hypocrisy into a dramatic light.

Almost every journal acknowledged that the opera was about a political event, despite the efforts of Scribe to focus interest on the love intrigue.[139] And for this reason, the *mise en scène* assumed a particular significance in clarifying the opera's implications both on stage and in the printed versions.[140] Knowing this, the regime, in the end, was forced to reach a ridiculous compromise that, in a double sense, cast political tensions in a revealing light. For a litter was to appear on stage in the ending in such a manner that the audience would see only the light from inside it and hence no discernible character.[141] The political symbolism of the Opéra, its function as political representation, here was clearly so significant that the regime could not allow this incident to pass. But, in the end, the effort of such belabored symbolic negotiations backfired, making the matter seem ridiculous and reflecting even more poorly on political authority.

As with *La Muette de Portici,* officials finally had to admit that, although a political embarrassment, the work was yet an artistic success. But it was again a success that could not be followed, a success that was far too dangerous, for given the audience's interpretive ground, its message was clearly a political threat. And so the fact that operatic reviews had come to serve as political statements, in the end, was directly to affect the future direction of the repertoire. If the role of the Opéra in political representation was originally responsible for the repertoire's innovations and strengths, now this role was to change and precisely the opposite was to occur. Given the nature of French grand opera as a complex kind of theater, and the institutional frame around it that gave it political meaning, the attempt to use it as image was proving futile. The bold new direction in using historical libretti, particularly from the nation's past, to "mettre en jeu les grands émotions" thus had to be consciously aborted.

And so began the period that contemporaries referred to as the opera's "decadence," one that lasted from about 1837 for approximately the next ten years. As we shall see, it was a period when success was elusive, largely because of officials' growing fears of the way in which certain kinds of works might now be read and responded to. The Opéra increasingly became no less than a dilemma for cultural officials, an institution from which, finally, the state tried unsuccessfully to dissociate itself. Amidst intensified contestation and another attempted assassination of Louis-Philippe (on June 26, 1836), the regime continued to turn its back on its "quasi-revolutionary" origins. Increasingly, it was being perceived now as not only politically conservative, but conservative in an empirical sense, without any ennobling principles, as well as being corrupt.[142]

Censorship pursued its established obsessions in the theaters with even greater rigor, and perhaps because of the political stakes, especially in the *grands théâtres*. However, even with these concerns, the regime was relatively indulgent with texts that did not invoke specific ideas and promised to "faire vibrer le public."[143]

This, then, was the period when the Opéra's decisions, to outsiders, often seemed without logic, so often did they appear to contradict its own artistic efforts in the most curious ways. But a closer examination will show that almost all of these contradictions issued from the administration's growing nervousness over current behavior in and around the Opéra.

The concept of grandeur, in its original sense, now began to disappear from the commission's deliberations about the advisability of presenting a work; and by the later 1830s it started to assume a different connotation, referring solely to external grandeur, to lavishness or pomp.

Throughout these years, in the wake of the mixed success of *Les Huguenots* and at a time of intensifying political tensions, violence at the Opéra sharply increased. Its file on "Désordres, Bruits, et Répressions" grew disconcertingly large, for it seemed that almost any excuse would trigger a show of discontent. One of the most violent disruptions occurred when a popular tenor, Poultier, was suddenly replaced by another, Raguenot (significantly, in *La Muette de Portici*). As reported by the Préfet de police:

A 8h½ et après le 1er acte de *La Muette,* l'acteur Raguenot qui doublait l'acteur Poultier, fit réclamer l'indulgence du public, aussitôt un tumulte se manifesta dans toute la salle. On essaya de jouer, le bruit continua avec plus de violence.[144]

[At eight thirty and after the first act of *La Muette,* the actor Raguenot who was the understudy for the actor Poultier, asked for the indulgence of the public, and immediately a tumult broke out in the hall. They tried to perform, [but] the noise continued with more violence.]

As he goes on to point out, the disruption spread gradually throughout the hall, from the orchestra to the parterre and finally to the loges as well. It lasted one and a half hours, making it necessary, in the end, for the police to expel the supposed agitators from the hall.

Perhaps because of the symbolism that now adhered to *La Muette de Portici* itself, the authorities immediately suspected some political manipulation. The director and commission, of course, were responsible for explaining this embarrassing disturbance, and also immediately suspected that it had been caused by agitators. A letter from the commission explained that Pillet, the current director, had done all he could to alert the audience well in advance about the substitution in the cast. And hence "il ne saurait être responsable du mécontent 'muet' réel ou factice que cette substitution a excité."[145] Such a nonverbal expression of displeasure, which used an artistic excuse with impunity while communicating a political message, increasingly worried the Opéra's officials. As in the Revolution, the Opéra seemed to be becoming an arena where political tensions could be given expression through indirect, hence legally acceptable, symbolic means.

The Préfet de police now sought to control other aspects surrounding performances, including the Opéra's publicity, to avoid providing further such excuses. He required that now all advertising, even that authorized by the minister of the interior, be presented to the Commissaire de police of each *quartier* before distribution.[146] But as soon as officials forestalled one pretext, another one seemed to arise, and generally around specific issues that carried politically symbolic implications. In particular, access to the Opéra now was becoming a sensitive issue, given the regime's original rhetoric about whom it was henceforth to address.

Both the price and distribution of tickets could now trigger either verbal or physical attacks outside the Académie Royale de Musique or inside its hall. An *arrêté* from the Préfecture de police points out that if the director sets the price of tickets too high, it could "faire naître dans l'esprit du public des doutes qui dégénèrent souvent en observations malvaillantes et même en discussions de nature à troubler l'ordre dans l'intérieur des théâtres" [instigate in the public spirit doubts that will often degenerate into malevolent observations and even discussions of such a nature as to disturb the order in the interior of the theaters]. Again, he explicitly points out that all possible means are to be taken to avoid any pretext for disorder in the theaters.[147]

Not only did the audience consider it its right to obtain tickets to the Opéra at affordable prices, but to obtain them fairly, with no ruses or favoritism. As evidence, we may cite an incident as early as 1837, when the public was frustrated in its efforts to obtain parterre tickets for the debut of a famous tenor, Duprez. After waiting on line for three hours, they began to threaten officials with violence, clearly transferring hostilities to higher authority, as reported by the Préfet de police:

Il est impossible de peindre l'exaltation du public, et les imprécations qu'ils faisaient entendre contre le Directeur et contre l'autorité pour être ainsi trompé dans son attente, et peu s'en est fallu que la salle fût envahie.[148]

[It is impossible to paint the excitement of the audience and the imprecations that they made audible against the Director and against authority for being thus cheated in its wait and the hall just narrowly missed being invaded.]

It was certainly not an easy moment to be the Opéra's director, and it is little wonder that there were several administrative changes in these years. Again, we must examine the actual position of the Opéra's director, observing the limitations now placed upon him and hence his almost inherently impossible task.

Duponchel had been coming under increasing criticism from the meddlesome commission, largely because of his frequent infractions in the Cahier des charges. But the public also resented the way in which he treated the Opéra's artists, even more so than Emile Véron, and finally opinion turned against him. The decisive incident concerned the situation of rivalry he created between the great tenors, Nourrit and Duprez, which led finally to Nourrit's suicide. In addition, the public resented his harsh treatment of the popular ballerina, Marie Taglioni, which, together with the fact that the Opéra was now losing money, led to his resignation.[149]

And so, as of June 1, 1840, Duponchel was removed as director and his financial association with Aguado accordingly dissolved. However, Duponchel remained at the Opéra, in charge of the scenic materials, and Léon Pillet assumed all the other functions, with Aguado's backing.[150]

Pillet, who was to run the Opéra from 1841 to 1847, came from a different background than his predecessors – a political one. The son of a *haute fonctionnaire,* he had become editor of the *Nouveau Journal de Paris,* a liberal publication that had been founded in 1827. With the advent of Louis-Philippe, Pillet became a faithful man of the government, and as a reward was soon given a succession of prestigious posts: first, as "maître des requêtes en service extraordinaire" in 1834, and then as "Commissaire royale près de théâtre de l'Opéra" in 1838.[151] The position as director was clearly yet another political favor, which probably prompted Wagner's remark that the Opéra was run by "political appointees, as a reward."[152] Neither an artist nor a true entrepreneur, Pillet, as a man of the government, must have seemed ideal to run the Opéra in a time of such political tension.

But again, the new director was to find himself plagued with the Commission de Surveillance, which was reconstitiued once more in the context of Pillet's Cahier des charges. It was even more powerful than before, and, significantly, once again it comprised almost all political figures, identified by the following titles: "MM. le Duc de Coigny, Pair de France; de Kératy, Pair de France; le Marquis de Louvois, Pair de France; Edmond Blanc; Pedre La Caze, député; Chaix d'Est-Ange, député; Armand Bertin; et d'Hennerville."[153] It is, perhaps, not insignificant that this group includes three peers, members of a body traditionally selected by the king in order to protect him from the "excesses" of the elected chamber.[154] And significant, too, is the presence now of Chaix d'Est-Ange, who, in 1832, had been the lawyer for the Ministry of the Interior that prosecuted Hugo's *Le Roi s'amuse*. The fines that this group was authorized to levy against the director, in the case of perceived infractions in his Cahier, were now startlingly high: each infraction could entail a fine of from 1,000 to 9,000 francs, taken directly from the director's deposit, within a period of three days.[155]

Certainly, pressure was being put on theaters of all kinds at this point, but the Ministry of the Interior continued to prosecute the infractions of the subventioned theaters with particular frequency. Léon Pillet was to have many problems with the authorities, but they centered on his purported artistic failings, both in the eyes of the commission and in those of the public as well. The director, however, was in no small dilemma, for the commission itself was aesthetically unsure, not certain of what it wanted, and often came near to dooming Pillet to failure. For what it wanted was contradictory, and no one realized that, perhaps, more than Pillet: it wanted external grandeur but with safely superficial subjects. It wanted, then, to "mettre en jeu" certain passions considered to be advantageous, while avoiding those politicized emotions and responses that were normally their concomitants. The Commission of Surveillance believed that the image of the monarchy could be protected by high standards of performance and staging, but the problem was, of what? The dilemma of the genre – the contradiction between its new historical definition after *Robert* and current political concerns – was becoming particularly acute. Once more, representation of revolts on stage was forbidden, a fact that may (despite the official explanations offered) account for the postponement of Meyerbeer's *Le Prophète*.[156]

We can already see the search for a safer subject in the famous case of the Opéra's purchase of the text, but not the music, of Wagner's *Flying Dutchman*. One must remember that it was at this moment that Wagner experienced the Opéra, perceiving it as a foreigner, and hence often misreading the institution's nature. All he saw was its quest for external grandeur and its curious artistic logic, as well as the apparent political favoritism shown in the appointment of Léon Pillet. Hence, undoubtedly to Wagner's delight, when *Le Vaisseau Fantôme,* with a French text by Paul Foucher and music by Dietsch, was produced in 1842, it failed almost unanimously to please.

The commission's disapprobation centered on the lack of grandeur in the production, which the artists involved undoubtedly realized would have been discordant with the opera's subject. In its report to the minister, the commission opined that it "n'a trouvé, ni dans les décors, ni dans les costumes et autres accessoirs, ce caractère de graveur et de magnificence, par lequel doit se signaler notre première scène lyrique, et dont le sujet ne pouvait disposer" [has not found in either the décors or in the costumes or other accessories the character of solemnity and magnificence by which our first lyric stage should be distinguished and to which this subject cannot lend itself]. It also complained that the painted décors were monotonous and so undetailed as to be considered not décor at all, but merely "un rideau d'attente." And perhaps even worse, in light of the audience's eagerness to find excuses for disruption, the vaunted *vaisseau fantôme* appeared only on the poster and not on the stage. Their report concluded with a warning that was to be delivered to Léon Pillet on their behalf about the necessity of improving his artistic efforts.[157]

But things were to get far worse for Pillet, who more and more became a scapegoat, caught between the impossible demands of the commission and those of the fractious public. The commission continued to accuse him of lacking concern for the Opéra's grandeur, and again their stress was on finding subjects that would be amenable to a grand *mise en scène.*

A case in point is that of the two-act opera *La Lazzarone,* with music by Halévy, performed at the Opéra in 1844. The commission was worried about the work almost from the beginning, pointing out "en raison même de la grandeur et de l'importance du théâtre, (l'opéra) ne saurait y être traité avec trop de réserve et de précaution." Again it was worried both about the possibility of audience ridicule and that certain scenes, if staged without appropriate pomp, might have a potentially dangerous effect:

Le premier regret exprimé par la commission c'est que l'action du *Lazzarone* se compose d'éléments dont la simplicité vulgaire n'est susceptible de produire ni gaité ni intérêt.

Enfin, dans la mise en scène de l'ouvrage, et particulièrement dans la cérémonie qui termine le premier acte, celle du baptême d'un cloche, la commission eut désiré . . . plus de pompe et d'éclat, ce que le genre ne comportait pas . . .[158]

[The first regret expressed by the commission is that the action of *La Lazzarone* is composed of elements whose vulgar simplicity is capable of producing neither gaiety nor interest.

Finally, in the *mise en scène* of the work, and particularly in the ceremony that ends the first act, that of the baptism of a bell, the commission wanted more pomp and *éclat,* which this genre does not allow.]

As we may recall in the case of *La Muette de Portici,* the Opéra's authorities inherently feared works that could be taken too seriously from the standpoint of their political message. This was now once again the case, for the commission went out of its way to discourage the production of any works it considered to be "triste et monotone."[159]

But success remained elusive, as a series of failures and short-lived works seemed to dominate the Opéra's stage in the early 1840s: Halévy's *Drapier* (1840), his *Charles VI* (1843), and Thomas's *Comte Carmagnolo* (1841) all failed to excite any real enthusiasm. And so by 1845 the commission offered the minister a bleak report on the current state of the Opéra and the prospects for the immediate future:

Dans les cinq derniers mois de l'année qui vient de finir, quatre ouvrages nouveaux ont été représentés . . . La commission éprouve le regret d'avoir à constater qu'aucun de ces ouvrages n'a obtenu le succès réel, soit qu'on les envisage au point de vue de l'art, soit qu'on les juge dans leur rapport avec la prospérité de l'entreprise.[160]

[During the last five months of the year that has just ended, four new works were presented . . . The commission regrets to have to state that none of these works obtained real success, whether one sees them from the point of view of art or judges them in relation to the prosperity of the enterprise.]

It is in response to this perception that we can begin to understand more fully the direction that the repertoire of the Opéra now began to take. At the Comédie-Française, the turn away from romanticism to classicism was well under way, having begun there, in fact, as early as 1835.[161] But given the dilemmas of the Opéra, one answer seemed to be to turn to modern Italian works, presented in French and performed with appropriate grandeur. Such was evidently the case with Donizetti's operas, given here in the early 1840s: *Les Martyrs, La Favorite,* and *Dom Sebastien.*[162] But the other answer, one we have also seen already in the late Restoration, was to turn to revivals of the grand works of the previous decade. As Wagner so acidulously observed, whenever a work at the Opéra now seemed to fail, *Robert le Diable* was soon to appear once again on its stage.[163]

But these revivals were hardly exact reproductions of the original works, for the semiological whole that determined their meaning and hence the character of the theatrical event was undergoing a change. Works conceived to embody grandeur in the original sense – to "mettre en jeu les grands passions" – were now to be merely externally or superficially grand. But once again this has to be seen in light of a larger theatrical culture in which revivals of pieces successful in the early 1830s were frequently provoking demonstrations. Audiences would often call out for passages that had been suppressed, throwing printed texts on the stage or demanding that political *chansons* be sung. Hence, from 1836 all pieces reintroduced into the repertoire had to be reexamined by the censors, now especially sensitive to the "jeu de la mise en scène."[164] For the Opéra, then, once politically resonant works had to be reshaped in such a manner as to activate certain kinds of emotions and simultaneously eliminate others. The goal seems to have been to draw attention away from the subjects, which could still be politically troublesome, and direct it toward the entertainment aspect. And so a different concept of grandeur was clearly emerging, along with a very different sense of the Opéra's potential political usefulness.

107

Figure 7. *La Muette de Portici,* n.d. (183?). Bibliothèque de l'Opéra.

Accordingly, the Opéra now often cut crucial scenes to further its redefined end, as was notably the case already with *Les Huguenots* in 1838. Another volatile work that the theater now tried to revive judiciously, one long put off because of previous disruptions, was *La Muette de Portici.* When it was finally performed again, in 1847, it was with *décors rajeunis* and with stunning new *divertissements.* Now all the public attention was apparently not focused on the subject itself but on the new team of Spanish dancers in "authentic" costumes in the spectacle scenes[165] (Figure 7).

But still the Opéra was not always successful: in fact, in its ardent attempt to escape potentially politicized responses to its productions, it encouraged precisely the opposite. One can see now not only how the director's limitations led to artistically ridiculous results, but how this led to the increasing spread of a certain political perception, as the regime well knew.

We can observe this dilemma clearly in the case of yet another revival of Halévy's opera *La Juive* in 1847. Here too we can see the effects of another probable strategy on the part of the state: its turning over of the Opéra to the city of Paris in October 1846. Although this change is often explained as an official attempt to transfer the financial burden, one can easily see this in a different way.[166] For no matter how much money the state seemed to pour into the Opéra, the institution appeared artistically paralyzed by the contradictions imposed upon it. Its image was no longer an asset, and now the only thing to do was precisely the inverse of 1831: to distance the regime from the Opéra. But even this goal was not easily attained, for the Opéra continued tenaciously to haunt the monarchy, as we can see in the case of *La Juive*.

On the occasion of the opera's revival in 1847 the press unleashed a veritable barrage of pungent, damaging satire. As one can see in Figures 8 and 9, real horses had apparently disappeared from the stage, perhaps a response to the increasingly serious financial plight of the Opéra. And this became an occasion for ridicule not only of the *mise en scène* but for virtually every aspect of the Opéra's current management (Figure 10).

Whereas the *esprit frondeur* had manifested itself heretofore in reviews of operas, it was now unvented in caricature, obtaining a special effect through the image. Again, commentary on opera here was deeply implicated in the political culture and in the dense web of understandings as to what was an effective political statement. Opera as a symbolic target naturally was pounced upon in the efflorescence of caricature that truculently attacked the prestige of Louis-Philippe. Moreover, not only were there relatively fewer obstacles to censorship in the visual image, but opera was an even safer or untouchable subject for ridicule.[167] As in operatic reviews, a range of trenchant political points could be made, but indirectly, obliquely, and sometimes for this reason, with all the more force. Again, like *mazarinades,* these were texts in which the element of political contestation is not inherent or transparent; the texts are rather vehicles for political responses. Such images, then, like *mazarinades,* must be decoded and seen as making several layers of potent political and cultural statements at once.[168]

As contemporary caricatures suggest, the tendency was to make only cosmetic superficial physical improvements, often with a patently ridiculous result. And more than ever, the new co-directors were made scapegoats, although still seen as retaining ties to the state, as evidenced in the acidulous caricature of the Opéra's actual curtain (Figure 9). Here we see not Louis XIV handing the keys of the Opéra (or the *privilège*) to Perrin and Cambert but a peasant *en sabots* handing them to Duponchel and Roqueplan.

109

Figure 8. Interior of the Salle Le Peletier during performance of opera *Charles VI* . . .

Figure 9. Caricatures from *L'Illustration*, 1847. Library of Congress.

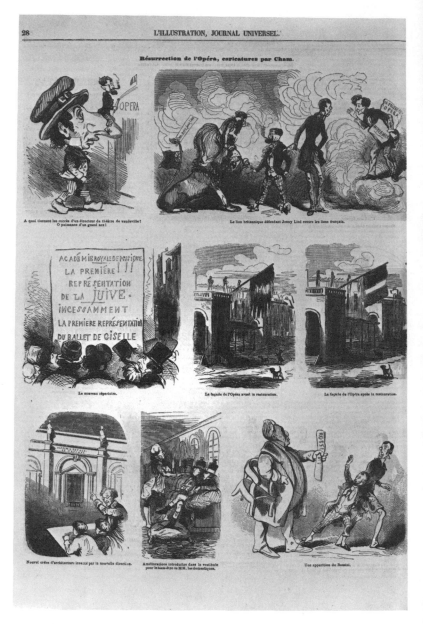

Figure 10. Caricatures from *L'Illustration*, 1847. Library of Congress.

This might also have been an allusion to the financial situation of the Opéra, now quite literally being starved, perhaps in the hope that it would die. Under Pillet's administration, the deficit of the Opéra had almost doubled, although the immediate reasons for his departure concerned his liaison with the singer Rosina Stoltz.[169] He was replaced now by the curious team of Duponchel and Roqueplan, who took over the Opéra's management on November 24, 1847. They inherited a bleak situation: a debt of 471,000 francs, with the extremely low subvention of 520,000 francs per year. The fact that the state now almost feared the Opéra is perhaps reflected here, as in another significant addition to their Cahier des charges: should any disruption or scandal result from a work that had been authorized, performances would promptly be suspended at the directors' own expense.[170] Inescapably, the Opéra had waxed from being a potential asset, a tool of image, as at the start of Louis-Philippe's regime, to being a liability, the opposition's tool.

The 1830s and '40s had seen a number of repeated but aborted attempts by independent entrepreneurs to found a competitive lyric theater in Paris. The state had refused to encourage the enterprise until the late 1840s, when it may have seemed just the answer to its difficult problem with the Opéra.[171] Not only would the new theater deflect attention away from the Académie Royale, it could promote a politically harmonious image, thus diverting the regime's opponents.

The new lyric theater was in many respects an inversion of the Opéra, not only in terms of repertoire but also of ambience and clientele. It was given the name Opéra-National, although not an official theater, and located a safe distance away on the popular Boulevard du Temple. Its founder, Adolphe Adam, conceived it as a theater for the people, where low ticket prices would now make it possible for even a worker occasionally to attend. Moreover, its ambience was not to be inimical to the lower classes, for it would deemphasize social stratification and the ceremony of operatic attendance. Indeed, this would have been impossible in the hall that Adam selected and then remodeled for this purpose, the former Cirque-Olympique.

If space speaks in the theater as a symbolizing agent, suggesting not only a relation between audience and stage but between theat-

113

rical and external reality, then the Opéra-National, just like the Revolution's Opéra, carried a message substantially different from that of the Académie Royale de Musique.[172] In its reincarnation, the old circus ring became the new theater's parterre, installed with *fauteuils,* and was, in turn, surrounded by floors of boxes and semicircular galleries. And the stage projected much further into the audience than in the other lyric theaters, thus increasing its sense of intimacy (as Figure 11 reveals).[173]

In contrast to the Opéra, the message projected by the new Opéra-National was one attractive to both the state as well as the audience, if for different reasons. The message, according to both sides, resembled that of the utopian, specifically Fourierist ideal, of a peaceful or conciliatory democracy, one at first vague in its political implications. For according to Fourier, opera was a symbol of a harmonious, cooperative society in which the classes joined efforts and all benefited from fulfillment and *le luxe.*[174] For the government, now, the stress on cooperation seemed particularly apt, as did the symbolic idea of spreading both culture and luxury to the recalcitrant mass. And even if it remained only a symbol, it could serve an important rhetorical role, as a token of good intentions, as had the Opéra of the late Restoration.

According to one of the new opera's supporters, the comte de Pontéculant, the theater was in addition, a means to regenerate the now menancing working class: it was a vehicle to sooth or calm it, a sort of *antidote lyrique* that would balance its "tormented, overstimulated" passions, exacerbated by the melodramas it attended. The new Opéra, on the contrary, would be both *doux* and *agréable,* providing good company for the workers and helping to instill them with "better morals."[175] And there seemed to be no danger here, as in the *grand opéra,* of a potential misconstrual and violent reactions to volatile works.

But there were tensions incipient from the very beginning over the intended and actual meaning of the new Opéra, for French workers read it in a more radical and politicized way. They saw a potential very different from that of the comte de Pontéculant— not the capacity for harmonization but rather for self-knowledge and expressive release. In a sense, they saw the deeper implications of Fourier's theories of the social function of opera, as opposed to the merely superficial elements of it.[176]

Figure 11. Performances at the Opéra-National, *L'Illustration*, 1847.
Library of Congress.

115

The new Opéra, some believed, would have a role in their political education; it would imbue them with a distinctive kind of insight as well as confer political status. At a time when even the *petit bourgeoisie* and the better off of the *classes populaires* could not elect deputies, and when other aspects of their *"vie associative"* were being repressed, such an Opéra seemed a small step forward. Given the Académie Royale as a point of reference, the alternative Opéra by comparison appeared to emit a progressive political message. If political opposition to the monarchy was already being expressed in operatic commentary, then the plans for an alternative theater were already serving a concomitant ideological function. Workers, in approaching the opera ideologically, saw more than the government intended in its sanctioning of the new Opéra, and their ideological construal of such decisions was increasingly the case over the next two decades.

Workers' journals of the 1840s had already begun to stress the fundamental social and political importance of access to the nation's high culture, including its art. Through the journals they read (or that were read aloud to them in groups), French workers were constantly reminded of the social importance of the arts and of their own unfair deprivations. One of their principal journals, *L'Atelier*, continually enjoined them to assert themselves in this domain, stressing that their *morale* should be part of that of the nation.[177] No more were they to be isolated, excluded from political discourse, a discourse communicated not only through words but through cultural symbols as well. Ostensibly because of its association with a national, political function, a small but significant group of French workers henceforth became deeply concerned with opera.

Indeed, because of its stress on the importance of workers' appropriating this political language, *L'Atelier* explicitly urged its readers to support the new Opéra: it stressed the importance of the theater's function of linking the real nation with the French state, that it could "mettre en lumière les faits glorieux de notre historie."[178] This sense of what it communicated symbolically was probably related as well to the fact that the journal had praised the spectacles of the Cirque-Olympique that involved the audience so intensely with the military glory of France. In this light, the new Opéra was an even more powerful form of political conception, for it could explain events and give insights into them in a far more incisive way. The new theater, then, would both teach and involve French workers in the nation's culture; it would impart to them a valuable patrimony in which they could now take pride. Already, the Opéra represented a powerful, if intangible, conceptual fusion, encouraging workers to make a considerable emotional investment in it.

Of particular significance for the future was that *L'Atelier* associated the Opéra with political participation, or with entry into the nation's larger political dialogue. For the Opéra was a means to develop political understanding, one relating to the reality of political symbolization through culture, so traditionally characteristic of France. French workers were to be able to read the messages that it sent and to respond in a similar language, or within the same terms of political discourse. This is not surprising given the fact that in the popular press prose was commonly used to express the imaginary, poetry being reserved for facts. If verse seemed to express "popular realities" more exactly, then the powerful language of opera could potentially do the same.[179]

At this stage however, there was not yet a desire to enter the Académie Royale itself, it no longer being as attractive as the alternative now provided. The Opéra that they sought to enter was a different kind of theater, presenting a different kind of art in a different social cadre. It was an art that dealt forthrightly with contemporary social and political issues, in the manner of the *opéra-comique* as opposed to the Opéra in eighteenth-century France. It stressed a clear and forthright language with the minimum of display and pomp, in a comfortable, accessible atmosphere where there were no rules to be learned (Figure 12).

The new Opéra, moreover, was one that promised to foster a new kind of dynamic between the audience and the stage, as differentiated from that now characteristic of the Académie Royale de Musique. It was indeed to serve the function originally projected in 1831 by the Opéra, to "mettre en jeu" the grand, noble passions associated with collective goals. For this reason, *L'Atelier* had no doubt that French workers would react enthusiastically to the new Opéra, and that they would make an apt and inspiring audience for it. And many, after all, had already been exposed to the *orphéon* choral societies, government-sponsored organizations that trained workers in the rudiments of music.[180] But more important was the seemingly inherent capacity of the

Figure 12. Performances at the Opéra-National, *L'Illustration* 1847.
Library of Congress.

workers not only to respond profoundly but to evaluate art intuitively, instinctively knowing the good from the bad:

> Le peuple n'ira pas entendre trois fois de suite l'exécution d'un morceau de musique pour . . . rechercher quelque défaut d'harmonie; non, le peuple n'a pas de science, mais en revanche il a le sentiment du bon, du bien; son coeur bat devant toute grande pensée noblement traduite, et c'est à cette heureuse passion qu'il faut s'adresser.[181]

> [The people will not go to hear the execution of a piece of music three times in a row . . . to search for some fault of harmony; no, the people do not have knowledge but in compensation they have the sense of the good; their heart beats before a great thought nobly translated, and it is this happy passion that it is necessary to address.]

The workers, then, decipher art in a manner fundamentally different from artistic dilettantes, who are concerned primarily with the inessential. We shall see the significant results of this fact very shortly, within the context of French workers' further exposure to opera in the Republic of 1848.

But already a dual reading was evident: *L'Atelier* applauded the first work presented for reasons substantially different from those of journals associated with other classes in France. Indeed, the first work performed was particularly apt for its interpretative mode, and it coincided with the social and political message that it saw in the theater itself. It was the story of two talented but impoverished artists, young aspiring men of the theater, who find themselves befriended by a simple and poor French worker. At a time of increasing concern over how workers were presented on the stage, often as drunk and ridiculous, this was a refreshingly positive image.[182] According to the plot, when the young artists' work was finally performed, they could not help but recognize the injustice caused by the contemporary theater's obvious discrimination by social class:

> Et nos deux jeunes auteurs, regardant les vilaines places à 50 c. où l'on a rélégué les porteurs de blouses derrière un luxe

prodigieux de barreaux de fer, témoignent très chaudement de leur reconnaissance.[183]

[And our two young authors, looking at the unpleasant places at 50 centimes to which they relegated the wearers of blouses behind a prodigious luxury of iron bars, warmly gave witness of their appreciation.]

Indeed, this parable was an apt projection of the theater's message in another sense: it was an Opéra for the nation's excluded, for artistic *débutantes* and the lower classes. And it was far different from the contemporary melodrama being decried by *L'Atelier* as well as the authorities, and which had become a vehicle for the diffusion of political ideas and particularly social contestation.[184] The bourgeois journal *L'Illustration* reported, perhaps incorrectly, "la sympathie que l'Opéra-National excite dans toutes les classes de la société Parisienne." But it did point out the conspicuous presence of "tous ces patients en blouse" who waited on line in inclement weather, some for over seven hours, for tickets.[185]

The Opéra-National, then, from the start was a theater with a dual appeal, responding to the ideological needs of two perceptibly different social groups. Because of the fate of French grand opera, it served authority as a new kind of image, as it did for the socially excluded, but in a significantly different sense. In both cases, however, the attack on grand opera and the projection of a counterimage communicated a political message, just as it did simultaneously in the thought of Wagner. But for French workers, it now served the special additional function of helping to make them more acutely aware of their own social, political, and cultural condition. And so, as we shall see, as we saw once again with *La Muette,* the Opéra was one of the images that helped forge the alliance that would foster a revolution.

The Opéra-National was not to last long, but workers' interest in opera was to endure, for they, like Wagner, found it a means of entry into the most profound social issues. Opera not only communicated a political reality to be deciphered socially, it could in itself be used as a conceptual and ideological force, as would be increasingly the case. And so already on the eve of the Second Republic we get a sense of the importance of an alternative opera, communicating a different social conception. And in time, indeed, it was to be Wagner's alternative that French workers would come to embrace, for one of the same reasons that stimulated Wagner – the connotations of the old Opéra. But clearly the aesthetic power of the operatic alternative in France was inseparable from its meaning within a particular cultural and social frame. Politics, then, played a role not only in defining and then transforming the art but in suggesting specific alternatives to it as the Republic loomed ahead.

3

RADICALIZATION, REPRESSION, AND OPERA: MEYERBEER'S *LE PROPHETE*

"Les gouverneurs ne dovient jamais perdre de vue que l'art peut se passer d'eux tandis qu'ils ne peuvent pas se passer de l'art."[1]

[The rulers should never forget that art can do without them whereas they cannot do without art.]

ACCOUNTS OF GOVERNMENT intervention in opera in France in 1848 are by no means lacking in existing histories of the Opéra.[2] And most historians would acknowledge that the state attempted to employ the theater for propagandistic purposes in support of the Republican ideological goal. But almost uniformly they approach this phenomenon as merely a transient one, both in terms of political manipulation of the Opéra as well as its after-effects. From this perspective, one that I have already elaborated on at length, the Opéra of 1848 is a brief aberration from an otherwise commercial institution.

This chapter will argue to the contrary that although the early Second Republic is a period in which the state's political use of the Opéra is most overt, it is one that we must see in the framework of continuity as well as change, or within a continuum of strategies, perceptions, and responses to opera in France.

As I hope to show, the Opéra of the Second Republic continued to serve the function of projecting an image that was to obscure political uncertainty and then contradictions; and that, again, this image underwent a transformation with the change in political direction, one clearly noted and indirectly responded to by the opposition to the regime. Here too the Opéra came to serve a political function that was not intended by providing a common framework for ideological debate among an increasingly broad social group. As a result, in part, of the government's merger of cultural spheres, or of its politics and art in the

Opéra, it here became the nexus for the contestation of social class.

And once more, the Opéra faced the problem of the delay between the conception and commission of works and their actual belated premieres in an unfortunate political conjucture. Moreover, here too the tactic initially devised for the Opéra was to backfire as a result both of unforeseen modes of construal and the Republic's political shifts.

It is from this perspective that I hope also to demonstrate that the history of the Republic's political uses or manipulation of the Opéra does not end in 1848: It affected another work that we have generally not seen in this connection, Meyerbeer and Scribe's opera *Le Prophète,* which premiered in 1849. The staging, the message, the utterance of the work, as well as its enduring aftereffects on political perceptions and operatic policy have to be seen in this light. The work said something different from what the Republic originally intended it to and from what the Republic of 1849 wished to communicate through it as well. Again, it became the matrix for a heated political debate that in turn helped to bring about a change in direction in operatic policies and intent.

Once more then, as in previous cases, we must begin by attempting to understand what the regime originally tried to articulate through opera and how its tactics thereafter changed; for this will help to explain the way in which the institution staged the work and the ways in which different groups construed its significance and constructed its sense.

If the regime that had come to power in 1830 confronted a complex political problem with regard to the symbolic role of the Opéra, that which replaced it did as well. For like that of 1830, the Revolution of 1848 was precipitous, but, in addition, it seemingly swept away an entire political culture.[3] The choice of symbols therefore now involved not only the problem of expressing an anonymous, collective, depersonalized and "desacralized" power, but also that of communicating directly with a new, unsophisticated electorate. Even more than before, images were charged with communicating political ideas and thus entered into a complex counterpoint with other modes of political discourse.[4] Symbolism, then, through both images and policies, assumed even more importance given its role in the political integration and education of the new masses. And once again, the problems of artistic and political definition were integrally intertwined as the nation attentively awaited the new regime's symbolic self-definition.

Historians have already studied the ways in which it chose its specific symbols – including political allegories and emblems – by returning to the vocabulary of 1830. And they have considered how it attempted to translate its message into terms of commissions and programs for the visual arts and through numerous ambitious programs of official patronage.[5] But here, as in other political images, the problem was pressing for other reasons too: the press immediately raised the question of the implications of the Republic for art and of the state's obligations. In fact, the former director of the Opéra, Emile Véron, was one of the first to openly criticize the Republic for its apparent lack of artistic action.[6]

Yet even greater complexities were involved in the question of the implications of the Republic for theater, including what it should encourage, what it should say, and what it should attempt to control. Undoubtedly the theatrical culture of the first revolution was very much in the minds of the officials who pondered the question of what the theaters could and should now do. Now as then the theatrical public of the great subventioned theaters was explicitly the nation and here specifically the broad-ranging new electorate. And for the theater, serving as the principal means of distraction and information for the illiterate in the first half of the nineteenth century, the question of how best to address it loomed particulary large.

Moreover, as contemporaries observed, the 1848 revolution "invaded" the theaters – from the boulevards to the official stages, it dramatized events almost as they occurred. For the moment, as in 1830, a receptiveness to historical tableaux and *allégories vivantes* seemed to cut across the classess, united by a "goût de la mise en scène."[7] And once more, as in 1789 and again in 1830, the boulevard spectacles fused with "the spirit of the masses" in a kind of *politique-théâtre;* as Hallays-Dabot, later the chief censor of theater for the Second Empire, was led to remark, the generation of 1848 almost seemed to have been "formed" by the theater.[8] Because of this pervasive theatricality, the government now faced a difficult task, and knew well the danger of leaving the stages free to run their own course. Not only then did a large number of treatises on theater begin to appear, but three successive government commissions were charged with making detailed reports – the first from the Conseil d'Etat, the second from the Ministry of the Interior, and the third from the Assemblée Nationale.[9]

The dilemma, of course, was how to free the theaters, in a symbolic sense, while still retaining a guiding role in order to assure the right effect. Officials understood well the importance of seeming to restore theatrical liberties, given the significance that they obviously carried in the wake of the preceding regime. As in the first revolution, they found the theater to be a convenient monitor of public opinion and of rapidly changing revolutionary sentiment. And so far a variety of reasons, they began with a law of theatrical liberties, thus abrogating the law requiring the submission of all manuscripts.[10]

The next major problem was to decide who was to set the new theatrical policies: was it to be government officials, private citizens, artists, theatrical administrators? The Conseil d'Etat instituted a committee to review the situation in the official houses, now in danger of closing because of the financial ramifications of the political upheaval. And later, in March 1848, the new minister of the interior, Ledru-Rollin, named a commission to make recommendations on theater under the auspices of his ministry. It comprised a representative of the goverment, the directors of the four state theaters, thirteen dramatic authors, three dramatic artists, and three members of the periodical press.[11]

But decisions concerning the theaters, in the end, were made upon the basis of immediate need, and perhaps because of political uncertainty not with a view to the potential long-term implications. The pressing task seemed to be to reinforce the connection of the major subventioned theaters to the state, or to reclaim them officially for the new Republic. Hence all subventioned theaters soon underwent a sharp metamorphosis, adopting their old revolutionary names as well as obvious external symbols: the *garde nationale* now kept the order in the place of the *garde municipale,* thereby strengthening the association or linkage between the official theaters and the state. But despite the government's apparent solicitude and concern with artistic symbolism, the major theaters, including the Opéra, were forced to close briefly in the early months of 1848.[12]

Of all the major theater closing, that of the Opéra was the most alarming in light of its immediate and successful response to the recent revolutionary events. Moreover, its importance as an instrument of political image became clear immediately, as did its special suitability to the particular needs of a socialist political power. For not only could it embody a vague idealism and evoke the "warm, eloquent, sentimental" spirit of harmony characteristic of 1848, it could serve as an instrument of political education, as in 1789.[13] And it was still a means for the government to establish its roots both in contemporary interests and emotions as well as its connection with the great or high cultural tradition of France. Finally, not only did the Opéra seem to concilitate different levels of culture, but because of its established repertoire it escaped the ideological vacillation of the other arts.

It was clear that the Republic's task in opera was to reclaim the grand repertoire for itself, and accordingly *La Muette de Portici* appeared soon after the revolutionary days. As in 1830, the opera, for contemporaries, seemed to be a "symbole même du soulèvement contre la tyrannie."[14] But when the Opéra reopened after a short hiatus, the problem was not so much what to perform, but how, symbolically and practically, to restructure the institution itself.

Officials were again concerned not only with the symbolism of operatic policy but with determining the kind of structure that would insure the desired results. Should the Opéra be governed directly by a representative of the state, or could it continue to be entrusted to a Directeur-Entrepreneur? While such a system might be less desirable symbolically, it nevertheless carried the potential practical advantage of lessening the financial burden on the state. Other questions concerned whether the Opéra should change its image substantially, deemphasizing the traditional luxury, or whether this was an essential and useful aspect. And finally the Opéra faced the problem of meeting the needs of the new audience it was to recognize, and of how or whether to integrate it with the *habitués* of the Opéra.

As usual, advice was in no short supply; as always, letters of suggestion abounded, two of which, the most characteristic, deserve to be quoted at length. The first is an unsigned "Projet d'une nouvelle organisation pour l'Opéra," which testifies to the special dangers seen in the potential closing of the Opéra:

Au moment où tout s'effraie, où la confidance s'ébranle, où une panique inconsidérée pèse sur la population, l'Opéra viendrait à suspendre ses représentations. Quel effet produirait sur les esprits timides cette sinistre nouvelle qui semblerait le symptôme effrayant d'une ruine universelle: l'Opéra lui-même ne peut vivre sous la République: la République a tué l'Opéra!

Telle serait l'impression publique que produirait cet événement, dont, comme de bien d'autres, la jeune République endosserais l'effet désastreux sans en avoir été la cause . . . L'Opéra est encore . . . une des gloires parisiennes. C'est le théâtre des plus grandes magnificences de l'art. La République, à son avènement, ne peut répudier le superbe héritage de luxe, d'élégance et de poésie qui lui a été légué . . .

Ce système nouveau nous le proposons: il est simple et nous parait infaillible.

C'est d'enlever l'Opéra à la spéculation privée, et d'en faire un établissement public, appartenant à l'Etat, administré sous sa direction et sous son contrôle . . .

The letter goes on to suggest:

représentations périodiques à prix réduit qui mettraient ce riche spectacle à la portée des classes populaires . . . C'est un beau tribun que la propagande républicaine doit se réserver pour elle seule; c'est là, par les triples attraits qui attirent, séduisent, et entraint l'âme, les yeux et les oreilles, c'est de lui qu'elle doit agir sur la population . . . [15]

[At a moment when everyone is frightened, when confidence is shaken, when a rash panic weighs on the population, the Opéra would suspend its performances. What effect would this sinister news that seems to be the frightening symptom of universal ruin produce on timid spirits: the Opéra itself cannot live under the Republic: the Republic has killed the Opéra! That would be the public impression that this event would produce, for which the young Republic would be held responsible without having been the cause . . . The Opéra is still . . . one of the glories of Paris. It is

127

the theater of the grandest artistic magnificence. The Republic, in its advent, cannot repudiate the superb heritage of luxury, of elegance and of poetry that have been bequeathed to it . . .

We propose this new system: it is simple and appears infallible to us.

It is to remove the Opéra from private speculation, and to make it a public establishment, belonging to the state, administered under its direction and under its control . . .

(The letter goes on to suggest)

periodic performances at reduced prices that would put this rich spectacle at the disposal of the popular classes . . . It is a beautiful tribune that Republican propaganda should reserve for itself alone; it is here, by the triple attractions that lure, seduce, and transport the soul, the eyes and the ears, it is by this that (the Republic) should act on the population.]

To shut the Opéra in a moment of confusion and panic would be disastrous, so closely are its glories identified with both the stability and spirit of the regime. Since the Opéra is such an important political mode of representation, responsibility for it should not be left to private speculation. An ineffable combination of civic *fête,* drama, and fantasy, its splendor, in the tradition of the *féerie,* can help to seduce the political public.[16] Using a Fourierist kind of imagery, the author points out the uses of such luxury to the political goal and image and in several different ways. Not only does it symbolize equal access to high culture and to material goods but it preserves a legacy of literature and splendor that is essential to political credibility.

Other letters warn against the danger of maintaining the Opéra as a private enterprise, and similarly cite past experience or the results to which it has led. One, written by a former inspecteur du chant, Duclot, points out that if the structure does not change the state should at least keep close watch over the entrepreneur.[17] As he observes, the state would still maintain the essential right to annul the *privilège* should the entrepreneur eventually betray its political trust.

But despite all this advice, other concerns in the end outweighed the obvious advantages of having the Second Republic run the Opéra directly. For officials had to keep in mind the state's other costly involvements in music or in more direct musical patronage outside of the Opéra. It was clearly concerned with sponsoring other kinds of music aimed at various cultural levels, which included a competition for the composition of patriotic songs in 1848. And the Republic, in addition, did take an active interest in concert life, was grateful for the concerts that Berlioz organized, and kept him in his sinecure as Conservatoire librarian.[18] And so, given the financial needs of the state as well as the essential need to ensure artistic continuity, Duponchel and Roqueplan were asked to remain as entrepreneurs.

As we have seen, this team had taken over the Opéra on November 24, 1847, inheriting Pillet's large debt and being given the small subvention of 520,000 francs. But as testimony to the official sense of the Opéra's inherent importance, the Assemblée Nationale voted an extra subvention of 170,000 francs (in addition to the annual subvention, now set at 620,000 francs).[19] Hence the year began well for the two directors, and within the first six months, despite the political traumas, they were able to show a profit of 100,000 francs. Wisely, they resuscitated the old repertoire – now resonant workers like *Robert le Diable* and *La Muette de Portici,* to which they slowly added new ones like Donizetti's *La Favorite.*[20]

So successful was the Opéra initially, and so compatible with the current political idealism, that the regime attempted to associate itself even more closely with the theater. To reclaim the Opéra, as in the First Republic, the state employed it as an important location for important ceremonies and announcements, thus reinforcing its symbolic significance. It was a locus for political redefinition, both outside its walls and inside its hall, a means for the state to project an identity and recognize a new audience or constituency. This use of art as politics, this attempt to effect a merger, was to have considerable ramifications later, but in quite unexpected ways.

A most telling example of the political goals that the state initially envisaged for opera is the ceremony that occurred in the small courtyard of the Opéra on April 2, 1848. The ostensible purpose of the ceremony was, as in the First Republic, to plant a

129

"liberty tree" in the Opéra's courtyard, thus christening it as a political domain. Major figures of church and state attended the solemn ceremony: Ledru-Rollin, minister of the interior; Morel, the curé of Saint-Roch; and Caussidière, the prefect of police. Perhaps this curious assortment of figures may be best explained in reference to the Fête de la Fraternité, to occur on April 20. Here, at the foot of the Arc de Triomphe, the "spirit of February" was to be symbolically expressed by the presence of officials of all kinds, along with the clergy and representatives of all social sectors of the population. If the "spirit of February" was the spirit of fraternity and cooperation of different social groups and functions, then the Opéra seemed to provide an ideal setting in which to express this. But it is important to note, in addition, that both ceremonies might well have been conceived as a preparation for the elections, set for Easter, April 23; it was then that universal suffrage would first be put into effect, and about which the government and other groups were notably nervous.[21]

In its ceremony, the Opéra's representative was one of its co-directors, Duponchel, symbolically mounted on horseback in the costume of the National Guard. This gesture in itself emitted a multilayered symbolic message concerning the Opéra's associations and the meaning of its conventions. As already pointed out, the National Guard now replaced the Municipal Guard at the major theaters, and thus this costume further emphasized the fact; and significantly, in the preceding month, on March 8, the National Guard was officially opened to all adult males, which perhaps increased the resonance here. Moreover, this attire made yet another kind of reference that emerges when we recognize the fact that Duponchel was here surrounded by a real processional body: a detachment of the National Guard, the Urban Guard on horseback, in their splendid ceremonial attire, almost as on the stage. In fact, this may have been meant to clarify further the meaning of the processions' on stage, as projections of the Republic's grandeur, thus encouraging the conflations that we have already seen. And to make this association between political and operatic grandeur even more strong, the Opéra adorned the courtyard with trophies of arms, which were also to appear on its stage.[22]

But beyond this, there was commentary to explicate the political symbolism of the Opéra, which, as we may have expected, employed the rhetoric of Charles Fourier. Since the "spirit of

February" included religious effusions as a prominent element, it is not suprising that the curé of Saint-Roch was one of the first to speak. He deftly skirted the issue of the radical or conservative implications of this particular image and referred to the Opéra simply and tritely as "the house of harmony."[23] The speech that followed, however, went beyond this vague invocation of harmony, being far more explicit about the Opéra's special political significance now. Ledru-Rollin delivered it, which was, perhaps, especially appropriate, he being a frequenter of the Opéra, having had a free press entry to it in the 1830s.[24] Hence he knowingly praised the nation's operatic patrimony, the core of which was the illustrious grand repretoire of the 1830s: Auber's *La Muette de Portici,* Rossini's *Guillaume Tell,* Halévy's *La Juive,* and Meyerbeer's *Robert le Diable* and *Les Huguenots.*

But even more significantly, perhaps, Ledru-Rollin went on to expatiate upon all that the nation could learn, historically, from these resonant works. There was no question as to their meaning now, for in the light of political circumstance their content was unequivocal – it could be ideologically stabilized. *La Juive,* for example, was about the dangers of religious fanaticism, whereas *Les Huguenots* concerned the contributions of Martin Luther. (*Le Constitutionnel* of course immediately noted the irony of the minister's praise of Luther in the presence of the curé of St.-Roch.) And in the context of these timely histories he then went on to describe another work: Meyerbeer's long-awaited *Le Prophète,* shortly to be premiered. Little could the minister foresee how problematic the political framework that he here set up would prove to be in the context of the Republic in 1849.

Yet for the moment, Ledru-Rollin was confident that the work would be a stunning success, just what the Opéra and indeed the nation needed so badly at this point. He was sure that Meyerbeer's prophet would be "the Messiah who would raise the fortunes of the theater, calling all of France and Europe to Paris."[25] His perspective, of course, was far more optimistic than that of artists like Berlioz, who by March had pronounced that cultural activity in the Republic was effectively dead. Perhaps it may have seemed so from the viewpoint of a creative artist, one far different from that of a politician concerned exclusively with rhetorical effect. The minister was sure that French grand opera was indeed far from dead, and he attempted to do everything in his power to

131

reassure Meyerbeer, who he feared might be frightened about the prospects for his work.[26] As we saw earlier, in the letters to the Opéra, many considered an operatic success to be a political reflection, an expression of vitality that would bolster confidence in a time of crisis.

But in spite of the great political importance that the government saw in the forthcoming premiere, it left the responsibility of how to present it to the entrepreneurs. Less concerned with means than ends, the state entrusted Duponchel and Roqueplan with maintaining the splendor of the Opéra and with broadening access to it. Indeed, this overriding concern coincided with what has been termed the period of the trial and failure of socialism, from February 24 to May 4, 1848.[27] The Opéra was part of a larger concern in this period with "les exigences populaires" and of a utopian stress on the poorest class and their cultural as well as their political development.

As in the First Republic, again, it was up to the theater's directors to prove their worthiness by demonstrating their patriotism by devising politically useful projects. And here once more, the desire to broaden access specifically to the lower classes for political reasons was not without precedent in France. There had been a long tradition in the eighteenth century of the "gratis" performance, or free performances offered by the theaters on the occasion of the great events in the life of the nation or the royal family. Such performances were considered to be signs of zeal and public spirit, and were expected of the royal theaters as well as the minor houses.

The Opéra thus necessarily participated in this practice in the eighteenth century performing most frequently either ballets or works of Lully, although with less frequency than the other theaters. *Petits gens* of all categories were said to attend (although this was probably predominately the better educated artisans), and such performances were routinely crowded, being in great demand. Comportment on these occasions was far different from that normally found in the grand or royal theaters, and certainly in the Opéra. The audience not only ate and drank, nor were they content merely to applaud: they often participated spontaneously in the spectacle, adding unexpected *intermèdes*. For their tendency was to see this *grand spectacle* as part of a national *fête,* hence inviting them to be actors as much as passive spectators of it.[28]

Such conflations could hardly be avoided, and as will soon become evident, continued in an altered form in the free performances in the Second Republic.

The Opéra's directors now responded immediately to their challenge, apparently knowing full well what could happen in the *spectacle* was not carefully planned in advance. With great political acumen, they lost no time proposing a plan for a new open-air summer theater, a "people's opera," on the Champs-Elysées. They conceived this new national opera essentially as an opera for the masses, to seat about 6,000 people, with tickets at the low price of two francs each. Perhaps the directors took political rhetoric more seriously than the politicians, but perhaps too they perceived the dual function that such a plan could serve. It could better their financial situation while playing an important ideological role; again, immediate needs took precedence over potential long-term effects. Although for the moment there seemed to be a consonance between the institutional structure (with entrepreneurs) and the Republic's political goals, this harmony was soon to turn dissonanat.

In tyring to translate the government's rhetoric into a concrete, politically attractive plan, the entrepreneurs no doubt believed that the open-air setting would help send a new kind of ideological message. As in the earlier Opéra-National, constructed from a former circus ring, the space for the lyric theater would speak in a fundamentally different way.[29] And its placement, away from the traditional theatrical centers, in a less urban setting, would not only support the ideological message of purity but facilitate safer and more effective surveillance. Once again, as with the Opéra-National, there would be a minimum of operatic etiquette and of separation within the audience or between the audience and the stage, which had been so dangerous in the first revolution. Such a theater, then, would not only be less costly in general to maintain, but could contribute to the *vulgarisation* of Republican ideals, attitudes, and spirit.

Certain state officials, in particular, were very enthusiastic about the directors' plan, especially those connected with the city of Paris and the National Workshops. For them, such an opera would serve both practical and ideological goals, at once communicating a political conception and employing or diverting unemployed French workers. Hence, in response to the

Opéra's request, on March 16, 1848, the Mairie de Paris wrote to Duponchel and Roqueplan: "Il est concédé à titre de location, aux citoyens Duponchel et Roqueplan . . . l'emplacement nécessaire pour établir dans les Champs-Elysées un théâtre d'été provisiore, destiné à la représentation d'opéras et de ballets"[30] [It is conceded for renting to the citizens Duponchel and Roqueplan . . . the necessary location to establish on the Champs-Elysées a provisional summer theater for the performance of operas and ballets].

And on March 22, the director of the Ateliers Nationaux in the Ministère des Travaux Publics responded to Duponchel: "Vous allez faire construire une salle d'Opéra d'été sur une vaste échelle, aux Champs-Elysées; cette idée est grande et belle. Je viens, comme directeur des atelliers nationaux, vous faire une offre . . . J'ai 25,000 [ouvriers] de toutes professions . . ."[31] [You are going to construct a hall for summer on a vast slope on the Champs-Elysées; this idea is great and beautiful. As director of the National Workshops I am going to make you an offer . . . I have 25,000 workers of all professions . . .].

For both officials, perhaps, the new opera promised to be a means to placate the increasingly restive Parisian workers through the impending long, hot Paris summer. Revolutionary elements in the clubs were already openly fighting the bourgeoisie, and by early March the influence of Louis Blanc among the "masses" was growing. Even now, popular disturbances were breaking out in the provinces as moderate and conservative forces were gaining in strength, which would culminate in their victory in the April elections.[32] There were those who already saw the project in view of this change of climate, preceiving its potential message more broadly, in light of the conservative tide. This included Ledru-Rollin, who finally refused to approve the plan, giving the reason that it would undoubtedly damage the Opéra's prestige. Already, the minister, with Lamartine, was beginning to play a conciliatory role, attempting to maintain the Republic in a certain ambiguity between socialism and reaction.[33] But according to his argument, it would make it impossible to maintain the traditional standards of luxury and spectacle so integral to the identity of this grand national theater.

The minister undoubtedly worried too about the message that it would send outside of France as well as that which would be sent to the increasingly divided political constituency. For what concerned him, he claimed, was that the regular audience would shun this new "popular" opera, considering it to be a sort of "théâtre de la foire." It is likely also that he feared the inherent ambiguity or volatility of the political message of this project for both French workers and the frightened bourgeoisie. For it would raise the explosive question of to whom the Opéra belonged, and whether the "people's" opera was indeed the same as the first lyric stage.

But the state in general was still eager at this point to attempt both to represent and to control the more radical aspirations of French workers through the imagery of the Opéra. There were safer means to do so than by constructing a new mass theater, and contexts in which the experience and audience dynamic could be more easily controlled. The operatic patrimony, officials believed, could be *vulgarisé* somewhat more safely through a program of distributing free tickets to workers for performances at the Opéra. By the end of March 1848, the minister of the interior decreed that a certain number of free performances should be held for "les ouvriers et petits artisans."[34] This meant, of course, that the Opéra was charged with the challenging task of arranging the *riche spectacle* of this theater so that it would appeal to the *classes populaires*. It would have to present the grand repertoire, the operatic, cultural patrimony of France, in such a manner so as to take into account the way that the new audience was likely to construe it, and to obtain the desired result. Perhaps knowing that its theatrical experience was limited largely to the boulevard theaters, the state left the problem of adapting the repertoire up to the entrepreneurs. Whether or not the directors knew what such an audience would grasp or what would be lost when it was exposed to such a cultural product, they knew that its political message would have to be strengthened.

The burden was hence on the Opéra, on the entrepreneurial and artistic imagination, to focus the ideological message present in the repertoire for the education of this social group. Clearly, given the significance of entering the Opéra, and participating in its *patrimoine*, it was no longer possible to make the kind of concessions that had characterized the Opéra-National. This theater, because of its lack of grandeur, in fact, had already failed, since, according to contemporaries, it had "sacrificed itself" to *actualité*. Like the other boulevard theaters, it reintroduced the singing of

135

patriotic songs, making its featured attractions naive tableaux like *Les Barricades de 1848*.[35]

The Opéra then, to the contrary, sought a far more complex political message, one that was indirect and synthetic, and for that reason, more inherently volatile. Officials must have already been well aware of how problematic the meaning of the grand works could be after the sobering experiences of *La Muette* and *Les Huguenots*. But still they were confident that the message of such works could be grounded in a manner so as to make the experience an uplifting and educational one for this group.

Predictably, it chose *La Muette* for one of the few performances of this type, a work with renewed political significance and also ties to the boulevard. The story, in fact, was already familiar to audiences who frequented such theaters, as were the use of the mime or mute and the specific repertoire of spectacular effects. It apparently did not occur to the Opéra that the audience might focus less on the political theme of overthrowing tyranny than on the social implications of the work now. It did, however, realize that it would have to make explicit not only certain political implications for the present but the political nature of the operatic experience itself.

To make the desired message of the work accessible to a popular audience, the Opéra tried to clarify the progression of the story or the meaning of each act; and it attempted also to clarify reasons for events in order to make the moral clearer, as well as to emphasize the topical connection with the recent revolution. As we have already seen, in the grand repertoire the treatment of the ending was frequently the most problematic point, for it was here that the *mettuer en scène* would have to clarify the work's point of view. We can recall from the opera's premiere that this could be done through the costumes as well as the décor and the physical movement or gestures of the characters on stage.

And the Opéra now realized the importance of equipping the stage with appropriate symbols, just as it accoutered its courtyard in the political ceremony that we have already observed. Through this technique, it could make the desired interpretive frame more clear, heightening and specifying the political aspect of the message and the character of a political *fête*. Again, in attempting to meet the pressing demands being made upon it, the Opéra may not have considered the long-range consequences

of such techniques – that it was associating the theater and repertoire with a political significance for workers and hence encouraging a specific manner of reading or construing its operatic
works.

A performance of *La Muette* was planned for April 9, 1848, just
weeks before the election of the Constituent Assembly, and the
triumph of moderates and conservatives. Interest in this specific
performance was accentuated in the press in view of the timing of
its production, so close to this political event, and in the midst of
a period of popular agitation in the streets. As in the first revolution, topical political issues inevitably impinged on the meaning
and significance generally seen in specific operatic works. *Le Constitutionnel* reported the details of the production, noting astutely
the way in which its political meaning was to be made especially
clear. The focus was on the ending, historically so problematic a
part of the work, the national, patriotic significance of which was
to be clarified by an appendage:

> Après *La Muette,* on exécutera ce jour-là *La Marseillaise en
> action:* entre chaque couplet, des scènes de pantomime et
> d'ensemble seront mimées avec accompagnement de cloches,
> de canon, de décharges de mousqueterie. Le couplet "Amour
> sacré de la patrie" [from *La Muette*] sera suivi d'une pièce
> chantée les choeurs et les premiers sujets.[36]

> [After *La Muette,* they will perform that day "La Marseillaise
> en action": between each "couplet" pantomime and en-
> semble scenes will be mimed with the accompaniment of
> bells, cannon, and the firing of muskets. The couplet
> "Amour sacré de la patrie" [from *La Muette*] will be fol-
> lowed by a piece sung by the chorus and the lead actors.]

Cultural levels were now to be fused to encourage a new politicized meaning: The patriotic panoply of the boulevard was to be
juxtaposed with the splendor of the grand repertoire. Dangerous
political implications, again, were to be canceled out by the splendor, which would provide a further link between a physical and
political grandeur. Moreover, specific selections from the opera
were to be clarified in their implications through the process of
concatenation with exegetical patriotic songs. In the end, reality

and art were to be fused as the characters from the drama step forward and join the audience, ritualistically, in the singing of a "revolutionary" hymn. Patriotic sentiments would thus be "mis en jeu" in a deliberate and careful way, further associating the grand repertoire with a national, political significance.

The response to these tactics was mixed, as we might expect in the political context: the traditional audience, now moving to the right, was evidently alienated by the projected *mise en scène*. *Le Constitutionnel,* soon to become a Bonapartist, imperialist journal, was notably far from pleased, seeing *La Muette* as a poor choice and the production too realistic:

> Ces scènces de révolte et de mort n'ont plus rien de nouveau pour la population de Paris. Et puis vos spectateurs de ce jour-là trouveront que vos figurants s'y prennent mal, et que cette révolte sur le marché de Naples est une révolte pour rire.[37]

> [Its scenes of revolt and death have nothing new for the population of Paris. And so your spectators for this day will find that your crowds do it badly, and that this revolt in the market of Naples is a revolt at which to laugh.]

A notable cynicism pervades the review, as well as an awareness of the literal nature of popular readings and hence a belief in the inappropriateness of this choice.

From the available evidence, however, this was not the response at all: the audience saw a different kind of reality, indeed a political and social one. Such performances did seem to succeed in the goal of fostering a sense of political participation, which is undoubtedly precisely what journals like *Le Constitutionnel* so feared.

But the apparent success of the program created both immediate and imminent problems: first, it presented a dilemma for officials charged with distributing free tickets. Given the symbolism of the Opéra as a locus of political recognition, insecurity and friction soon arose over the priorities to be observed in distribution. As before in the Opéra's history, such tickets were intended to be (and were understood to be) political rewards, a form of symbolic recognition and hence of status. In the form letter sent out to leaders in the different *arrondissements,* the minister of the interior made the criteria absolutely clear:

> Citoyen Maire – – –J'ai l'honneur de vous transmettre– – – places pour la représentation nationale qui doit avoir lieu demain au Th. de la Nation. Je recommande à toutes vos attentions leur distribution qui devra être faite par vous-même, et, de préférence aux ouvriers, aux habitants peu aisé de l'arrondissement digne de cette faveur.[38]

> [Citizen Mayor– – –I have the honor of transmitting to you– – –places for the national performance that is to take place tomorrow at the Théâtre de la Nation. I call all your attention to their distribution, which should be done by you yourself, and giving preference to workers, to the less welloff residents of the arrondissement worthy of this favor.]

As in the Restoration, *entrées de faveur* were being revived, and again they carried a political meaning and so were once more actively sought. Myriad letters from public servants complained of being unduly slighted or of having been promised tickets that were never delivered, with serious results. In the often violent behavior that surrounded such incidents we can see, again, a transfer of meaning, a case of the projection of political tensions onto disputes over the Opéra. For example, in one letter from an unidentified official to the Ministère des Travaux Publics, the following incident is relayed:

> J'ai reçu une lettre du Citoyen Gornet, Maire du XI arron-dissement, me disant que vous lui avez announcé qu'il m'avait été remis, par vos ordes, 500 billets pour la représentation de l'Opéra . . . Le citoyen Gornet m'adressait, en outre, quelque mille ouvriers de son arrondissement pour leur dis-tribuer ces billets . . . il m'a été remis seulement vingt-quatre billets que j'ai distribués suivant les indication qu'on m'avait données.[39]

> [I received a letter from Citizen Gornet, mayor of the elev-enth arrondissement, telling me that you announced to him

139

that by your orders, I had been sent 500 tickets for the performance at the Opéra . . . Citizen Gornet addressed several thousand workers from his arrondissement for the distribution of the tickets . . . I was sent only twenty-four tickets, which I distributed according to the indications that you gave me.]

But other incidents abounded that testify to the importance accorded the Opéra and attendance at its performances, seen as a political symbol and right. Significantly, at a time when workers' rights and political power were failing, as debates on the National Workshops began, tension was growing. It had been increasing steadily since April 16, and immediately after the election that took place on April 23 disturbances in the provinces broke out.[40] On the very day that the debates on the National Workshops began, the mayor of the city of Batignolles-Monceaux complained of exclusion to the minister, arguing that his city was really part of Paris.[41] Certainly, attention was focused on Paris because of the ideological ferment there, but entry into the Opéra was a theoretical issue that transcended corporeal attendance. Again, we can recall that already journals like *L'Atelier* in the early 1840s were raising the workers' consciousness about culture, including the Opéra.[42] It had explained to its readers the importance of attending theaters like the Opéra-National as a way of overcoming their sense of isolation, inferiority, and political impotence.

Workers throughout France had been told of the importance of appropriating a broader culture that would allow them to grasp and enter legitimate political dialogue, or to speak in a politically recognizable way. Connected with this was the theme of entering the nation's heritage, its cultural patrimony, which invloved, first, education, or the appropriation of the necessary tools, and, thereafter, instruction.[43] For this reason, workers were exhorted to shun the debased and dangerous literature spread by *colportures* in the countryside or in urban *cabinets de lecture*. Popular drama was a special concern since, as recent studies have shown, theater generally occupied an important place not only in journals but in commercial reading rooms.[44]

And so it is not suprising that because of this concern, in addition to the current political stakes, *L'Atelier* supported the Republic's efforts in the theater:

Le théâtre étant devenu pour ainsi dire un besoin de notre époque, le public peu aisé était réduit à demander aux scènes inférieures le plaisir que les autres lui refusaient. Or, l'enseignement fait dans les petits théâtres est presque toujours détestable: une littérature de mauvais goût grossièrement épicée, des idées fausses, des sentiments malhonnêtes ou tout ou moins exagérés.[45]

[The theater having become practically a need of our time, the less affluent public is reduced to asking the minor theaters for the pleasures that the others refuse them. Yet the instruction in the minor theaters is almost always detestable: a literature in bad taste, grossly spiced, the ideas being false, the feelings dishonest or more or less exaggerated.]

The major theaters now seemed to promise not only a more adequate culture but political understanding and recognition, to this point denied the working class.

Certainly such performances appealed to familiar experiences while slowly integrating new ones, resulting in a complex synthetic experience that transcended either ritual or art. And if, as we have seen, the *chanson* was a poetic means to comment on actuality, then such performances could well have been perceived as another kind of poetic response to the political world, again more accurate than factual description. This may, in fact, be part of the reason why, even before the formation of clear political movements among the "popular classes," one finds a "diffuse familiarity" with political reality, or a unique way of apprehending it.[46]

And not only the message, but the experience of workers in the Opéra must have been both familiar and unique, relating to established traditions yet provocatively adding new elements to them. They undoubtedly transferred other cultural experiences as well as their indigenous approaches to art in a manner so as to alter the operas' content and the nature of the theatrical experience. A largely workers' audience, first, must have created the kind of sociability with which workers were already familiar in the context of other musical gatherings. As we can see in Figure 13, the popular concerts presented in the "Salle de la fraternité" and other such assemblies were more than simple, isolated aesthetic experi-

Figure 13. "Concert Populaire," Salle de la Fraternité, *L'Illustration*, 1849. Library of Congress.

142

ences. The associations were inherently social, as they were in the popular *goguettes,* or singing societies, that united art with political commentary and mutual aid.

Indeed, the bourgeois *L'Illustration* (in Figure 13) might well have misunderstood the event it was depicting graphically by calling it a "concert populaire." It is more likely that it was one of the special meetings of a *goguette* in which a woman ceremoniously assumed "la présidence." This occurred on solemn occasions, with the woman normally dressed in white and wearing a blue or red ribbon to identify her coveted function. Such meetings were often devoted specifically to the aid of a sick comrade, others being "séances de bienfaisance," mixing music with some sort of mutual aid.[47]

But the social element entered also into the content of the art, as Proudhon observed, noting that a popular audience generally abstracts the social core of a work. As he pointed out, in popular art there is a close exchange between art and life: one feeds off the other, determining what is significant and what is real.[48] Observers of the workers at the theater, like Balzac, also noted their distinctive disposition, the way they construed reality and involved themselves experientially in the works. As he remarked, in the melodrama the suffering of the actors is real for them. They see real blood on the stage, and continually draw connections to their own lives. "Aesthetic distance," then, in the workers' experience of theater, was minimal, a fact clearly to have considerable repercussions in their approach to opera.[49]

The experience gained in 1848 through such national indoctrination in opera, even if brief or obtained secondhand, was to be of enduring significance for workers, The Opéra, for a small but significant group, had become an avenue of political perception, and it was shortly to become a mode of political communication or expression. Even if brief, then, it is unlikely that such experiences were quickly forgotten, so widely were they reported and so repeatedly were they stressed.[50] In 1848 the Opéra, for workers, was a means to achieve integration – a cultural integration that simultaneously and integrally prepared for political entry. The *orphéons* may have provided education, but the Opéra offered "instruction" or essential insight and understanding of the social and political world. But this harmonious image of the Opéra, as we shall see, effectively masked certain irreconcilable

143

The Nation's Image

tensions that were shortly to erupt. For when the political situation began to reverse, bringing a policy change, the dynamic established through indoctrination could not be so easily expunged.

It is essential to understand the sequence of political events that henceforth was to determine the future of the Republic, since they determined the nature and the rhythm of changing policies concerning opera. First, the meeting of the constituent assembly, in May 1848, marked the end of what historians have called the Republic's "revolutionary phase." The fall of "popular" leaders and the growing hostility to socialism were then followed soon after, in August, by the election of political moderates. By June the battle of classes was overt, leading ineluctably to the bloody revolt that was repressed by "the forces of order" and then followed by their angry retaliation.[51] And so by December the political mood was such that the forces of repression could triumph conclusively as Louis Napoleon was officially elected the president of the Republic. With the splintering of the fraternal Republican ideal, new political alliances began to form; notably, the most radical Republicans now fused overtly with the workers' movement. Hence with the decimation of the moderate Republicans after the election, the battle lines were unequivocally drawn between the forces of the Right and the Left. This dialectic of radicalization and repression that chracterized the Second Republic was inevitably to impinge on policies concerning the arts in France.[52]

By early 1849, official policies in the visual arts and indeed the very language of patronage underwent a notable shift. The government now commissioned religious paintings not by but for the working class, and official orders for then became "stereotyped and perfunctory." The goal was apparently to strip equivocal subjects of their ambiguity, to give them an unmistakable meaning "in the service of antisocialist propaganda." Concomitantly, the Louvre now repudiated its bold new plan of reorganization and returned to being, as contemporaries phrased it, a mere depository for *grandes études*.[53]

And other symbolic alterations worked simultaneously with these changes, such as a concerted effort to de-Republicanize and thus deradicalize civic décor. In general, the tendency of all these policies was to reintroduce a distinction between popular art, or

144

art for the people, and that intended for the social elite.[54] That which was aimed at the former, above all, was not to be equivocal in meaning but unambiguous, stable, and hence inherently safe in its implications.

The repression, of course, presented a difficult problem in operatic policy, for it involved a marked cessation of a dynamic already set up. Given the political message of bringing workers into the Opéra and the difficulty of controlling construal of its works, all programs of operatic indoctrination abruptly ceased. And certainly there was fear of riot in any gathering of this sort, especially when successful theatrical scenes were becoming models for popular demonstrations.[55] *Politique-théâtre* was still as alive as it had been in 1848, motivated now, perhaps, by the government's tactics in its *théâtres politiques*.

Although it was certainly not difficult, in effect, to exclude the newly initiated French working class from the hallowed halls of the Opéra through prohibitive ticket prices and social ambience, given the awareness of its political message, it was now impossible to exclude them from involvement in an indirect manner or from participation through discussion of operatic debates. In this sense, officials were unable to reverse the dynamic set up in 1848: the government, from this perspective, was again the ironic victim of its own success.

No longer could it quell French workers' interest in a theater that they now astutely read in terms of its implied political message. Although other kinds of political restrictions could now be imposed on French workers, the Right could no longer suppress the symbolic constituency of the public of the Opéra. Workers were more than ever aware of the importance of engagement in the nation's culture, and especially of the symbolism as well as the information to be gained through it. As a result, they still claimed the right to engage in commentary on the nation'a major theaters, to respond to the political message they read as it was conveyed in theatrical terms. The Opéra was, then, once more a realm where power was elusive and vulnerable, and where another kind of power or tactic of delegitimization could be introduced.

It was in this specific context that the state was now to confront one of the inevitable dilemmas resulting from the exigencies of the institution itself. As in the case of *Les Huguenots,* the public had long been awaiting an opera commissioned in an earlier period

145

and thus under very different political circumstances. The work in question now was perhaps the worst possible opera under the current conditions – Meyerbeer's *Le Prophète,* the work so avidly awaited in 1848. In the early months of the Republic, an opera about revolt was still a plausible, indeed a useful subject for presentation on the Opéra's stage. In fact, it was probably intended to be analogous in function to *La Muette* in 1830 – a means to invoke, indirectly, patriotic sentiment and revolutionary enthusiasm.

The text of the work, as we may recall, was prepared in the period of political tension that followed the production of *Les Huguenots,* which probably led to even greater ambiguity in its presentation of the story. Scribe had completed the libretto as early as 1838 and Meyerbeer the score, in its essentials, in 1840. Given the fears of the Opéra in this period, there might well have been concern over its safety, although the reasons publiclly given for its delay were practical and logistical. (Meyerbeer was said to be unhappy with the artists available under Pillet's administration.) And so the work was not put into production until the early months of the Second Republic.

As Ledru-Rollin had hoped, rehearsals began in 1848, with the famous stars of the Opéra, Roger and Viardot, in the leads. But the premiere did not take place when expected because of endless complications involving the engagement of the singers and the composer's exacting rehearsal requirements. Needing an operatic success so badly for both political and financial reasons, the Opéra was now as solicitous of Meyerbeer as it had been insulting under Véron.[56]

The opera, then, was ready for its premiere at a most politically inopportune time, scheduled now for April 16, 1849. It was a period of intensifying social fear in which the bourgeoisie felt intimidated, a feeling being fostered further by imaginative literature, especially novels. This undoubtedly influenced fears of the content of theatrical presentations, which led officials immediately to survey leading personalities concerning their opinions about liberty in the theaters. Auber, the composer of *La Muette,* was a supporter of the establishment of censorship, and Scribe, his librettist, of censorship with certain modifications. But finally, on January 28, 1849, on the request of the Directeur des Beaux-arts, preventive censorship was reestablished in the theaters.[57]

Certainly there was an awareness that *Le Prophète* would be read with a political subtext; the events thought likely to provide it are not difficult to discern. In some cases, they related to specific incidents or actions that seemed to have direct counterparts in the opera itself. Only the month before had occurred the trial of those implicated in the uprising of May 15, 1848, when a crowd had boldly invaded the Assemblée Nationale after a political demonstration in favor of the Poles (now a group whose plight was highly symbolic for the extreme left). Soon after, on April 30, 1849, was to follow the first action by French troops in Rome in defense of the pope against the republicans there.[58] These events, as we shall see, were to help provide the opera's frame, which was to interact with the tensions also being generated by the impending general elections. Moreover, the premiere occurred in the midst of another worrisome event – a virulent outbreak of the cholera epidemic in Paris, which again claimed many lives. Had the work been performed when originally scheduled not only would the *mise en scène* have been different, but clearly so too would have been the political subtext and interpretive frame.

Now, in April 1849, the public awaited the work with great anticipation, for a number of factors converged to focus a remarkably wide interest upon it. Not only was it politically topical but the regular public of the Opéra was starved for a serious new opera of both musical and theatrical substance. At the Opéra, the only other recent premiere was a ballet, *Le Violon du Diable*. There was a work of Halévy at the Opéra-Comique and the second act of *La Vestale* at the Conservatoire. It was precisely because of the need for an operatic success within this context that the Opéra went to extraordinary pains to present a work of lavish grandeur. Berlioz remarked not only about Meyerbeer's courage in allowing the premiere to take place at this moment but on the Opéra's special pains on the occasion of its premiere.[59]

For all these reasons, one cause of worry for the Opéra, as undoubtedly for the state, was how the meaning of the ambiguous work might now be construed. Everyone knew, of course, that it was about John of Leyden and the Anabaptist revolt, but there was great uncertainty as to how its political implications could be read. Moreover, the public was unsure of what the regime would attempt to say through the work, or how the meaning of the historical event would be presented on this national stage.

Partly from curiosity, no doubt, the first forty performances

147

immediately sold out, and even soon thereafter only those with extraordinary resourcefulness or connections could attend. Hence the press followed the opera closely, disseminating information about it, attempting to present its message to those not able to attend the theater.

As we shall see, again the opera's meaning was the subject of intense debate, it by no means being clear from Scribe's artful handling of the opera's plot. And as with *La Muette,* the nature of the hero could be interpreted in several ways, as could the character and motivation of the people in the crowd. Finally, as in *La Muette* and *Les Huguenots,* Scribe sought to heighten the personal drama to deflect attention away from the more controversial aspects of the plot. In this case, Scribe apparently drew certain elements from Pushkin's *Boris Godunov,* particularly the story of the "false Demetrius" who ascended to the throne of Russia but was confronted by his humbly born mother.[60] The libretto that Scribe produced and that the Opéra confronted in 1849 raised a number of immediate and highly sensitive questions. (See Appendix.)

Once again, as in *La Muette,* the same points of ambiguity recur, particularly the relative guilt of the nobles compared to the eventual fanaticism of the crowd. But of significance now is that the Anabaptists clearly incite insurrection by using their skills in rhetoric and thus provide a clear dramatic focus. And the peasants, as opposed to "the people" depicted earlier in *La Muette,* are easily taken in by them as well as being cowed by authority. But Jean (John of Leyden), like Masaniello, is still represented as on the side of order as is the figure of his mother, which undoubtedly assuaged official fears. Yet as in *Les Huguenots,* the final attribution of social guilt would become conclusive only in connection with both the musical style and the *mise en scène.*

Before examining the latter, it is important to look more clearly at what Meyerbeer abstracted from the style as well as the content of Scribe's libretto for *Le Prophète.* The essential issue in understanding Meyerbeer's endeavor is the way in which he attempted to capture the particular force of the specific drama. Indeed, in this work we see another aspect of the range of his musical dramaturgy and the facility with which it adapted itself to the different libretti at hand. For once again the composer attempted to suit his music to the pace and flow of the text, one very different in both respects from that for *Les Huguenots.*

As contemporaries soon observed, if *Les Huguenots* was essentially a chronicle like its literary model, *Le Prophète* rather more closely resembled a pamphlet. Indeed, Meyerbeer composed it relatively quickly and at the height of his command of the genre, having had a good deal of operatic experience now in France. Knowing the requirements of such a libretto, he made the work tight and highly compact with a continual and focused dramatic flow and a new use of the mosaic effect.

Here Meyerbeer employs the eclecticism that we have noted in *Les Huguenots* but in a manner so as to further the flow and contrasts of the literary text. Again he tries to project the drama, now a melodramatic intrigue, to make it more legible and eloquent, to add more color, direction, and force.

The opening scene is an apt example of the clarity and concision of Meyerbeer's style and the way in which it relates to both textual conventions and the nature of the *mise en scène*.[61] It is prefaced by a short overture that presents the dominant colors of the drama, or those that are to be associated closely with the major characters. He then begins the opening chorus with an attempt at visualization, or a suggestion of context and atmosphere that immediately evokes a scenic equivalent. Here he deftly suggests the soft breeze of the text through rhythm and orchestral color, but the music continues only as long as the dramatic situation requires.

The orchestra then makes a smooth and concise transition to Berthe's *cavatine* (added after the work's premiere at the insistence of the soprano). But Meyerbeer ingeniously makes it into the traditional solo continuation or interpolation generally included in the opening chorus of French operas. Although it is an independent number that can be extracted for solo performance, it still fits neatly, like a mosiac, into the continuous flow; and like a mosaic piece, it fits integrally into the artistic whole yet retains its integrity and luster even when removed. The subtle rhythmic transition that leads into it makes it appear a logical development from the chorus, one calculated precisely in terms of color, weight, and size.

To suggest a simplicity or innocence of character, Meyerbeer saves most of the gratuitous vocalism for the end, choosing to translate the imagery of the text (the palpitations of the heart) into rhythmic terms. As in Lully and the French tradition that Meyerbeer studied assiduously, virtuosity still stands outside the drama or the most intense dramatic points. The final flurry of vocal display serves to carry the movement forward and to lead directly into the next subtle orchestral transition. Here he makes the continuation seem logical by picking up on a rhythmic connection with the preceding number while simultaneously reintroducing the local color that foreshadows the action to come. Then, in the following scene, a dialogue between Berthe and Fidès, Meyerbeer displays his skill as a composer of traditional, rich, highly flexible French recitative. But eclecticism returns, for as in previous works where the text suggests it, he lapses into the more naturalistic, intimate manner of *opéra-comique*.

Another feature of the score is that, as in Auber's *La Muette*, the emphasis is on the chorus, one of the dominant characters again being the people. Here, of course, the character of Fidès, one of considerable dramatic weight, somewhat counterbalances its dominance, or so it may have appeared to officials. But clearly, the *mise en scène* was intended to make the character of this body more clear and to add emphasis to its sinister implications, thus avoiding the phenomenon of *La Muette*. For in accordance with the tendencies already noted, the staging was intended to make the opera, like visual art, help further antisocialist propaganda in France. In addition, the Opéra was well aware, as were state officials, that far more people would read about the work and its effect than see it in person. Not only would there be printed *mise en scènes* that would further clarify its meaning, but illustrations would appear in numerous publications in addition to reports in the press.

As Figure 14 suggests, the Opéra continued its quest for historical accuracy conveyed through painstaking detail in the magnificent sets designed by Cambon. Of course, engravings of the sets were quick to appear in journals, those in *L'Illustration* coming out only twelve days after the work's premiere.[62] For not only was the opera considered politically to be of great moment but one whose final message depended heavily on the *mise en scène*. Hence the proliferation of illustrations of it now, which immediately increased even further the public resonance of the work and its political implications.

Although the Opéa was already running a heavy deficit, being solicitous of Meyerbeer for reasons we have seen, it nevertheless

Figure 14. Performance of *Le Prophète*, Act IV. *L'Illustration*, 1849. Library of Congress.

151

Figure 15. *Le Prophète*, costumes by Paul Lormier. Bibliothèque de l'Opéra.

spared no expense. But again, as in *Robert le Diable,* the lavishness of the production was here made possible through the additional appropriation of special funds for it by the state. This *subvention exceptionelle* in 1849 made it possible that 250 of the 680 costumes be entirely new, in a financially strained period.[63] As we can see in Figures 14, 15, and 16, their detail was particularly great; and if this was lost on the Opéra's vast stage, it could be captured in illustrations of them. If such historical accuracy was now a means

Figure 16. Costumes, *Le Prophète*, 1849. Bibliothèque de l'Opéra.

of creating a distance from the violent events, it remained a matter of credibility and status at the Opéra. Visual and dramatic reality were still equated in the Opéra's conventions, just as they had been in the late Restoration and under Louis-Philippe.[64]

The Opéra also took similar pains with the spectacular elements of the work, again perhaps hoping that they would serve to defuse the more explosive aspects of the story. Most noteworthy here was the Opéra's first use of electricity on its stage, obtained in this case by a carbon arc to suggest the rising sun.[65] But it also lavished attention on the *divertissements* in the work, particularly on the skating scene, which here clearly served a dual function: first, it brought actuality into the opera by incorporating an element of contemporary life, since Meyerbeer was said to have gotten the idea by seeing ice-skaters on the Champs-Elysées.[66] But it is important to recall as well that this spectacle was juxtaposed dramatically with a provocative scene of tension and violence in which the peasants threaten their noble prisoners. Here they brandish realistic weapons, as indicated explicitly in the printed *mise en scène*, scrupulously recorded by the *régisseur* of the Opéra, Palianti.[67]

But the *mise en scène* also reveals another element in interpretation or clarification intended to make the opera a means to serve antisocialist propaganda. In the face of imminent, clearly implied murder, the heroes are obviously the aristocrats, who, according

153

to descriptions of their acting, comport themselves with heroic bravery. The *mise en scène,* in addition, clarifies the intended characterization of the people as a violent mob in search only of personal gain and not motivated by ideology or a sense of justice. And again, given the authorities' general fear of manipulators or inciters, it is not suprising to find this fear projected onto the *mise en scène*. While the Anabaptists give their first sermon, suspicious-looking figures are shown gradually to infiltrate the crowd in order to suggest a conspiracy that is instigated from the outside. It is significant too that this was a period of continuing trials of popular leaders and thus one particularly clouded by an obsession with "responsibility."[68] And one must remember as well that other references to current or recent events were likely here, especially the invasion of the National Assembly and the plot to kill the pope in Rome. Finally, the opera includes a vivid, explicit scene of looting, undoubtedly intended to evoke the recent looting of the Hotel de Ville. For all these reasons, the work was one of particular theatrical force, but one, again like *Les Huguenots,* that would create, not solve, political problems.

The analogies suggested were by no means lost on either the audience or the combative press, divided here between publications that supported or challenged this interpretation. The implicit message of the opera, as communicated in part by the *mise en scène,* was, for the press, a political one and hence their responses were thoroughly politicized. Reviews continued to be a particularly trenchant means of political articulation in addition to being aesthetic commentary; indeed the two were inextricably bound.

Filtered through such a political perception, the work was not about a religious phenomenon or movement but rather about fundamental class and social issues. Commentators immediately recognized the peculiar political aptness of the work, after noting the ironic timing of the composer's other French operatic premieres. And frequently they stated with confidence that the work in question was conclusively about either "communism" or "the social revolutions of the sixteenth century."[69] As in the reviews we noted of the premiere of *La Juive,* it was precisely those political and historical elements suppressed in the libretto that the press here chose to stress. And as in the original reviews of *La Muette de*

Portici, each faction emphasized different details and interpreted events in different ways.

Operatic commentary, here again, as in the contemporary political *chanson,* was a mode of commenting on reality, of reacting to events, one that, once more, would influence grand opera's fate. Now more than ever, each journal employed a complex political-aesthetic amalgamation to define its own specific position and trace the broad contours of its political stance. *The power of the opera as an image lay in this amalgamation,* in this inextricable fusion of aesthetic and political perception, as experienced in 1849.

As one might expect, the reviews of the opera that appeared in the contemporary French press used it to cast the tensions of the political world in a theatrical, a dramatic light. Central were the issues of what is considered the legitimate action, who betrays whom in the work, and what are the real causes and the consequences of the actions.[70]

The moderate and official press had no doubts as to the opera's contemporary relevance, or that the appropriate framework in which it was to be discussed was both political and historical. Not only did the bourgeois *L'Illustration* publish lavish engravings of the work but by way of preparation it ran a long article on its interpretation of John of Leyden.[71] Here he is clearly a radical revolutionary of the Left, and thus numerous connections are drawn between the political situation as seen in the opera and that of the present.

Not suprisingly, given the current political tendencies, the official newspaper, the *Moniteur Universel,* labeled the opera unequivocally an "antisocialist drama." Since May 1848, communists, socialists, and democrats had been grouped together as *"rouges,"* and partisans of a democratic-social republic were referred to as "socialists." Now, given the fear that peasants, in addition to workers, were becoming "red," the "party of order" was actively engaged in popular propaganda against socialism, depicting "reds" as "monsters in the moral and intellectual order."[72] If earlier, Ledru-Rollin had seen historical lessons in the grand repertoire, now we find the assertion that these social truths can be better communicated in no other way. The paper explicity equates Anabaptism with contemporary socialism in France, and hence John of Leyden's revolt becomes the product of misguided fanaticism:

Au 16e siècle, comme aujourd'hui, les ennemies de la société, au lieu de chercher à améliorer, à guerir . . . ont pour système perpétuel de lâcher la bride aux passions les plus remuantes, aux appétits les plus cupides, et de promettre satisfaction aux besoins les plus exagérés . . . [73]

[In the sixteenth century, like today, the enemies of society, instead of searching for a means to ameliorate, to heal . . . perpetually gave reign to the most agitated passions, to the greediest appetites, and promised satisfaction of the most exaggerated needs.]

The people here become enemies of society, who thwart the possibility of social harmony, who indulge in greed, in exaggerated demands as well as in unreflective passion. Because they are clearly presented as, in essence, outside society, their revolt is similarly presented as one that is without justification.

Journals like *Le National,* originally liberal and now antisocialist and antirevolutionary, were, however, more moderate in their assessment. Again, as in the reviews of *Les Huguenots* that stressed the issue of historical truth, *Le National* claimed that if correctly construed, the work was "a striking mirror of France's history." Accordingly, the opera captures the fanaticism of the sixteenth century with a powerful, unique coherence to be found in no other source. But although it vindicates the people in the opera, the journal does attempt quite clearly to distance the case of the present from that of the past, when oppression was quite ostensibly the case:

Le caractère de l'insurrection et les causes qui la produisent sont donc ici très clairement indiqués, et l'on voit que tous les excès de la lutte qui va commencer ne seront que la conséquence naturelle des excès de l'oppression.[74]

[The character of the insurrection and the causes that produced it are here very clearly indicated, and one sees that all the excesses of the battle that is going to begin are nothing but the natural consequence of the excess of oppression.]

The Left, in a sense, inverted the right-wing press's view of the opera by claiming that the laws of society had not been broken by

156

the peasants and that there was indeed an analogy between past and present. The radical left-wing workers' press was the most trenchant in its reviews, taking a defensive position, seeing French workers being represented in the opera. We may observe this intense engagement in the opera, or rather in the politicized commentary about it, in no better source than Pierre-Joseph Proudhon's own political journal, *Le Peuple*. Despite the discouraging political development for proponents of the Left, Proudhon remained in his writings profoundly concerned with the "social question."[75] As Figure 17, a caricature that appeared in *L'Illustration*, reveals, above all through the use of distortion, many considered it a dangerous, inflammatory publication.

For *Le Peuple*, comment on the Opéra was both its right and its obligation, for it represented a political reality that had to be deciphered and responded to. And especially in a time of political repression, when other avenues of political expression were forcibly closed, operatic commentary presented an important and powerful alternative. This was, in fact, a moment when the socialist press, having to follow a tactic of indirect propaganda, was always searching for new and effective forms.[76] And again like the popular political *chanson*, it provided a store of cultural images to which it ascribed political meaning in an incisive, evocative, and now sophisticated mode of political speech.

Proudhon's journal had attentively followed the opera's progress for months, immediately recognizing the special political significance of its impending premiere. And undoubtedly a substantial number of its readers recognized this as well, particularly those in Paris who underwent the indoctrination of 1848. Moreover, a certain range of its readers must have had a genuine interest in its artistic aspects, having been exposed to operatic and choral pieces in the *orphéon* societies. *Le Travailleur*, in 1848, for example, had reported the performance of excerpts from Meyerbeer's operas as well as works by Beethoven and other great composers.[77]

Reminiscent of the government's efforts with *La Muette* in 1848, the review in *Le Peuple* attempts to make the political subtext clear in a clever manifestation of the *espirit frondeur*. The approach is still imaginative; in a sense, it assumes the mode of discourse that it saw in the opera itself—at once political and dramatic. Such a blending of fact and fiction, moreover, may not have seemed foreign to the

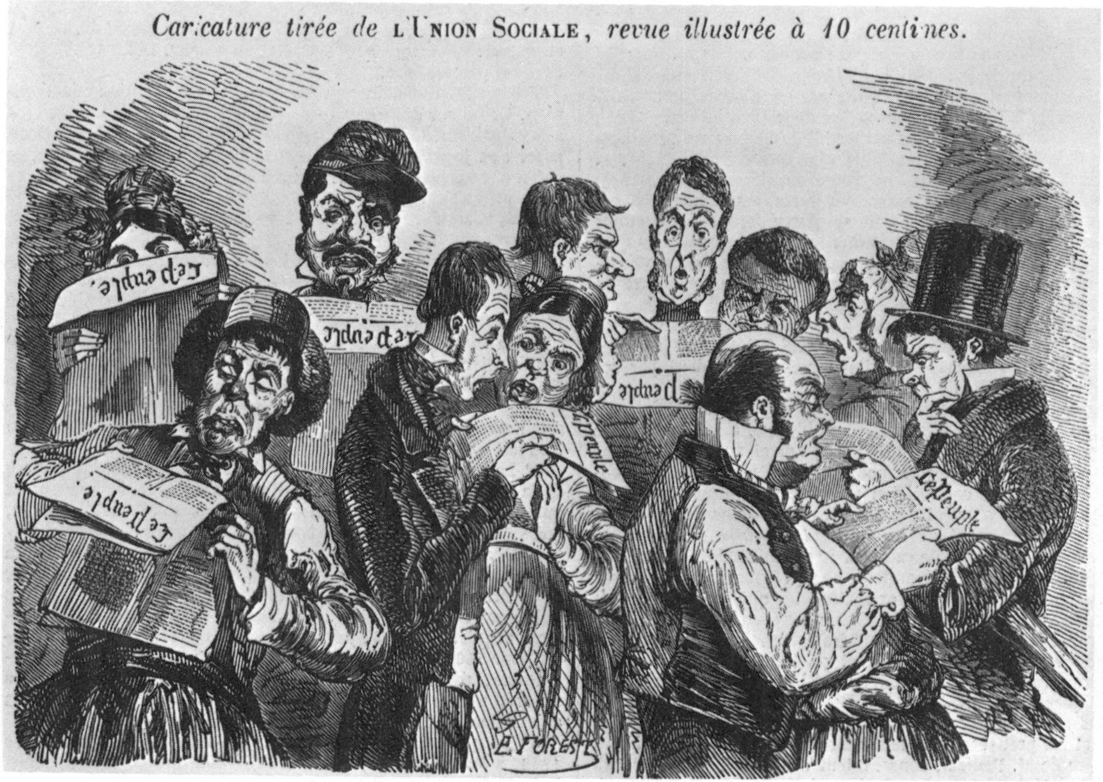

Figure 17. Caricature from *L'Union sociale*, "The People Reading *Le Peuple*." *L'Illustration*, 1849. Library of Congress.

journal's readers, who were seeking an authentic form of political enlightenment from it. Again, nineteenth-century workers' journals often used prose and verse interchangeably, poetry often being used for facts, as a more accurate way of expressing popular realities. Poems, songs, and melodramas, for them, were not isolated objects of culture but rather forms of civilization that made workers more aware of their condition. Such a review, then, was a conceptual source, just as opera itself could be, something that would "mettre en lumière" an otherwise intangible social reality.

The review assumes the form of a fictional letter designed to answer the questions posed about the opera by a candidate in forthcoming elections who must remain in "the electoral field of battle."[78] The candidate needs to know about the opera, to derive political information from it, and hence he begins by posing questions about the nature of the presentation at the Opéra. He knows that the *mise en scène* in this theater will provide clues to the meaning intended and that the Opéra's conventions should clearly be construed in a political sense. Indeed, previous discussions in *Le Peuple* had already, in a general way, considered the false political messages being generated in this theater by the state. (*Le Peuple* noted the reprise of "imperial" pieces on the official stage, which thus used the Opéra in the people's name for what was really a political *fête*.)[79] Like audiences at the premieres of *La Muette* and *Les Huguenots,* it suspected contradiction at the Opéra, or the projection of an image that was, in fact, false.

The reply to the "candidate's" questions is clearly a challenging one to decipher, for using the language of revolutionary politics it interprets the story within its ideological frame. And, in addition, it tries to vindicate the people from the slander of the staging and the right-wing press, going on to suggest an alternative view of their past, their present, and their future:

Vous connaissez . . . l'histoire de ces terribles révoltes qui signalèrent la fin du moyen-âge. A la voix de Luther, les esprits et les bras brisèrent leurs fers: les fronts couchés par la féroce oppression féodale se relevèrent, et regardèrent le ciel: ils y lurent confusément les mots de liberté, d'égalité, de fraternité; mais la loi divine entrevue, ils ne pouvaient la formuler et l'appliquer. C'était à nous que cette tâche était réservée. Nos yeux, comme ceux de nos pères, ne sont point affaiblis par de longues ténèbres; notre paupières ne s'abaissent point devant la lumière, et d'impures illusions, filles de la lumière et de la vengeance ne troublent plus notre cerveau. Le premier cri des opprimés du cloître, des déshérités de la glèbe, fut un cri un guerre et de sang; aujourd'hui il est la voix même de la discussion quotidienne qui prêche le pardon, la concorde et la fraternité. Jean de Leyde . . . écrit, il discute, il est représentant du Peuple; il ne reste de son passé que la cage de fer dans laquelle les gens du parti de la suppression . . . voudraient l'enfermer.[80]

[You know . . . the story of the terrible revolts that signaled the end of the Middle Ages. To the voice of Luther, spirits and arms broke their chains: brows, lowered by the ferocious feudal oppression, raised themselves again and looked at the heavens: there they read confusedly the words liberty, equality, and fraternity; but the divine law foresaw that they could not formulate and apply it. It was to us that this task was reserved. Our eyes, as those of our fathers, are not lowered before the light, and impure illusions, daughters of light and vengeance no longer trouble our minds. The first cry of those oppressed by the cloister, the disinherited of the soil, was a cry of war and blood. Today it is the voice of daily discussion that prescribes pardon, concord, and fraternity. John of Leyden . . . wrote, he debated, he was the representative of the people; all that remains of his passing is the cage of iron in which the men of suppression . . . would like to enclose him.]

The dialogue here with the right-wing press is, of course, aggressively direct: the review attempts to show that the people at present are different from their predecessors. As in *L'Atelier* earlier, there is obviously still a deep concern with the way in which the people are presented in works of art. And in the attack on feudal oppression one can also see the expression of certain continuing traditional themes, here those already rooted in popular folklore.[81] But in general, the people today, it argues, having the advantage of enlightenment, are rational and pacific and aware of how to obtain their ends through legitimate political means. The social truth of the opera, then, is the inverse of that claimed by the right-wing press both with regard to the people and to their leader, in this case, John of Leyden. And so from the perspective of this reading, the opera historically is partially false: its representation of Jean and the extrapolations made about his followers are, it claims, untrue. Here, once more, we can trace a continuity back to the reviews of *La Muette de Portici*: to the issues of historical truth, the verisimilitude expected of opera, and how the people are depicted on stage.

Obviously, this reading ignores the generic frame of Scribe's libretto, recasting the shape, the scope of its meaning, and emphasis that it implies.[82] For the libretto here becomes something else — material for interpretation, a vehicle of political self-definition and reflection on the historical past. The review is no exercise or diversion: It is a means to articulate, trenchantly, a political stance in a manner eminently accessible to all the political interlocutors involved. Aesthetic distance has evaporated, for the opera here is a social and political text, a complex mode of utterance that calls for an equally synthetic response.

Opera, as we see, was still a vehicle of conception and understanding, and in this sense a valuable means of grasping an otherwise ineffable social reality. In addition, it was an avenue of political participation in France, for workers could be excluded physically and yet through commentary they could enter its symbolic domain. Perhaps, then, it was a part of the phenomena responsible for the sustained opposition among workers in the streets of Paris, still continuing in June 1849. Or perhaps too it participated in the renewal of the terms of political debate that historians have perceived as simultaneously occurring elsewhere the very same month. Before this date, conservatives challenged the legality of the democracy in France, but after June it was the political "radicals" who questioned the legality of the regime. But finally, perhaps, this phenomenon was also one that played a role in sustaining a continuing sense of optimism despite further arrests after the June demonstrations.[83] Like *La Muette*, the spirit of contestation expressed around the work could carry a certain symbolic force that played a not unimportant role. The government, significantly, reacted now far more decisively than in the mid-1840s, preparing the ground for the major shift in emphasis that was to characterize Second Empire opera.

The Republic was now in a curious stage, and so too, then, was the Opéra, for it was a Republic in name alone, one functioning without Republican leaders. Already, important symbolic changes were occurring in institutions, changes begun, in fact, immediately after the election of Louis Napoleon as president. This had been precipitated by the perception that Republican rites were no longer in accord with the mores now apparently characteristic of a large percentage of the population. Many institutions, as well, no longer seemed to be in harmony with the larger political mood, and this included, in a prominent way, the Opéra.[84]

But by 1850 we can see an attempt to transform the Opéra's ambience, for *Le Prophète*, like *Les Huguenots*, had revealed the theater's potential danger. The state now tried first to clarify the issue of whom the Opéra was for – not directly, but symbolically, through a series of subtle changes. The Opéra again became one of "the exclusive realms of splendor where the privileged of society celebrate great voices."[85] Once a symbol of the Revolution, the Opéra was now diametrically its opposite: a locus of entertainment, the domain of the nation's social elite.

To implant this message symbolically and to reclaim the great works of the repertoire, to stabilize and reshape their meaning, it soon revived *Le Prophète*. Few could have missed the significance of the fact that this was the work selected for performance at the Opéra on the occasion of the Prince President's official "entry." Before long, symbolic changes in the hall reinforced this redefinition, and the royal box returned, placed again ceremoniously in the center.[86]

Already, however, the new president, who was concerned with the political education of the masses, knew the potentially serious results of denying workers access to the great lyric patrimony of the operatic stage. Henceforth we can observe a marked attempt to find an alternative lyric outlet, and particularly to make the *orphéons* a "théâtre lyrique à tous."[87]

As we shall see, however, workers again saw a different potential here, just as had been the case already in the Opéra-National in the late 1840s. But the state was now well aware that this utopian image had inherently radical as well as conservative implications, that it could mean very different things at once. Indeed, it was to be within the framework of these choral societies, in the Empire, that a challenging alternative conception of national lyric theater arose. If political ideas were still being integrated with traditional, folkloric forms in the countryside, then in the city a related phenomenon was occurring there. For available outlets like the *orphéon* were also being actively imbued with political content, resulting in a potent blend that was only to gain in force.

The Opéra had certainly come full circle from being the home of an exalted, social art to one of superficiality, aesthetic falseness, manipulation, and contradiction. And this image of the Opéra was to be incorporated integrally in a political perception that would merge in an increasingly inextricable manner with a sense of the repertoire's worth. The doctrine of "l'art pour l'art" was thus not the only aesthetic response, in the light of the political events, to the Republic's original goal in art.[88]

In a sense, opera, by 1852, was approaching "drama" in Wagner's sense: it was, for at least a part of the population, a mode of social awareness, experience, and exchange. And so, if political and aesthetic conceptions, by this date, were joined in Wagner's thought, so too were they fusing in France, where his alternative was soon to find fertile ground.

4

POLITICIZED ATTACKS ON GRAND OPERA AND THE GENESIS OF ALTERNATIVE MODELS

Le théâtre n'enseigne pas plus la morale, qu'il n'enseigne l'histoire ou la philosophie. C'est indirectement, en ennoblissant les instincts sensibles de l'homme, retenus jusque-là dans les liens de la nature physique, qu'il affranchit l'intelligence elle-même et la rend capable par cette initiation à la beauté, de concevoir également la vérité rationelle, la justice et la science.

[The theater doesn't teach morality any more than it teaches history or philosophy. It is indirectly, in ennobling the sensitive instincts of man, held back to this point by the ties of physical nature, that it frees the intelligence itself and by this initiation to beauty, renders it capable of conceiving moral and rational truth equally, justice and knowledge.]
LE PEUPLE 14 FEVRIER 1869

THERE IS HARDLY an existing account of grand opera that fails to establish the significant point that the repertoire endured, with amazing tenacity, throughout Second Empire France. One cannot deny the facts concerning the emphasis obviously placed on this body of works, the frequency of their revivals, or the scenic lavishness with which they were staged. But again, the questions I raise concern the relation between the Opéra's function and the development of the genre, or the transformation that it underwent.

My purpose here is to establish that, as opposed to the conventional perspective that sees the Opéra as appealing to a bourgeois public as a spectacle of entertainment and exhibition, throughout the Empire the theater continued to be a realm of political representation, and this affected the theatrical nature as well as the significance of the grand repertoire. Again, the Opéra was structured so as to make a specific symbolic point as well as

164

to produce the kind of art that the state now deemed to be politically useful. The Opéra continued here to serve as a tool or symbol of political compromise, an image to obscure contradictions but one that ended by magnifying them instead. The period of the repertoire's aesthetic demise was thus not the end of its political meaning or of politicized modes of construal and attacks against the genre in France.

But this is not only the period of the repertoire's physical transformation, it is one in which attitudes toward it, both aesthetic and political, now ostensibly harden: it is the period of grand opera's disrepute among specific social groups who are united in their opposition to the cultural hegemony of Napoleon III's regime. Concomitantly, it is the moment of their articulation of an alternative model or of a new kind of grandeur now strongly influenced by the stylistic conceptions of Wagner. Hence for several reasons, the premiere of Wagner's *Tannhäuser* in Paris in 1861 is a valuable case study and an appropriate point at which to conclude. Through this event we can best understand not only the social and cultural associations that the genre had assumed and thus among whom it first lost its aesthetic credibility; in the commentary on Wagner's *Tannhäuser,* in addition to certain seeds of later symbolist thought, we see a debate concerning the role of opera in an egalitarian social order. Here again the political and aesthetic fuse in the context of a specific tradition—that of the operatic-political speech that lay originally behind grand opera's rise.

As we have seen, from the moment he assumed power, Louis Napoleon was well aware of the symbolic message of opera and the importance of reshaping the institution immediately. The Emperor was cognizant that his pressing task in the wake of the Second Republic was to use the Opéra to project a different image of egalitarian culture. Further testimony to the weight he attributed it, moreover, lies not only in his frequent attendance but in his own intervention, within the new structure he imposed, in its internal affairs.

For Napoleon III, the Opéra (now the Académie Impériale de Musique) was once again to be placed in a politically crucial symbolic position in France. It was not only to convey a sense of the Empire's relation to France's great past and thus to emphasize the regime's legitimacy, its basis in a democratic conception; it was now to help foster an alliance between old and new social forces in France, and specifically between the opposing, still contentious aristocratic and democratic traditions. On a political level, the contradiction was between a sense of legitimacy conceived as hereditary and one based on national sovereignty, although at first, in the great plebiscites, they coincided.[1] But this tension remained a symbolic problem, made more complex by the fact that one faction viewed the Empire as a regime of "nouveau-riche upstarts" devoid of any distinguished ancestry. The aristocracy considered the emperor himself to be "mal élevée, peu cultivé," and thus only superficially admitted to society because of his office.[2]

And so the Empire, like the July Monarchy, although it claimed to be linked to the future, still wished to use the Opéra to maintain a vital connection with the cultural past. As was the case with Louis-Philippe before, Napoleon did not make a total break from the political past or attempt to change the fundamental locus of power in French society. And so, if official culture here too was to sustain specific conventions and traditions of the old political order, it was again for a calculated political goal.[3]

But the contradictions of the Empire in the realm of operatic imagery were a projection of yet other political contradictions in the new regime. Proudhon noted the inevitable contradictions that existed in a regime with elements of reform, based on universal suffrage, but also on a conservative and clerical alliance. Historians, too, have pointed out the inherent contradiction between political institutions modeled on those of the first Empire and the new emperor's more progressive ideals. Certain tensions were perhaps inescapable since Napoleon III aspired both "to end the revolution" recently experienced and to avoid reaction, to meet new needs.[4]

The Opéra was by no means to project the image of a bourgeois enterprise, anymore here than it was to have done in 1830, under Louis-Philippe. It was rather to incarnate the nation's patrimony, the treasures of its cultural past that were now, theoretically, to be the property of all the people of France. But there was again an inherent contradiction between such rhetoric and actual fact, for the Opéra projected accessibility on one level but denied it on another. Its implied and actual audiences were, in effect, now quite distinct, the former existing only in rhetoric and never expected to enter the hall.

In opera, the Empire was clearly to avoid the image of its immediate predecessor, or of the Second Republic's "people's opera" and the political ideals that it fostered. Figure 18 testifies to the general perception of chaos surrounding the occasions on national holidays when the general populace was admitted free to the hall. The Empire limited free performances to celebrations of national *fêtes* for which it consistenly deployed the grand repertoire with lavishness, pomp, and great expense. All the Parisian theaters, in the tradition of the "gratis" performance that we have noted earlier, opened their doors free to the public on these occasions. The national theaters, of course, were provided with an additional subvention to do so, but the Opéra was consistently accorded by far the most generous funds.[5] But despite this rhetoric for the rest of the year the Opéra was the province of a very small group: the nation's patrimony was, in effect, actually experienced by a small elite.

The Opéra now, as many years before in the eighteenth century under the ancien régime, returned to a consecrated repertoire to evoke a grander, more heroic past. Now, as then, it provided the context for the nation's elite to "celebrate itself in culture," to experience together its socially privileged role. Its audience largely comprised the *grande* and *petite noblesse,* political figures, foreign diplomats, and other notable persons, including those without title.[6] But evidence of both the Opéra's sense of its audience and the significance of attendance may also be found in ticket prices, policies of free entry, and the conventions of operatic comportment.

Ticket prices undoubtedly discouraged the attendance of more modest social groups, ranging from poor 2.50 franc seats to 16 francs by the later 1860s. Free entries were now greatly expanded, making the Opéra an enclave of the political elite in addition to being, as in the Restoration, the ostensible "house of the court." Entries were hence routinely granted to *aides de camp* of the emperor and to ministers, senators, and prefects of the Empire as well.[7] Indeed, a large official presence characterized the Opéra from the Empire's very first years as, concomitantly, did the careful control of seating arrangements, drawn up in detailed charts. It is therefore not surprising that Napoleon often concerned himself

Figure 18. Opéra, rue Le Peletier, "La fête du 15 août—l'entrée de public au spectacle." Bibliothèque de l'Opéra.

168

personally with the Opéra, frequently intervening in even its more mundane internal affairs.[8] In this sense too the Opéra seemed to have returned to the model of the Restoration, which, as we can clearly observe, was generally the case in its structure as well.

In organization, the Opéra reverted to the system characteristic of the Bourbons: although the emperor meddled, it was directly responsible to high state officials and run by internal directors who had little say.[9] As we shall see, by now the message of the Opéra's administrative structure was deeply embedded in the political consciousness of certain groups, often determining responses to its productions.

In general, the Empire ensured a greater control of the major or subventioned theaters through a fundamental shift in the chain of command or surveillance in the bureaucratic hierarchy. By a decree of 1854 the emperor ended the Opéra's status as an "entreprise privée" and placed the director under the orders of the Ministre d'Etat et de la Maison."[10] Roqueplan briefly continued as director, but resigned several months later, realizing perhaps how unprofitable and exasperating the new structure was likely to be. He was replaced by François Crosnier, an autodidact and son of *concièrges* at the Opéra, briefly a director of the Opéra-Comique and a deputy (a government candidate) from the Loir-et-Cher.[11]

But the controlling body behind the Opéra was no longer a Commission of Surveillance, although a commission continued to exist, with reduced powers, as we shall note. Because of the prevailing sense of the necessity of the smooth and safe functioning of the Opéra, its superior direction fell to the Ministre de la Maison de l'Empereur, Achille Fould. It was now the minister who intervened in almost every conceivable detail, no aspect of the Opéra's functioning being too small to escape his vigilant attention. It was he, instead of the commission, who complained about aspects of artistic performance; he personally approved the repertoire and watched over the budget, the appointment of artists, repairs in the hall, and ticket prices. Not only did he have a major role regarding the choice of repertoire, he often reproved the director for his choice of singers, freely offering his artistic judgment.[12]

Although the minister held essential power, there was still a *commission supérieur,* which nominally was to serve the same function as the old Commission of Surveillance. It took care of the mundane affairs with which the minister did not choose to concern himself, and significantly was now composed entirely of political figures: "Troplong, Président du Sénat; Baroche, Président du Conseil d'Etat; le Comte de Baciocchi, Premier Chambellan, Surintendant des Spectacles de la Cour, de la Musique de la Chapelle et de la Chambre; Roucher, Vice-Président du Conseil d'Etat; le Comte Morny, député, ancien ministre; Chaix d'Estange, avocat, ancien député; de Gautier, Secrétaire Général du Ministre de la Maison de l'Empereur."[13] Notably absent now is representation by journalists and men of letters: the new commissioners were "men of the government" who had no doubt as to the Opéra's role.

The Opéra's director was clearly constricted in his prerogatives by this structure, the only advantage of the situation being the generosity of the Opéra's funding. Although the institution's actual administration was under the Ministre d'Etat, its subvention returned to the Liste civile, as was the case in the Restoration. This remained the system until 1866, when, under the "Liberal Empire," the Opéra returned to the former system of a Director-Entrepreneur. But even then it retained its large subvention from the Liste civile, in addition to another generous subvention from the state. In 1854 the annual subvention was 800,000 francs; by 1866, it had reached the considerable sum of 100,000,000 francs.[14]

The Opéra, in short, was a tightly, indeed a rigorously controlled institution, run more or less directly by officials or bureaucrats of the French state. Nothing about it was left to chance, from the assiduously drawn up seating charts to the detailed statutes concerning the claque, to the repertoire or the *mise en scène.* Once again, the aim of this control was to insure a certain kind of theater: a specific mode of audience sociability and a particular conception of theatrical grandeur.[15]

The larger determining conception, however, was the Opéra's inherently dual function. Like the regime that sustained it, it was to have a popular radiance while still appealing to a glittering elite. In addition, it was to be the home of an authoritative, reproducible art, the splendor of which, of course, could rarely be matched on any other stage. The Opéra, then, was to be inspiring and at the same time politically safe; neither *savant* nor *populaire* in itself, it was to be accessible and yet august. We shall presently see what these ideals implied for the treatment of the repertoire, both in terms of its presentation and the place of the established grand works.

As a contemporary observed, "L'Opéra n'est pas un théâtre d'essai, destiné à représenter les oeuvres d'auteurs nouveaux, mais bien celles dont le mérite ou la renommée ont été consacrés par le temps, ou celles encore d'autres contemporains dont la réputation s'impose à l'opinion publique" [The Opéra is not a theater for trials, meant to perform the works of new authors but those whose merit or renown has been consecrated by time, or those (works) of other contemporaries whose reputation asserts itself on public opinion]. He goes on to point out that, given its now conservative function, many referred to the Opéra in a derogatory way as "une musée historique pour l'art musical."[16] As we shall observe very shortly, however, although this was the dominant impression, new works did enter the repertoire, if erratically or with no clear plan.

The Académie Impériale de Musique being the home of authorized art, the seat of artistic innovation became the reincarnation of the Opéra-National, the new Théâtre-Lyrique. Not grand but lyric, a kind of musical equivalent of the *Salon des Refusés,* it was the new theater for the Opéra's excluded, for the nonelite public and artistic *debutantes.* It was the Théâtre-Lyrique that premiered the great original operas of the Empire, such as Gounod's *Faust* in 1859 and Berlioz's *Les Troyens à Carthage* in 1863. In opera then as well as in painting, the Empire handled artistic innovation in a similar way: it was relegated to more experimental institutions and given only a modicum of state support. As a condition of its small subvention, which barely covered half the cost of renting the hall, the Théâtre-Lyrique was obliged each year to present a three-act opera composed by one of the younger "lauréats de l'Institut."[17]

But the Opéra, beyond its function as museum, icon, and home for the Empire's elite, also has to be seen within an even broader cultural plan. For it served yet another function and another distinctively political role as a part of the Empire's scheme of social and political control through stratification.

As in the First Empire, the Opéra was now integrated in an obvious manner in a comprehensive scheme of social and cultural

171

The Nation's Image

classification and surveillance. The Opéra, if not exclusive in its content, was exclusive in its audience and ambience. As we have noted, the repertoire was a common patrimony, but it was to be experienced in different ways. No more was there to be the dangerous merger that earlier had worried Ledru-Rollin, for now there was a clear demarcation between social recognition and social status through opera.

In this context, then, it is less the general theatrical culture that is so essential to see in order fully to understand the Opéra than it is the structure of official culture. As at the end of the July Monarchy and the last days of the Second Republic, the Opéra's excluded were assigned another domain in which to experience the lyric patrimony of France. Here, as before, the government wished to avoid the inappropriate symbolic message of bringing the people in the Opéra and of risking an uncontrollable reading. In addition, there was a broader fear, given the growing "democratization" of knowledge, that the people were prone to "an exaltation of passion," to sensualism and hence to "moral anarchy." Popular singing societies for this reason were being forced to go underground or become hermetic as the "*chanson politique et sociale*" was consciously "strangled."[18]

The Second Empire responded to these fears in the domain of literature by counteracting the effect of the *colporteurs* by spreading "good reading" in the countryside.[19] In the domain of music, as in the Republic, the *orphéon* societies were now to play an analogous role, fulfilling a cultural need through less politically volatile means. Emile Véron himself, now having been elected as a government candidate, promoted the use of music for this end, as a tool to palliate and placate in a time of dangerous democratization. Using the same rhetoric as had been employed for the Opéra-National, Véron, in the light of the Republic, stated these concepts in the following revealing terms; "Et d'abord, la musique n'a rien de révolutionnaire; elle représente au contraire la discipline: un orchestre est plus discipliné qu'un régiment . . . La musique charme l'esprit et touche le coeur, elle adoucit, elle tempère la rudesse des moeurs démocratiques"[20] [First of all, music has nothing revolutionary; on the contrary it represents discipline: an orchestra is more disciplined that a regiment . . . Music charms the spirit and touches the heart, it softens, it tempers the roughness of democratic manners]. This, of course, does not include

172

opera, with its unstable political message and its uncontrollable semiotic complexity with which officials were familiar by now.

As a substitute, the *orphéon* societies served an essential function, as they had begun to at the end of the Second Republic. They did perform the resonant works of the *patrimoine,* the grand repertoire, such as *La Muette de Portici,* but in a special "edition populaire." It is significant that such a collection prominently omits those pieces (such as the "seditious" barcarolles) that were obviously considered inapropriate or dangerous to such a group.[21]

Because of these same concerns, the state now encouraged musical *réunions populaires,* which emitted a safe utopian message, the conservative one of Fourier. Hence the Empire not ony commissioned large-scale patriotic works like Berlioz's cantata *L'Impériale,* but encouraged concerts that would make the "music of the masters" accessible to each social class. This was to be done in appropriately segregated and hence controlled social settings, and often in more relaxed, informal open-air performance contexts. Each group, then, had its own domain, as the *Revue et gazette musicale* observed, noting the proliferation of concerts, like those of Pasdeloup for the *tiers état.*[22] The elite not only had the continuing Société des Concerts du Conservatoire but, above all, the Opéra as its distinctive and privileged domain.

We can see the central role of the Opéra, in both the senses described above, not only in terms of usage but also in the symbolic, semiotic domain. It is highly revealing that a map of the capital's theaters in 1867 places the new Opéra, then under construction, concentrically at their center. By its very placement it was clear not only who the Opéra was to be for but the social, cultural, and political messages that it was intended to carry.

It is especially revealing to find that, apparently at the emperor's express demand, it was to be installed across from a major artery connecting it with the Comédie-Française and the Tuileries Palace. Since the Louvre was now the official residence of Napoleon III, the effect of the plan was undoubtedly to strengthen the association between the Opéra and the court. But just as significant, this placement also perhaps indicated just which elites it was for, since it was situated in the heart of both a thriving business district and an elegant residential neighborhood. Haussmann's new boulevards, moreover, linked the Opéra to other major cultural monuments, such as the Arc de Triomphe, but also to the railway

stations and to the stock exchange.[23] The new Opéra's very placement, then, makes a telling statement about Second Empire culture and about the place of the Opéra in its peculiar configuration
of political interests.

But just as revealing as the placement of the new Opéra is its
design and the plan employed, one that similarly had to reconcile
several symbolic and functional needs. The first and most immediate need, that which launched the project itself, was the need for
greater security in the wake of attempts on the emperor's life.
Undoubtedly it was with symbolic significance, as before in 1820,
that Orsini had attempted, in 1858, to assassinate the emperor on
his way specifically into the Opéra to hear a performance of *Guillaume Tell*. The Opéra still being a prominent cultural frame for
power, it was the perfect place to make a symbolic point, especially in view of the now complex symbolism of Rossini's opera.[24]

The program for the Opéra's construction was *mis en concours* in
December 1860 and understandably included the specification of a
porte Impériale. Within a month officials were inundated with 171
proposals, but the criteria for the choice soon made the inevitable
winner clear. All the designs submitted faced the task of resolving,
on a semiotic plane, the contradictions of the institution itself, or
the different functions it was to serve. Again, the Opéra was to be
an icon or emblem accessible to all of France, an immobile crystalli-
zation of spirit and grandeur to be appreciated from afar. It was,
then, to be a "people's palace" and at the same time a frame for
authority, a realm of assembly for the elegant world, and a museum for theatrical art.

Significantly, the emperor himself, long an aspiring amateur
architect, took a personal interest in the Opéra's design and even
conceived his own plan. But he was probably forced to admit, in
the end, that his more functional, iron-based structure did not
emit the appropriate message as clearly as did the selected design.[25]

Perhaps it should be no surprise that the winner came from a
humble social background, part of the very constituency to which
the image of the new Opéra was aimed. Charles Garnier was born
in a workers' district in Paris, on the rue Mouffetard, the son of a
blacksmith and a lacemaker, who, because of his talent, was admitted to the Ecole des Beaux-arts.

In his plans for the Académie Impériale de Musique, Garnier
had an infallible guide: an intuitive sense of the complex ideologi-

cal and social functions the Opéra was to serve. Here again, artistic perception and expression perhaps were able to accomplish coherently what calculated policy decisions, made by officials, were unable to do. For Garnier the Opéra was a social center in a multifaceted sense, a realm of sociability for the "power elite" and a beacon of grandeur to all of France.

The architect hence confected a "brilliant and sumptuous composition of the social spectacle," indulging the impulse for pomp and recognizing the protocol of operatic attendance. If the exterior was to be as lavish and historically detailed as a typical grand opera set, the interior was to allow the perambulating public itself to be "mis en scène"[26] (Figure 19).

The exterior that Garnier designed was far different from that of the existing Opéra and indeed from all the buildings that the Paris Opéra had previously inhabited. As Figures 20 and 21 reveal, the old Opéra was a Palladian *palazzo* ensconced in a dense web of buildings and streets, its entrance unemphasized and practically designed. But for Garnier the exterior message was to be as important as the interior, indeed a projection of the values and vision of grandeur that informed the *mise en scène*. His structure, although it used iron as a basic supporting material, nevertheless masked its structural function with a lavish neo-Baroque facade.[27] But beyond this, Garnier emblazoned his vision in a vocabulary of decorative forms, apparently chosen intuitively from current associations with "opera-going."[28]

Garnier hence translated his sense of the social experience and grandeur of the Opéra as well as of the character of the repertoire itself into architectural and decorative equivalents. The Opéra he designed, just like its repertoire, was indeed a "musée pour l'art musical," as much a projection of image and patrimony as the works to be performed on its stage.[29]

The repertoire in question was both old and new, here in two different senses. Certainly, new works were not excluded–those of Gounod and Verdi were performed in these years–but the French works added to the repertoire all generally proved to be short-lived. (They included Auber's *Marco Spada* and *Cheval de bronze* [1857], Halévy's *La Magicienne* [1858], and Felicien David's *Herculanum* [1859].) The repertoire largely comprised revivals, but revivals in a special sense–those that refocused the nature and

175

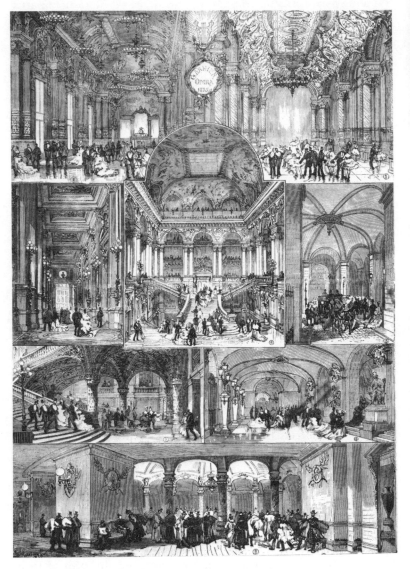

Figure 19. Opéra-Garnier, vues intérieurs. Bibliothèque de l'Opéra.

Figure 20. Opéra-Le Peletier, façade et intérieur. Bibliothèque de l'Opéra.

content of the works in subtle but significant new ways. For like the new Opéra, their style and content were adapted to a complex function; the repertoire, like the building, was to serve a distinctive cultural and political end.

Contemporaries characteristically noted the disproportionate emphasis upon décor, costumes, and *mise en scène,* and the tendency to judge a triumph solely upon this basis. The triumph, however, as we have seen, could not have been a monetary one but a triumph of prestige, of official approbation, on which the director now depended. For this reason one finds the same quest for exactitude in the historical detail of the *mise en scène* and in the focus on vocal execution that also characterized the Bourbon Restoration. For now, as then, the concern was with political credibility through official image, the Opéra's stage still being a primary locus for such political symbolization.[30]

And so once more, as in the late Restoration, in the midst of fear over *actualité* the boundaries between fantasy and reality were, for deliberate reasons, blurred. There was clearly an awareness of the kind of dynamic that could occur, given both the symbolism of the Opéra and the symbolic disposition of the elite audience itself inside the hall. Authenticity in historical detail was no longer sought in the interest of realistic experience: now it was a fetish and a distancing mechanism to frame, safely, the historical past. Scenic detail thus often approached a kind of Meissonier-like realism, or the opposite of a realism of social forces, a realism of emotion or feeling.

One may observe, then, the Opéra's tendency to aestheticize, to euphemize the grand repertoire, to eviscerate it, to control its meaning through a strategy of substitutions and cuts. Such was already the case with the revival of *Les Huguenots* in 1853; critics noted the many deletions and the shifting emphasis toward *divertissements.*[31] When revived again in 1868 it was with a splendid new décor, particularly for the provocative third and fifth acts, by Desplechin and Cambon. Widely noted as well were the elegant new costumes introduced for the dancing scenes, more impressive than ever before and hence drawing the public's attention to an even greater degree. The ballets in general played a prominent role in shifting not only the focus but also the cultural tenor of the works, the kind of spectacles they were considered to be.[32]

One finds a similar case with the once incendiary *Le Prophète* (revived in 1860 and 1869), first with a new *mise en scène* and then with new *divertissements.* In 1869 all attention centered on the famous "Ballet des patineurs," which now featured an attractive and brilliant pair of skaters imported by the Opéra from England.[33] And another revolutionary opera reappeared in 1868 as well: Rossini's *Guillaume Tell,* apparently to commemorate the composer's death. The press described the performance as a "représentation solenelle," a ritualistic performance, and now ostensibly in more than one dimension . To claim Rossini as an integral part of the cultural *patrimoine* of France, a bust of the composer was placed in the center of the hall and ceremoniously crowned with laurel. When *L'Avenir National* referred to *Tell* and *Les Huguenots* as "two pages from history," it was now referring not to their content but to the cultural history of France.[34]

But yet another revival, and perhaps in this context the most revealing of all, took place in the 1860s: that of *La Muette de Portici.* Again, not only did the Opéra give the work an entirely new scenic presentation but the critical commentary similarly mused on its place in France's political past. It was now a charming relic, accorded a selectively accurate *mise en scène* in a curious approach to historical accuracy, as Figure 22 reveals. As opposed to the original sets we have seen, the aim was an academic kind of realism, one now interspersed with fanciful ruins, making it credibly accurate and yet remote. It was a controlled kind of realism, now consciously devoid of the quality of *actualité* once so integral to the aesthetic and political force of the grand repertoire. The Opéra's realism, like that of the earlier Restoration's opera, was a realism that evoked a fantasy, a dream world that was safely remote from the present.[35]

But the once explosive opera was refashioned (or refocused) outside the stage as well, and not only through the arrangements for the *orphéons* that we have seen. By far the largest volume of instrumental arrangements date from the Second Empire, almost all of which also deemphasize the works' original points of dramatic strength. Most are "fantaisies de concert," or "polkas brillants" on themes from the work, and range from pieces for organ to saxophone and piano four hands.[36]

Given the shift to fantasy, Théophile Gautier made an apt observation: that despite its pretensions to historical accuracy, the Opéra strove for precisely the opposite: "L'Opéra est le seul refuge de la poésie et de le fantaisie . . . La grossière réalité n'y est pas admise . . . rien d'actuel, rien de véritable; on est dans un monde enchanté"[37] [The opéra is the only refuge of poetry and fantasy . . . Gross reality is not admitted . . . nothing actual, nothing real; one is in an enchanted world].

Figure 22. Reprise de *La Muette de Portici*, Act V, décor de Cambon et Thierry. Bibliothèque de l'Opéra.

181

In conjunction with this, commentary about these works underwent a concomitant change, as we have already noted in the specific case of *La Muette de Portici*. No longer do we find an ambiguity of message hotly disputed in the contemporary press, for the question was no longer one of the historical relevance or significance of these works. It was now easy to summarize their meaning: *Robert le Diable* was not about the divided soul of France, as discussed at the time of its premiere, but rather about "la Catholicisme légendaire." *Le Prophète* was no longer about the nature and causes of social revolution but now rather simply about "les chimères et les utopies." According to the *Journal Officielle,* the common theme behind all these works was not political controversy but now rather simply, religion.[38]

But if the French grand repertoire was undergoing reinterpretation, so too was the achievement of its noted master, Meyerbeer. By the 1860s Meyerbeer's greatness no longer lay in his ability to bring an historical text alive but the way in which his music embodied the preeminently French trait of eclecticism. It was no longer the dramatic force of his style, his attentiveness to the qualities and pace of the text that aroused critical (or critics') admiration, it was rather his "wise synthesis." No longer an original genius, Meyerbeer was now instead the "great conciliator," who like all great artists of modern France, brought breadth and universality to his art. According to the secretary of the Académie des Beaux-arts, Meyerbeer's eclecticism was a complex, refined language, one that suitably "pleases our times." Moreover, he goes on to claim that this is a particularly French point of view, and hence advances the idea that in becoming eclectic Meyerbeer became truly French.[39]

Despite the fact that Meyerbeer was German, making his home in Berlin and rarely in Paris, his work, in essence, now belonged to France. Indeed, contemporaries noted the irony that the grand works, the core of the repertoire, now perhaps more than ever, were the product of foreign composers writing for France.

The Opéra's officials, as we saw, believed that only authorized masterworks should be produced, and hence only established composers should be allowed to write for the Opéra. Even if foreign, and perhaps in part for that reason, they were considered safe or had been observed and were duly consecrated by success elsewhere before being called to the grand stage of France. And so both Meyerbeer and Verdi were awarded membership in the nation's Legion of Honor, much to the dismay of French composers who felt their territory was being usurped. Although composers like Charles Gounod and Félicien David briefly gained access to the Opéra, their musical language and dramatic conceptions seemed more appropriate to the Théâtre-Lyrique.

The Opéra was still, and perhaps more than ever, the nation's exalted, first lyric stage, and as such had no use for the musical or dramatic innovations of France's younger composers. Since younger, innovative artists could not rest artistically immobile as the Opéra's needs demanded, once again as in the Restoration the Opéra was forced to look outside of France. To keep similar grand works in the repertoire, to add to the small existing supply, it had to seek out those composers still willing or able to find meaning in its theatrical conventions.

And so, for all the reasons developed above, at least two different groups in Second Empire France had a clear understanding of what the Opéra was, of its political and cultural functions. Here there was increasing dissatisfaction for diverse but intersecting reasons that together made the Opéra a target once again for a complex cultural and political critique.

A study of attacks on the Opéra and the specific terms in which they were couched can provide us with even deeper insight into its evolving and complex social meaning. Negative responses to the Opéra's presentations and policies were far from passive and they still carried political meaning: the so-called *esprit frondeur* endured. Antagonists continued to respond to the symbolism of the Opéra with a similar set of terms, but now finally proposed an alternative conception that was to gain significant conceptual power.

For this very reason, it is at this time that Wagner's conception of opera found such fertile new ground in France and among an otherwise incongruous cultural alliance. For Wagner, as we shall see, appealed to the Académie Impériale's excluded—to those excluded both in an artistic and creative as well as in a social sense. It was, in part, as a result of the antagonism between the "fossilized" institution and the creative and political world confronting it that this particular faction took shape.

A significant number of the opposition forming against the Empire's opera comprised its innovative artists, not only in music but in literature and the visual arts. They naturally brought their tensions, their sense of artistic truth and reality, as well as their tactics and aesthetic terms to bear on the Opéra. Their image of the Opéra was harsh and trenchant, an image communicated simultaneously both by commentary (strongly influenced by the realist movement) and in actual artistic content. And it is in this framework that artists as diverse as Richard Wagner and Jacques Offenbach were similarly involved in the process of undermining the credibility of grand opera as a genre in France.

Perhaps the most revealing documentation of the operatic opposition of the Second Empire is a painting by the young Eduard Manet completed in 1862. His *Music in the Tuileries Gardens* is both a subtle and incisive statement not only about the identity but also the tactics employed by this operatic opposition culture.

Assembled on official ground, ostensibly to hear one of the Empire's many safe or popular concerts, is a seemingly curious assortment of figures. But their real coherence derives from the fact that several were vocal commentators on the operatic culture of the Empire and had, in some manner, involved themselves with it. Moreover, several were figures simultaneously outside and inside the establishment, or those who through their marginal official connections attempted to undermine official culture from within. The "music" of the painting's title thus plays with a powerful and provocative ambiguity: the issue of whose music is being referred to – that of the establishment or that of this group.

Outside the cognoscenti this allusion was lost or perhaps overshadowed by the striking artistic innovations now beginning to appear in Manet's technique. And so when the picture was first exhibited in 1863, it was not the implications of the subject itself to which critics vociferously objected. Since there were ample precedents for such a physical grouping of figures in journals like *L'Illustration,* the incisive point made by their specific choice could well have been lost. Rather, it was the nature of the style, the neglect of exact definition, the avoidance of traditional academic attitudes, half-tones, and shadows that aroused complaint.[40]

But the threat of Manet's style in the work had an analogy in the subject he depicted, since both painter and his subjects had recently been decried for their dangerous "realist" tendencies. Among the figures presented the terms of deprecation had indeed been similar: almost all had been labeled not only realists but concomitantly democrats. However, in the mind of Manet, beyond such a linkage (which in several cases was not actually true) there was another clear, illuminating filiation, one that we must also try to see.

All the figures but one were known to have been supporters or sympathizers of Wagner in France, and hence of the musical style or operatic alternative for which he stood.[41] All of them linked an artistic and operatic to a cultural and political critique, thus confronting the cultural hegemony of the establishment in its own subtle cultural terms. The figures prominently included here are, first of all, Jacques Offenbach, the increasingly popular composer of satirical operettas; Champfleury (Jules Fleury), the realist novelist and author of books on popular music (the *chanson*), visual art, caricature, and most recently, Wagner; Charles Baudelaire and Théophile Gautier, recently established as "Wagnerites," having come to the German composer's defense in the wake of his Parisian premiere.

Offenbach, although he was known to have detested Wagner, nevertheless helped prepare the way for the alternative that Wagner offered by comically attacking the older model.[42] He began a subtle subversion of the artistic credibility of French grand opera, mercilessly exposing what it had now become in Second Empire France. Offenbach knew very well the range of what could be said through an operatic critique as well as the special power of the comic language that he employed.

Ironically, then, despite their differences, Offenbach and Wagner were the composers who were first sponsored and then decried by the political-cultural establishment. For it learned that despite his comedy Offenbach's message was a serious one, and it is the way that this message was communicated that we must now attempt to elucidate.

From the very start of his career, Offenbach employed a characteristic tactic: that of pretending to serve the establishment with comic diversion while in fact doing a good deal more. We can see the distance between the artistic goals that Offenbach expressed in public and those that become evident by analyzing his works from the beginning of his career. Offenbach's first appointment as conductor at the Comédie-Française in 1849 apparently taught him much about the manipulation of official rhetoric, as evidenced in his application to the minister of state to open a theater in 1855:

My intention would be to present "harlequinades," panto-
mimes in one or more acts . . . I would be aiming to introduce Paris to the genre of the Italian *fantoccini,* modified to
suit French taste, and to offer new and original amusements
of a kind to please those of cultivated intelligence and the
general public. In addition, I would put on *tableaux vivants,*
reproducing the most beautiful subjects of historical painting, and finally, plays for two or three characters with new
music . . . The use in this sort of show of music composed
with skill and care would not only result in giving an unac-
customed emphasis to a particular kind of popular entertainment, but would also offer a fairly wide opening to any
young composers who might come along to try their
strength.[43]

Clearly, Offenbach was aware of how to appeal to the Empire's
cultural plan, relating his goals to those of traditional as well as
contemporary popular art. At a time when popular theaters were
being razed on the boulevard, Offenbach offered one that seemed,
from the standpoint of the authorities, to be both practical and
safe. Like the Opéra-National, it would cater to the nonelite as
well as to young artists, although the appeal of its products would
transcend any one social class.

What Offenbach did in the end, of course, is far different from
what he overtly claimed, for his goal in part was to expose what
lay behind so much of Second Empire culture. One target was
thus French grand opera—its language, its subjects, and its conventions, but as a means through which to unmask a subtle amalgam of political and cultural traits.

Numerous studies have already treated Offenbach's parodies of
Meyerbeer and especially his witty, irreverent references to *Les
Huguenots* in his *Ba-ta-clan.* But if Offenbach did more than simply
parody the style and conventions of the grand repertoire: there
was a message in the way he did this, particularly in his use of a
technique of inversion.

"Carnivalization," or a turning upside-down of the official
world, had long been an element of popular or indigenous folk
culture in France. It often involved parody of ceremonies as well
as vulgar obscenity, in addition to exaggeration and parodistic
inversion of accepted or normal behavior.[44] Although such tech-

niques had been consciously repressed by the authorities, especially since the French Revolution, they had reappeared in other forms in the course of the nineteenth century. Satirical journals like *Le Charivari,* which often employed this technique, appeared "as another vehicle for exposing the rampant hypocrisy of Orléanist politics."

But they also reappeared in literature, most notably in the writings of Gustave Flaubert, and above all in his famous and scandaluos novel, *Madame Bovary.* Significantly, Flaubert employs one form of this technique in particular scenes in the novel, including notably the scene that takes place at the Opéra in Rouen. The cacaphonous tuning up of the orchestra here becomes the metaphor for *charivari,* the derisory use of noise to ridicule such individuals as remarried widows, partners of unequal age, or *maris battus.* The scene at the Opéra, of course, is intended to bring about the meeting of Emma, the Madame Bovary of the title, and her future, disappointing lover, Léon. But the scene at the Opéra is also symbolic of vacuous social convention: Flaubert describes with relish Emma's gullible, naive reactions to the grand *mise en scène*:

Elle n'avait pas assez d'yeux pour contempler les costumes, les décors, les personnages, les arbres peints qui tremblaient quand on marchait, et les toques de velours, les manteaux, les épées, toutes ces imaginations qui s'agitaient dans l'harmonie comme dans l'atmosphère d'un autre monde.[45]

[She did not have enough eyes to contemplate the costumes, the décor, the characters, the painted trees that trembled when one walked, and the velvet caps, the coats, the swords, all those imaginations that were aroused in the harmony of another world.]

Flaubert's deeper message through such treatment of grand opera in *Madame Bovary* is one, in fact, to which Jacques Offenbach was to make an explicit reference. In *Orphée aux enfers,* he not only attempts to further Flaubert's point but to respond specifically to the accusations against the novel made at its trial the previous year. It is perhaps, then, not without significance that Manet's depictions of Offenbach and Baudelaire in his painting are symmetrically balanced, each head outlined against an inclining tree trunk. For both Flaubert and Baudelaire had been tried for offenses against the "public morality," but in Flaubert's case the accusation had been based on a matter of literary technique. Flaubert had jettisoned the traditional narrator who served as a point of moral orientation—the "reasoner" in bourgeois drama, who anchored the moral perspective from inside the play.[46]

This is precisely what Offenbach's librettists, Hector Crémieux and Ludovic Halévy, chose as a trenchant vehicle of satire to run incisively throughout the work. The reference is unmistakable from the very first lines of the opera, and then continues to appear throughout it as a connecting thread:

> Qui je suis? Du théâtre antique
> J'ai perfectionné le choeur;
> Je suis l'Opinion publique,
> Un personnage symbolique
> Ce qu'on appelle un raisonneur.

> [Who am I? In the antique theater
> I perfected the chorus;
> I am public opinion,
> A symbolic character
> That one calls a reasoner.]

The carnivalization of the trial is evident in the fact that Public Opinion speaks from a standpoint almost opposite to morality in the conventional sense. But other references to the novel continue to appear throughout the work, making it a carnivalization of the social world behind the trial.

Previous commentators have seen a parody of Napoleon III and his court in the work, in its message that "the great and powerful can ride roughshod on public opinion with impunity"; and they have also noted that Orpheus and Eurydice are presented here not as "star-crossed lovers" but rather, for comic effect, as "a nagging married couple."[47] One can, however, easily see Eurydice as a comic Emma Bovary, insuperably bored with her life and hence in search of romantic adventure. Offenbach, moreover, reinforces the carnivalization in his musical setting, one which satirizes, parodies, and exaggerates the operatic language of this social world.

He parodies, for example, the mosaic-like idiom associated with Meyerbeer's works, especially the historical quotation originally intended to "mettre en jeu" noble and patriotic sentiments. We can see this in his witty invocation of the "Marseillaise" as well as in his reference to historical styles, most notably that of Gluck. This extends to the scene of revolt, by now a commonplace in French grand opera, which here becomes a particularly ridiculous, ineffectual revolt of the gods. And he concomitantly parodies the pastiche effect that frequently resulted from the insertion of more popular numbers into the mosaic, for *actualité*. Offenbach well knew how easily this technique could be pushed into parody and hence takes every opportunity to do so, emphasizing the resulting dramatic incongruities. The conventions of the language had so lost their meaning, their dramatic rationale, that Offenbach knew the audience was already inclined to see only their ridiculous shell.

But there was soon another context in which opponents of grand opera in France were able to confront the social, political, and cultural conventions for which it stood. This time it involved a movement from a critical, negative satire to the projection of a positive alternative of a national operatic culture. As we shall see, in the process of commentary and reflection on the implications of Wagner's work, this alternative was eventually linked to the musical style of Richard Wagner.[48] Again it was the political context that gave Wagner's style such meaning, but the style itself was to have its own "engendering effect" on political conceptions. The figures involved in this process are those who are present, with Offenbach, in Manet's work: the writers Champfleury, Charles Baudelaire, and Théophile Gautier.

The debate over Richard Wagner began as the result of a kind of irony endemic to the nature and structure of the Opéra in Second Empire France. For the performance of Wagner's *Tannhäuser* resulted from the intervention of political authority, in this case of Napoleon himself, who saw the French premiere as a political tactic.[49]

Wagner had returned to Paris in 1860, some years after his first visit, with the hope that he might find a more favorable atmosphere for his work, or at least financial success. And Napoleon III had begun a policy of domestic liberalization, or the "Liberal Empire," in which he became more conciliatory to the Left. In 1859 he issued a decree of clemency for revolutionaries of 1848 that in essence made France "possible again for men with radical backgrounds." As with *La Muette de Portici,* such a political liberalization was to be responsible for an ultimately "dangerous" artistic innovation.

And as with Rossini in the Restoration, Wagner was a useful image himself because of his political ambiguity, someone who had participated in the revolution in Dresden but still admired "authoritarian rule and the myths and symbols of monarchism." Hence his supporters in France included members of both the Left and the Right, many of whom, it is significant to note here, sometimes collaborated in opposing the regime.[50]

And unlike his previous, disastrous visit in 1839, he now came with powerful contacts that included the socially prominent German colony in Paris. Chief among these was the influential Princess de Metternich, who had been briefly engaged to Napoleon but was now married to the Austrian ambassador. Napoleon was trying to court Austria's favor, having alienated it through his Italian policy, and hence when the princess appealed to him on Wagner's behalf he acquiesced. Typical, then, of his character, as noted by incisive observers such as Zola, the emperor could be stubborn but was also capable of surprising audacities.[51]

But Napoleon had a number of political reasons for supporting Wagner's premiere; it was now consonant with the Opéra's policy to perform French versions of "grand" foreign works. For clearly by the late 1850s the grand repertoire of the thirties was finally losing favor, with the number of performances of the most legendary among them now declining.[52] The additions had largely been Italian: Verdi's *Trouvère* (in French translation) in 1857, Bellini's *Roméo et Juliette,* in 1860, and Rossini's *Semiramis,* in the same year. And so, although the German work was forcibly imposed on the Opéra's director, Royer, it seemed a plausible addition to the now weak repertoire.[53]

Royer was told to spare no expense, and the opera was consequently allowed an unprecedented period of six months for punctilious rehearsal. As Figure 23 shows, it was staged conventionally as a grand opera, with a *mise en scène* that observers described with amazement as "une luxe incroyable."[54] Further to ensure the

Figure 23. *Tannahäuser,* 1861, décor Act III. Bibliothèque de l'Opéra.

work's success in Paris, the Opéra offered Wagner extensive counsel, the majority of which he rejected, creating considerable tension with the Opéra's management. For not only did he refuse advice concerning the conventional placement of the ballet, he refused to hire the claque, preferring to replace it with his own group of friends. And much to the Opéra's consternation, Wagner proceeded to promise free tickets that normally sold at the highest prices to his substitute claque.[55]

As in the case of *Le Prophète,* excitement and rumors preceded the work, word of which undoubtedly crept out from the rehearsals to which selected guests were invited. Of special concern were the rumors that some kind of disruption would most likely occur, a cabal having been formed against Wagner that he stubbornly refused to combat. Indeed, Wagner had lost support among some of his Republican admirers who saw him as associated far too closely with Napoleon III. *Le Siècle* openly warned that "trouble was brewing" at the Opéra, but it was also fomented by disenchanted Legitimist sympathizers on the Right.

This primarily involved the Jockey Club, comprised largely of young aristocrats who antagonistically demanded the customary ballet in the second act. Again, participating in a long tradition of searching for pretexts for politicized demonstrations, they chose perhaps in the case of Wagner the most obvious one. When Wagner, instead, added a short ballet to the Venusberg scene, trouble was sure to occur, which the minister of state conscientiously did his best to avert.[56] And undoubtedly worried about the possible dynamics in the hall at the first performance, the administration took special pains to draw up a carefully organized seating chart.[57] Hence the hall was inherently politicized by expectations and physical disposition, in addition to the general knowledge concerning the political circumstances of the performance.

It was in this context that the performance unfolded amidst a glittering *assemblée choisie* in a tense and crowded hall on March 13, 1861. Accounts of the first performance attest to the drama of the situation, and to the manner in which the events in the hall interacted with those on the stage. Once more, as in *La Muette,* it is important to see how this drama unfolded, in light both of those present at the premiere and those who learned of it outside the hall. And it is important to remember that the regime's opponents were again prepared to damn the opera on any plausible artistic pretense, just as in the Restoration and July Monarchy. In addition, of course, there were members of the audience whose reaction was more purely to the style, who were disoriented by the way in which the opera created expectations of, but ignored, most of grand opera's conventions.

Apparently, on the first evening all went normally until the Venusberg scene, which the audience found long and boring and which ushered in a notable change of mood. Laughs soon followed and increased in volume throughout the scene of the song contest, and aside from the marches in the second and third acts, and the "Song to the Evening Star," the audience condemned all the rest.[58] Perhaps we can comprehend the initial disruption if we recall that the Opéra's *mise en scène* was that of a conventional grand opera, which created a certain set of stylistic assumptions. These the music did not fulfill, except in those isolated numbers that could loosely be assimilated to the conventions of the grand repertoire.

Otherwise, Wagner's music communicated in a different way, together with the text, one essentially foreign in nature to the grand tradition. And so for some in the audience the most disquieting sections were those that abandoned any reference to the principles of musical form and dramaturgy that they knew. There were complaints of the "longues mélopées," the "sonorités à outrance," as well as the "interminable" recital of the trip to Rome.[59]

For the second performance, on March 18, Wagner made numerous cuts, but all in vain because the opposition had been steadily building since the first performance. This time the audience expressed hostility not only through laughter and noisy murmurs but by whistling belligerently on noise makers that resembled the sounds of animals. Perhaps there was reference here to the tradition of *charivari,* and maybe a reference to the sensualism of the musical language, with the person exposed or derided being Napoleon III.

Without a claque to combat this disruption it gradually grew more chaotic, especially at the moment when the emperor and empress ceremoniously entered the hall. As was traditional, they arrived for the opera at the end of the second act, and the audience who saw them, respecting the established convention, immediately applauded. But those who did not see them arrive interpreted the applause as an "anticlaque," and in response redoubled their whistling so that the music was virtually inaudible.[60]

The third performance, on March 24, was only slightly less tumultuous. The Opéra had scheduled it for a Sunday to escape "the systematic hostility of the subscribers." But the notorious Jockey Club, which along with the other men's clubs of Paris claimed the first ten rows of the orchestra, arrived and belligerently undermined the performance. Shortly after the third presentation, by mutual consent of Wagner and the officials of the Tuileries palace, the opera was withdrawn "to avoid further scandal." The Opéra substituted it with Verdi's *Trouvère,* which was met by a practically empty hall, forcing the Ministre d'Etat to recommended that it be followed by a one-act ballet.[61] The Opéra, having been ridiculed, in effect, for ignoring its own conventions, evidently felt the need to reassert them again, but now more strongly than ever.

But the event was far from over, for, as happened with *La Muette de Portici* and so many operas that followed, the process of commentary was now to begin. Still to emerge was clarification of the political meaning of these interlocking dramatic events, or those that had taken place in the hall both on and off the stage. In viewing this process, two particular factors should be kept in mind: that the state attempted to distance itself from the composer, and that the political alliance against the work disintegrated.[62]

Conservative or establishment figures attempted to imply that the Opéra had made an honest mistake, and that this mistake had been corrected by the removal of the work from the stage. For one of the most prominent conservative spokesmen, François-Joseph Fétis, the events at the Opéra were no surprise, given his previous impression of Wagner. Already in 1852, Fétis had believed Wagner to be politically seditious, branding him a "realist, positivist," and hence a "democrat," an adherent of the "socialist school of Proudhon."

For Fétis, Wagner's was an art that abjured the quest for any higher ideal, appealing to man's sensuous nature and hence unleashing "dangerous passions." Another conservative, Paul Scudo, averred that Wagner's music was calculated to incite, to "violente des passions au lieu de les évoquer avec aménagement."[63] As we may recall, this is precisely what officials feared most in the context of opera, especially when it was made available to the lower classes of society. Both critics, then, had already noted the affinity of Wagner's style with the ideals of radical democracy or egalitarianism, on which the Empire's proponents were now to seize.

It was precisely on this basis that the democratic and realist novelist Champfleury (the pen name of Jules Fleury) leaped to Wagner's defense. For conservatives this was no surprise, given Fétis's observations, and since they identified Wagner's supporters as "les écrivains médiocres, des peintres, des sculpteurs sans talent, des démocrats, des républicans, des esprits faux" [mediocre writers, painters, sculptors without talent, democrats, republicans, false spirits]. Champfleury, to them, must have seemed to incarnate several of these attributes at once, since he had already engaged in the realist cause on behalf of various works of art in different media. Most notably, he had defended the work of Courbet, seeing a democratic statement in his bold, aggressive technique, his monumental treatment of popular sources and subjects, and his socially realistic depictions.

But Champfleury was equally an advocate of contemporary caricature as another mode or genre through which to attain the same culturally critical end.[64] For Champfleury, then, realism in visual art was a mode of perception or a way of defining and perceiving truth that distinguished it from official culture. And hence it implied not only how the artist should represent the social world, but also asserted what the artist had a right to represent. It was a question, then, of whose culture or values should be projected on a monumental scale, or be allowed to make a public statement in the people's name.

For Champfleury, such an aesthetic had implications for two kinds of music: first, the traditional popular *chanson,* literally the art of the people of France. This premise he elaborated in detail in the preface to a collection that he brought out along with the composer Weckerlin, *Chansons populaires des provinces de France.*[65] In his penetrating analysis, Champfleury redefines the nature of the popular *chanson,* seeing in it not a reflection of the naive or childlike, as cultural officials had recently claimed, but rather a manifestation of a trenchant popular realism, an ability to "see things as they are" and to describe them in an authentic, independent mode of discourse. Like his ally Proudhon, Champfleury had no qualms about calling it realist art, for it was incisive, honest art that was rooted in social existence – art that "meets a need."[66]

But realist art was something more as well when applied to music, for it had clear implications for modern music, according to Champfleury. Realist music here was that which communicated on a more direct and powerful plane and thus both represented the emotions of and appealed to a far broader social spectrum. For Champfleury, Fétis was right in labeling Wagner a democrat and realist for he did seek to authorize the instinctual, a characteristic he saw in the mass, and to elevate it in status. Wagner, for him, in *Tannhäuser,* communicated on a new emotional plane, introducing thereby unprecedented depth, immensity, and grandeur into musical expression. In this, Théophile Gautier concurred: "Il se fondait sur l'instinct, il en appelait aux formes élémentaires de l'émotion, il prétendait pénétrer dans le monde de l'inconscient, afin d'atteindre aux sources primordiales de la sensibilité"[67] [It was founded on instinct, it called forth elementary forms of emotion, it claimed to penetrate the world of the unconscious in order to reach the primordial sources of sensitivity.]

For Champfleury as for Max Buchon and Edmond Duranty, both editors of realist journals, these qualities were aspects of realist art. For realism was that art which addressed not just visible, external social reality but also collective emotion, an equally important aspect of social reality.[68] An "exaltation of passion" and sensualism was thus to be desired in this context for it expressed and released what was egalitarian or authentically and truly shared. Wagner's was a style of opera that was thus desirable for the French national stage since it was one legitimately based on the cultural reality of modern France.

Hence, again participating in a tradition we have traced from the Opéra-National, Wagner's music was projected as a counter-image, one now associated with authentic democratic representation. We find this articulated most clearly in the writings of a wealthy and learned doctor with a strong interest in music, literature, and politics, Auguste de Gasperini.[69] For Gasperini, who had heard Wagner's music in Germany and had seen one of his operas in the 1850s, there was no question as to the political implications of his operatic model. In the context of French politics, this model was an authentically democratic paradigm, a true representation of the social order as it ought to be. It was a model associated with liberty and release, with precisely the kind of expression that officials of the Empire were attempting to expunge in all aspects of culture.

Liberty, here, for Gasperini was the opposite of manipulation: it was the capacity for autonomous social action and for an independent conception of society and culture.[70] Like Proudhon, Gasperini was absorbed with defining where authentic liberty lies and with promoting the release of true community, very much along Wagner's own lines:

Le mouvement musical auquel Wagner a associé son nom est essentiellement démocratique; je n'en voudrais pour preuve que ce passage d'une lettre à Berlioz, où Wagner dit expressément que l'oeuvre la plus achevée est celle que saisit "immédiatement l'intelligence la plus ordinaire" . . . Au lieu de s'amoindrir en des mains frivoles qui asservissaient au profit de quelques-uns, il tend à se tourner du côté des masses, à s'inspirer des foules, pour les inonder à son tour de ses clartés purifiantes . . . le temps est venu où le drame lyrique, dans son expression la plus haute, appartiendra à tous les peuples at relèvera de l'humanité tout entière.[71]

[The musical movement with which Wagner has associated his name is essentially democratic; I would want no better proof than the passage from a letter to Berlioz where Wagner says expressly that the most accomplished work is that which seizes "immediately the most ordinary intelligence" . . . Instead of diminishing in the frivolous hands tied down to the profit of a few he tends to turn to the masses, to be inspired by the crowds, to inundate them in his turn with his purifying clarities . . . the time has come when the lyric drama, in its highest expression, will belong to all the people and will rise from all of humanity.]

What Gasperini called for was in a sense precisely what was already beginning in France: an appropriation of the Wagnerian model and its political implications by a small but significant group of French workers. Long aware of operatic symbolism and now especially atuned to its message and the unique conceptual synthesis that it could articulate, they were becoming more and more interested in Wagner. Given the treatment of the grand repertiore that we have seen in works like *La Muette de Protici,* it was not suprising that it was losing its attraction for this group, among others: nor that, as a recent study has observed, there was an increasing and palpable fascination with Wagner and the regenerative power of his art within the context of the *orphéons.*[72] Selections from his operas found their way often into regional programs and discussions of his ideas were not uncommon in their proliferating journals.[73]

Moreover, it is significant that in the first workers' libraries in France, such as the "Bibliothèque des amis de l'instruction" (founded in 1861, in Paris), scores of operas, soon to include Wagner's, already occupied an important place. Despite the fact that most users of the library could not read these piano-and-vocal scores, they were nevertheless symbolically present as something about which one should know.[74] For opera was still "instruction," so important to French workers, as we have seen: it was knowledge and understanding of a complex sort and a reality of the political world. If at the start of the Empire workers were concerned with their material condition and by the end were turning to their human condition, opera was once again relevant.[75]

But given such concerns and awareness, their interest in opera now was not just in the messages it relayed from the state, messages then to be decoded in commentary. Opera, in addition, could serve as a positive tool for the political opposition and thus as a valuable and necessary conceptual force. As one journal observed, depriving French workers of access to music was a notable way of maintaining them in a culturally dependent, insensate, childlike state:

> La musique est le premier des arts, parce qu'elle est compréhensible pour tous. Un beau monument, une belle pièce de vers, une belle statue, un beau tableau, ne produiront aucun effet sur une nature inculte. Un beau morceau de musique réveillera dans l'esprit et dans le coeur de l'homme le moins cultivé des sensations et des sentiments dont il ne se rendra pas comte, mais auxquels il lui est impossible de se soustraire.
>
> C'est cependant cet art par excellence qui est le plus négligé à Paris. C'est peut-être là qu'il faut chercher le secret de la dépravation des moeurs qu'on remarque dans les couches inférieurs de la population parisienne.[76]

[Music is the first of the arts because it is comprehensible to all. A beautiful monument, a beautiful piece of verse, a beautiful statue, a beautiful painting, will produce no effect on an untutored nature. A beautiful piece of music will awaken in the spirit and the heart of the least cultivated man the sensations and the sentiments for which he cannot account, but from which it impossible to shield himself.

And yet it is especially this art that is the most neglected in Paris. It is perhaps there that we should search for the secret of the corruption of morals that one notices in the lower strata of the Parisian population.]

Noticeably absent from Paris was a musical theater for French workers, which as we have seen, many now considered one of the most important means of "instruction." The ends of both education and instruction were still individual liberty and social equality, and to a certain extent this implied a cultural fusion of classes.[77] As the epigraph to this chapter suggests, they believed that the beneficial effects of theater lay in the way it "ennobles" the instincts, frees the intelligence and hence leads to truth.[78] Such beliefs, then, explain the increasing importance being attributed to the foundation of a lyric theater that would be open to workers, one now to be both independent and "grand" in scope. Indeed, the development of such plans became not only an idiom of political speech but an integral element within a coherent alternative political program.

Workers were well aware of what could be communicated to political power through the defense of certain operatic models and the concomitant attack on others. By projecting an alternative grand opera they were entering at once into political discourse while retaining their own integrity, actively conceiving a different frame.

No longer content with the *orphéons*, in 1865 *La Réforme théâtrale* overtly proposed that a new "people's opera" be built at last in Paris. (Significantly, this was three years before the emperor was to sign a law authorizing, under certain conditions, popular *réunions publiques*.) It was to be a grand opera, one that would seat 3,600 people and would be located in the heart of one of the city's most populous districts. Like the earlier Opéra-National, it was to serve both a cultural and a social end, being at once "le théâtre des débutantes et l'Opéra à bon marché."[79] As in the Opéra-National, there was no desire to present the conventional grand works: the innovative works to be performed were not just substitutes to be tolerated but ones valuable in their own right. They would, moreover, be authentically grand, an expression of the true vitality of France, a real projection of the nation's energy and its authentic cultural base.

The ideals of the early 1830s, in a sense, here once more reappear but now as the property of those deprived of power and defining themselves against the state. The subsequent political use of the Opéra had helped to bring this situation about, and had led eventually to the discrediting of the existing national lyric theater. By the 1860s asserting a new and coherent conception of a new political culture required asserting a new Opéra and a new repertoire. Aesthetic and political ends were here thus as closely, as inseparably bound as they were in the original development of the grand paradigm under Louis-Philippe. An aesthetic-political fusion then was partly responsible for both grand opera's rise and for the antagonism that it finally incurred, and its eventual decline in France.

Ironically, by the time that the new Opéra opened in 1875, the institution was losing its former political function and the grand works were increasingly being met with indifference.[80] They were treated almost as relics, but now not even inciting the fervor or the political antagonisms they had so tangibly in Second Empire France. The new Opéra was indeed a "museum" for them both in its exterior and on its stage, but it was no longer the nation's "image," a political vehicle that politicized its art.

CONCLUSION

THE HISTORY of grand opera that I have traced has revealed, I hope, many things, but perhaps most clearly that the "story" behind the genre is not simply that of the French bourgeoisie. Grand opera was not "engineered" by entrepreneurs in order specifically to appeal to this class; as art it was not a simple compromise between tradition and innovation for this end.

The evolution of the repertoire is one we have seen within the context of a different kind of social phenomenon, or rather set of interacting phenomena, to which I referred at the start of this book. Most fundamentally the Opéra served a subtle political function, one of a complex nature that affected the repertoire on several different levels at once. I hope to have shown that the Opéra in these years was a politically symbolic institution and that this influenced simultaneously institutional decisions as well as the audience's interpretive frame.[1] The repertoire was thus politicized by reference, a fact that helped to imbue it with a distinctive force. It did engage and challenge, although in different moments in different ways. The fact that its "frame" has since disappeared, leaving only the outer integument, has led to a basic misunderstanding of the genre's conventions and the way in which they once made sense.

If there is a story behind the grand repertoire, I have proposed that it is the story of what happened both in terms of political exchange and artistic production in certain "public" institutions of culture. For such institutions were designed to serve an indirect image-making function; this was true of the Opéra in this period and in a sense still is today. It continues to be a cultural reflection of the current political leadership, which continues to articulate a political vision through the language of operatic policies and plans.[2]

201

The Nation's Image

From this perspective, the story of grand opera is related to that which historians are now beginning to trace in the realm of political symbolism and its cultural construal and actual use. It is becoming apparent that we must analyze the attempt of the state to meet symbolic exigencies, but also to recognize where and why it failed, and what this failure inadvertently opened up.[3] Certainly, such insights are important not only for an understanding of the historical past and the cultural world as it then was but also to what is continuing to occur today. A subtle political exchange still transpires through such avenues of institutionalized culture, not only in democracies but in regimes that balance rhetorical concessions with political control. Politics through cultural practices and through the language of culture endures, and it is the historical study of this phenomenon that can help sensitize us to it today. Grand opera, as so many vehicles still do, functioned not as propaganda in an overt sense: its message could not be easily reduced to conventional terms of political discourse. The grand repertoire hence became the matrix for an often ineffable political transaction, a unique dialogue between political groups, and a means of apprehending complex realities. For the art had a certain "engendering" quality: it gave positions a distinctive tonality that at moments functioned in the interests of power and at others acted against it.[4]

A further conclusion that I might thus propose is that to divide the realm of politics from that of culture or to see institutions only as repressive tools, as the Opéra has shown us, is a distortion.[5] Such intermediate institutions, or those imbued with a "personalité morale," did exist historically and played significant political roles in the nineteenth century. They dispensed a culture calculated to project an image that would inspire and reconcile but the very vagueness of which encouraged different groups to assimilate and construe it differently. In the Opéra, as we have seen, assimilation of a national political culture and protest against it coexisted in a variety of complex ways. The Opéra, because of this function, became a part of the "language" of politics, one of the forms or "languages in which political discourse and discussion were actually carried on."[6]

But we must, of course, consider grand opera not only as politics but also as art, and pose the question of the kind of art and theatrical genre it was. I hope to have shown that at its most powerful grand opera was integrally engaged in a direct, provoca-

202

tive dialogue with the real or actual political world. If all historical drama makes "a pretense at engaging with reality,"[7] then this is especially true of the politicized stage of the Opéra in these years. And it is for this very reason, along with broader changes in taste, that it was a powerful genre at specific moments in its history but in others lost theatrical force.

Again, it was Mikhail Bakhtin who noted the "relative independence of aesthetic texts" from the immediate historical context in which they were originally experienced. For such texts are not as "locally dependent as other forms of utterance": they retain a meaning that can deepen in other interpretive frames.[8] But texts like those of French grand opera, again like *mazarinades,* although slightly less so, gained their most complete vitality in the context of a specific social function or use.

While this is true to a particular degree in the genre that I have examined, I hope also to have suggested its implications for our understanding of other musical genres. Indeed, related studies are now being conducted using other cases, including the performance of Handel's oratorios in the eighteenth and nineteenth centuries and Italian romantic opera.[9] There is an increasing awareness that as a performing art music's meaning can be integrally affected by its performance context and interpretive frame. And in this sense, the analysis of musical forms within their social and cultural contexts are now becoming as integral to studies in historical musicology as in ethnomusicology. The issues of function and framing are equally integral to both fields if we are to understand musical experience fully, as both cultural and aesthetic experience.[10]

Through grand opera, then, I hope to have established that cases exist in music history in which cultural history cannot be dismissed or separated from historical musicology. After a period of the dominance of a formalist approach, it is time to search for a balance, to recognize the necessity of studying both formal properties and their cultural environment. And cultural history, as the field traditionally concerned with understanding "fusions," must also continue to include the study of art in its map of the "cultural landscape."[11] In its study of how cultural products are inscribed in social existence and experience and how they act on each other, it cannot afford to exclude the domain of art. To penetrate the cultural landscape, to arrive at more satisfying or revealing designs, we must not force the arts into established functions or categories, but use them heuristically, see what they suggest. Social functions and experiences interact in art no less than in other cultural realms and often in ways that are uniquely revealing, as in the case of grand opera in France.

NOTES

All archival references are to the holdings of the Archives Nationales and the cataloguing of series employed there.

INTRODUCTION

1. For a more extensive discussion of this tradition and of this particular concept see Jane F. Fulcher, "Current Perspectives on Culture and the Meaning of Cultural History in France Today," *The Stanford French Review,* Spring 1985, pp. 91–104.

2. Michael Holquist and Katerina Clark, *Mikhail Bakhtin: A Biography* (Cambridge, Mass.: Harvard University Press, 1984), p. 207; and Samuel Kinser, "Chronotypes and Catastrophes: the Cultural History of Mikhail Bakhtin," *The Journal of Modern History,* June 1984, pp. 301–310.

3. On the concept of "popular" Romanticism, see James S. Allen, *Popular French Romanticism* (Syracuse, N.Y.: Syracuse Univ. Press, 1981); and William Croston, *French Grand Opera: An Art and a Business* (New York: Kings Crown Press, 1948), pp. 130, 4

4. *The New Grove Dictionary of Music and Musicians,* 20 vols., ed. by Stanley Sadie, s.v. "Opera, France," p. 583. For other related perspectives see Catherine Join-Dieterle, "*Robert le Diable:* le premier opéra romantique," *Romantisme* 1980, p. 148; and Karin Pendle, "Eugène Scribe and French Opera in the Nineteenth Century," *Musical Quarterly* 57 (1971), p. 541.

5. See Heinz Becker, "Die historische Bedeutung der Grand Opéra," in Walter Salmen, ed., *Beiträge zur Geschichte der Musikanschauung im 19. Jahrhundert* (Regensburg: Bosse, 1965).

6. See the Archives du Théâtre Nationale de l'Opéra, AJ^{13}1 à 1466. *Inventaire* par Brigitte Labot-Poussin, Conservateur (Paris: Archives Nationales, 1977).

7. Jack Lang, *L'Etat et le théâtre,* Thèse pour le doctorat en droit, Université de Nancy (Paris: Librairie Générale de droit et de juripru-

205

dence, 1968), pp. 154, 322. Relevant studies have already been done on such theaters as the Comédie-Française. See Nancy Nolte, "Government and Theater in Nineteenth-Century France: Administrative Organization for Control in the Comédie-Française" (Ph.D. dissertation, University of Akron, 1984). Nolte argues that while the Comédie-Française was "a relatively independent society of actors" at the beginning of the nineteenth century, it came to be "totally dominated" by the government with respect to control of its repertoire through both censorship and other means.

8. François Fûret, *Penser la Révolution française* (Paris: Gallimard, 1978).

9. Robert Darnton, "Revolution sans Revolutionaries," *The New York Review of Books,* Jan. 31, 1985, p. 22.

10. Marie-Hélène Huet approaches the theater of the French Revolution as part of "the network of political communication," in *Rehearsing the Revolution: the Staging of Marat's Death 1793–1797,* trans. by Robert Hurley (Berkeley: Univ. of California Press, 1982).

11. See Henri Lagrave, *Le Théâtre et le public à Paris de 1715 à 1750* (Paris: C. Klincksieck, 1972), pp. 210–13. On the Opéra in the later seventeenth century see Robert Isherwood, *Music in the Service of the King: France in the Seventeenth Century* (Ithaca, N.Y.: Cornell University Press, 1973).

12. William Weber, "*La musique ancienne* in the Waning of the Ancien Régime," *The Journal of Modern History,* March 1984, p. 86.

13. Ibid., pp. 61, 75.

14. See Elizabeth C. Bartlet, "Etienne Nicolas Méhul and Opera During the French Revolution, Consulate, and Empire: a Source, Archival and Stylistic Study" (Ph.D. dissertation, University of Chicago, 1982).

15. Marvin Carlson, *The Theater of the French Revolution,* pp. 98; 171–2.

16. Carlson, p. 92, cites the case of the many plays based on the king's attempted escape to Varennes. On spectacle, and particularly the use of a volcano, see p. 177.

17. Ibid., p. 192.

18. Ibid., p. 173.

19. Ibid., pp. 218, 222, 256; and see François V. A. Aulard, "La querelle de *La Marseillaise* et du *Réveil du peuple,*" in *Etudes et leçons sur la Révolution française,* 3e série (Paris: Félix Alcan, 1902).

20. For a more complete discussion of the expression of public opinion in theater see Marie-Hélène Huet, *Rehearsing the Revolution.*

1. *LA MUETTE DE PORTICI* AND THE NEW POLITICS OF OPERA

1. Cited by Jean Gourret, *Les Hommes qui ont fait l'Opéra 1669–1984* (Paris: Editions Albatros, 1984), p. 119.

2. See, for example, Karin Pendle, "Eugène Scribe and French Opera in the Nineteenth Century," *Musical Quarterly* 57 (1971).

3. Catalogue to *Le Spectacle et la fête au temps du Balzac* (Paris: Maison de Balzac, 1978–79), p. 20.

4. For an illuminating, if biased discussion of the Opéra's structure and direction under the Restoration, see Emile Véron's *Mémoires d'un bourgeois de Paris* (Paris: Librairie Nouvelle, 1856).

5. See the Introduction to the *Inventaire* of F^{21} 4523–4710, Censorship of the Parisian Theaters, p. iv.

6. Gabriel Vauthier, "Le Jury de lecture et l'Opéra sous la Restauration," *La Revue Musicale* 1910, p. 63.

7. For a discussion of the earlier Bourbons' political use of the Opéra, see Robert Isherwood, *Music in the Service of the King: France in the Seventeenth Century* (Ithaca, N.Y.: Cornell University Press, 1973).

8. Françoise Waquet, *Les Fêtes royales sous la Restauration ou l'ancien régime retrouvé* (Paris: Arts et Métiers Graphiques, 1981), pp. 2–18.

9. Jean Gourret, *Les Hommes qui ont fait l'Opéra*, p. 115; Rey M. Longyear, *"La Muette de Portici,"* *Music Review* 19 (1958), p. 38; Danièle Pistone, "L'Opéra de Paris au siècle romantique," *Revue internationale de musique française,* janvier 1981, p. 17.

10. Catherine Join-Diéterle, "La Monarchie, source d'inspiration de l'Opéra à l'époque romantique," *Revue d'histoire du théâtre* 4 (1983), p. 433.

11. As stated in $AJ^{13}180$, Letter from the Académie Royale de Musique, Paris, 20 mai 1831, from Cavé, Secrétaire de la Commission de l'Opéra. For further information, see Nestor Roqueplan, *Les Coulisses de l'Opéra* (Paris: Librairie Nouvelle, 1855), p. 21; Eugène Briffault, *L'Opéra* (Paris: Ladvocat, 1834), p. 413; Louis Desnoyers, *De l'Opéra en 1847: à propos de Robert Bruce: des directions passé, de la direction présente* (Paris: Imprimerie de E.-B. Delanchy, 1847), p. 69.

12. Alphonse Royer, *Histoire de l'Opéra* (Paris: Bachelin-Delflorenne Editeur, 1875), p. 24; Emile Véron, *Mémoires d'un bourgeois de Paris* (Paris: Librairie Nouvelle, 1856), p. 292; Eugène Briffault, *L'Opéra* (Paris: Ladvocat, 1834), p. 445.

13. Gordon Wright, *France in Modern Times* (Chicago: Rand McNally Publishing, Inc., 1974), p. 97.

14. William Weber, *"La musique ancienne* in the Waning of the Ancien Régime," *The Journal of Modern History,* March 1984, p. 78.

15. Béatrice Froger et Sylvaine Hans, "La Comédie-Française au XIX siècle: un repertoire litéraire et politique," *Revue d'histoire du théâtre* 13 (1984), pp. 260 ff.

16. Maurice Albert, *Les Théâtres des boulevards (1789–1848)* (Paris: Société française d'imprimerie et de librairie, 1902), p. 260; and James Bil-

lington, *Fire in the Minds of Men: Origins of the Revolutionary Faith* (New York: Basic Books, 1980), p. 88.

17. Peter Brooks, *The Melodramatic Imagination* (New Haven: Yale University Press, 1976), p. 15; Germain Bapst, *Essai sur l'histoire du théâtre* (Paris: Librairie Hachette et Cie., 1883), p. 543.

18. Pierre Martino, *L'Epoch romantique en France 1815–1830* (Paris: Hatier, 1944), pp. 86–8.

19. Quoted in Lionel de la Laurencie, *Le Goût musical en France,* Paris, 1905 (Genève: Slatkine Reprints, 1970), p. 158.

20. René Dollot, *Une Chronique de la Restauration: Stendhal correspondant des revues anglaises (1822–1829)* (Grenoble: Imprimerie Albier, 1943–44), p. 55.

21. For a discussion of eighteenth-century reforms, see William Weber, "*La musique ancienne,*" p. 86.

22. This quotation is from $AJ^{13}180$, "Quelques observations sur l'Académie Royale de Musique. Necéssité d'un régéneration dans le système de chant et décorations" (1825); and see $AJ^{13}116$, Letter to La Rochefoucauld, Administrateur des Beaux-arts, 7 Sept. 1825, from Gimel, "Confidentielle."

23. Jean Gourret, *Les Hommes qui ont fait l'Opéra,* pp. 114–15. Lubbert, perhaps the most creative, came from a position as Inspecteur de la lotterie au Ministère des Finances, but having a passion for composition, he took courses in harmony and composition. In 1823 he brought out a "failure" at the Opéra-Comique.

24. See Nicole Wild, "Un Demi-siècle de décors à l'Opéra de Paris: Salle Le Peletier 1822–1873," in *Regards sur l'Opéra.* Centre d'Art, Esthétique, et Littérature (Paris: Presses Universitaires de France, 1976), pp. 17 ff.

25. As Coudroy points out, *Le Courrier de l'Europe,* on 23 November 1831, gave the following definition of the diorama: "grand tableau placé de façon que l'on puisse varier l'intensité et la direction du lumière pour produire successivement des effets différents aux yeux des spectateurs placés dans l'obscurité. Le diorama date de 1822." It goes on to describe the effect as one "de la belle et bonne peinture, de la vérité, de l'art grand, de la grande nature." Marie-Hélène Coudroy, *Les Créations de Robert le Diable et Les Huguenots à la Critique* (Conservatoire Nationale Supérieur de Musique de Paris. Thèse de Musicologie, 1979), p. 85.

26. Théodore Muret, *L'Histoire par le théâtre 1789–1851* (Paris: Amyot, 1865), p. 277; Bronislaw Horowicz, *Le Théâtre de l'Opéra* (Paris: Editions d'Aujourd'hui, 1946; reprint ed., Editions Pierre Horay, 1976), p. 147; Germain Bapst, *Essai sur l'histoire du théâtre* (Paris: Librairie Hachette et Cie., 1883), pp. 512, 515.

27. The *Bibliothèque bleue* is not an easy phenomenon to describe, and thus I am grateful to Roger Chartier for the following condensed explanation: Books intended for a large, predominantly "popular" public were printed principally at Troyes between the beginning of the seventeenth century and the middle of the nineteenth century. Covered in paper (generally blue) and sold by *colportage* (peddling) in cities and in the countryside, they were in small format and adapted to this new public. The texts were religious, literary, or poetic, and some dated from the Middle Ages; they had already been edited but were here reedited for a specifically "popular" audience. For more information see Roger Chartier, "Livres bleus et lectures populaires in *Histoire de l'edition française* (Paris: Promodis, 1984), Tome II, *Le livre triomphant 1660–1830. Ogier le Danois* was a logical choice, given the tendency of the Restoration to emphasize the most prestigious moments of the monarchy's past, since it was set in the time of Charlemagne.

28. See Emile Véron, *Mémoirs d'un bourgeois de Paris,* and Adolphe Jullien, *Paris dilettante au commencement du siècle* (Paris: Librairie de Firmin-Didot et Cie., 1884), p. 47.

29. For information on the minor theaters, see Adolphe Jullien, *Paris dilettante,* and Théodore Muret, *L'Histoire par le théâtre 1789–1851.*

30. Ibid.

31. Pierre Brochon, *La Chanson sociale de Béranger à Brassens* (Paris: Les Editions Ouvrières, 1961), p. 15.

32. See *Le Globe,* 26 juillet 1827.

33. Odile Krakovitch, *Hugo Censuré: la liberté au théâtre au XIXe siècle* (Paris: Calmann-Lévy, 1985), p. 101.

34. Brochon, *La Chanson sociale,* pp. 16–18, 31.

35. $AJ^{13}180$, "Quelques observations sur l'Académie Royale de Musique," 1825.

36. Préface to *La Vie de Rossini* par V. Del Litto (Lausanne: Editions Rencontre, 1960), p. 19.

37. For the intellectual background to this change of paradigm, see Stendhal's *Racine et Shakespeare;* for the musical background, see Alphonse Royer, *Histoire de l'Opéra* (Paris: Bachelin-Delflorenne, 1875), pp. 131–2.

38. See the explanation given by Rey M. Longyear, in *"La Muette de Portici,"* pp. 38–40. Hanslick asserts, on the other hand, that the impetus behind the work was the Opéra's possession of a good mime. See Eduard Hanslick, *Die Moderne Oper* (Berlin: A. Hofmann, 1880), pp. 123–37.

39. The work was one of the revolutionary period, entitled *Les Deux Mots.* See Gustave Choquet, *Histoire de la musique dramatique en France* (Paris: Librairie Firmin Didot Frères, 1873).

40. Carafa, Michele Enrico, 1787–1872. Italian-born composer, active in France for most of his career. He was a close friend and collaborator of Rossini, and settled in Paris in 1827. Later, in 1838, he became director of the "Gymnase de Musique Militaire," a short-lived orchestral society. Hector Berlioz, *Memoirs*, trans. and ed. by David Cairns (London: Panther Books, 1970), pp. 532–3, 546.

41. Krakovitch, *Hugo Censuré*, pp. 247, 36–7.

42. AJ^{13}1050. Académie Royale de Musique, *La Muette de Portici*, 14 août 1827 (Autorisé). Comité de censure des pièces de théâtre.

43. See the Introduction to *Fonds de la censure pour les théâtres Parisiens de 1800 à 1830. Inventaire analytique*. Archives Nationales, Paris, p. xx.

44. See the advertisement for such excerpts in *Le Constitutionnel* 1 jan. 1828. The separate pieces of the work were printed successively as soon as possible, apparently without distinction, for, again, as symbols they were all important. So too, perhaps, were the *quadrille* and *contredanse* "sur les plus jolis motifs de l'opéra," arranged for the piano with the accompaniment of flute, violin, or flageolet *ad libitum*, at the low price of 3 francs, 75 centimes, clearly for "popular" consumption.

45. *Le Consitutionnel*, 11 jan. 1828.

46. See *Receuil des costumes de tous les ouvrages dramatiques représentés avec succès sur les grands théâtres de Paris* (Paris: Vizenti, n.d.) and "Opéra Comique, Décorations originales de 1822 à 1829," Bibliothèque de l'Opéra.

47. See Gabriel Vauthier, "Le Jury de lecture et l'Opéra sous la Restauration," p. 13.

48. Krakovitch, *Hugo Censuré*, p. 32.

49. For example, see Karin Pendle, "Eugène Scribe and French Opera in the Nineteenth Century" (thesis, Univ. of Illinois, 1970), pp. 557; 546–7.

50. See Longyear, p. 247.

51. Report (undated) in AJ^{13}1050, Théâtre de l'Opéra-Comique, *Masaniello ou le pecheur napolitain*, Opéra en 4 actes.

52. AJ^{13}1050, Académie Royale de Musique, *La Muette de Portici*, Opéra en 5 actes, 14 août 1827. Autorisé, Comité de censure des pièces de théâtre. (Illegible words are indicated by a question mark.)

53. AJ^{13}1050, report on *La Muette de Portici*, 21 juillet 1827.

54. F^{21}969, *La Muette de Portici*, report of 8 août 1827, signed A. de Charget.

55. Carlson, p. 145.

56. Karin Pendle discusses the influence of *opéra-comique* in dramatic technique and the character types in *Eugène Scribe and French Opera in the Nineteenth Century*, pp. 542–3.

57. Nicole Wild, "Un Demi-siècle de décors à l'Opéra de Paris," p. 17.
58. It is important here to be aware of the many contexts in which ideas were associated with images in this period. This includes the practice of illustrating *chansons* and selling the illustrations separately as a kind of transcription or visual analogue, with a certain level of realism communicating the ideas intended. For example, see the advertisement for illustrations of the *chansons* of Béranger in *Le Constitutionnel* on January 11 and 15, 1828.
59. Maurice Agulhon discusses the significance of the Phrygian cap at length in *Marianne au combat: l'imagerie et la symbolique républicaine de 1789 à 1880* (Paris: Flammarion, 1979). It is also interesting to note that *Le Globe,* on 5 mars 1828, criticized the costumes of *Masaniello* as being of a "caractère incertain."
60. Froger, "La Comédie-Française," p. 269.
61. The previous year (1827) it had presented *L'Ultimo giorno di Pompei.*
62. For a description of the premiere based on contemporary accounts, see the Bibliothèque de l'Opéra's *Album de l'Opéra. Principales scènes et décorations les plus remarquables des meilleurs ouvrages représentés sur la scène de l'Académie Royale de Musique* (Paris: Challomel, n.d.). For the most factual account of the events surrounding the subsequent performance in Brussels, see James Billington, *Fire in the Minds of Men: Origins of the Revolutionary Faith* (New York: Basic Books, 1980), p. 156.
63. M. P. Bondois, *L'Histoire de la Restauration* (Versailles: E. Aubert, 1889), pp. 126–7.
64. Krakovitch, *Hugo Censuré,* p. 32.
65. Claude Bellanger, ed., *Histoire générale de la press Française* Vol. II (Paris: Presses Universitaires de France, 1969), p. 77.
66. See the issue of 2 mars 1828.
67. The issue of 2 mars 1828.
68. The issue of 1 mars 1828
69. The issue of 2 mars 1828.
70. *Le Globe,* 5 mars 1828, p.246; the *Gazette de France,* 2 mars 1828, p. 2.
71. For publication information on this collection, see note 62 above.
72. The issue of 2 mars 1828, p. 2.
73. *Mise en scène de La Muette de Portici* par Solomé, Act V scène vi. Bibliothèque de l'Opéra.
74. For example, a work presented as the victory of order over anarchy would be read instead as promoting love of the fatherland. See Carlson, *The Theater of the French Revolution,* p. 55.
75. For background on the *mise en scène,* see Marie-Antoinette Allévy, *Edition critique d'une mise en scène romantique* (Paris: Librairie E. Droz,

211

1938); and for a discussion of this event, see Victor Hallays-Dabot, *Histoire de la censure théâtrale en France* (Genève: Slatkine Reprints, 1970; Réimpression de l'édition de Paris, 1862), p. 279.

76. It received 100 performances in less than a year at the Opéra, drawing great crowds, which still failed, however, to pull the opera out of debt. *Le Consitutionnel,* 14 avril 1828, reports a debt of 800,000 francs, despite the subventions given the Opéra. See $AJ^{13}120$, Letter from the Maison du roi, Dept. des Beaux-arts, from l'Aide de camp du roi chargé du Dept. des Beaux-arts, 1 mars 1828.

77. $AJ^{13}120$, Letter from the Maison du roi, Dept. des Beaux-arts, to Lubbert, 9 juin 1828.

78. Vincent W. Beach, *Charles X of France: His Life and Times* (Boulder, Col.: Pruitt Publishing Co., 1971), p. 265. And see $AJ^{13}122$, Letter from the Ministère de l'Intérieur, Direction des Sciences, Lettres, Beaux-arts, Librairie, Journeaux, et Théâtres, 1 Oct. 1829.

79. *Nouvelle Biographie générale* (Paris: Firmin Dido Frères, 1968) Vol. 37–8, p. 950.

2. THE POLITICS OF GRAND OPERA'S RISE AND DECLINE

1. Report of the Commission of Surveillance, 1 mars 1831, $F^{21}4633$ »3.

2. John Merriman, ed., *1830 in France* (New York: New Viewpoints, 1975), pp. 1–3.

3. Ibid., p. 4, and see Alfred Cobban, "The 'Middle Class' in France, 1815–1848," *French Historical Studies* V (Spring 1967), pp. 46–7, and Thomas Beck, *French Legislators 1800–1834* (Berkeley: University of California Press, 1974), p. 137.

4. Pierre Brochon, *La Chanson sociale de Béranger à Brassens* (Paris: Les Editions Ouvrières, 1961), p. 26.

5. See Roger Williams's discussion of this period in *The World of Napoleon III* (New York: Free Press, 1965).

6. J. J. Weiss, *Le Théâtre et les moeurs* (Paris: Calmann-Lévy, 1889), p. v; and see René Rémond, *The Right Wing in France: From 1815 to de Gaulle* (Philadelphia: Univ. of Pennsylvania Press, 1971), p. 104.

7. Sebastien Charléty, *La Monarchie de Juillet* (Paris: Hachette, 1921), p. 7.

8. René Rémond, *The Right Wing in France: From 1815 to de Gaulle,* pp. 104 ff.

9. Significantly, the words were by Casimir Delavigne and the music by Auber.

10. For the background of popular symbolism, see Maurice Agulhon, *Marianne au combat* (Paris: Flammarion, 1979), and see also *Juillet 1830,* Musée Carnavalet, 8 juillet–2 novembre 1980, catalogue.

11. Merriman, *1830 in France,* p. 3.
12. Charléty, *La Monarchie,* p. 8.
13. For a discussion of this point of view, see Albert Boime, *The Academy and French Painting in the 19th Century* (New York: Phaidon Publishers, Inc., 1971).
14. Rémond, pp. 114–16; p. 145.
15. Cobban, "The Middle Class," p. 49.
16. See Chapter One for the background in the 1820s; on the issue of the unintended radical interpretation of symbols, see Agulhon, *Marianne au combat.*
17. Léon Rosenthal, *Du Romantisme au Réalisme: essai sur l'évolution de la peinture en France de 1830 à 1848* (Paris: Librairie Renouard, 1914), p. 3.
18. Arno Mayer, *The Persistence of the Old Regime: Europe to the Great War* (New York: Pantheon Books, 1981), p. 189.
19. See James Billington, *Fire in the Minds of Men,* and René Rémond, *The Right Wing in France,* p. 160.
20. Maurice Agulhon, *1848 ou l'apprentissage de la république* (Paris: Editions du Seuil, 1973), p. 7.
21. Germain Bapst, *Essai sur l'histoire du théâtre* (Paris: Librairie Hachette et Cie., 1893), p. 566. And see *Robert le Diable,* Théâtre National de l'Opéra, 2 juin–20 septembre 1985, Catalogue de l'Exposition par Martine Kahane, p. 14.
22. See *L'Illustration,* 18 Sept. 1847.
23. La Rochefoucauld reputedly fought the idea vigorously. See Pierre Bossuet, *Histoire des théâtres nationaux* (Paris: Editions et Publications Contemporains, n.d.), p. 157. This is opposed to the argument that claims the dominance of financial interests, as seen in Jean Gourret, *Les Hommes qui ont fait l'Opéra 1669–1984* (Paris: Editions Albatros, 1984), p. 15, and William Croston, *French Grand Opera: An Art and a Business* (New York: Kings Crown Press, 1948).
24. See $F^{21}4633$, Report of the Commission, 1er mars 1831.
25. Pierre Bossuet, *Histoire administrative des rapports des théâtres et de l'état,* p. 157; Georges Bureau, *Le Théâtre et sa législation* (Paris: Paul Ollendorff, Editeur, 1898), p. 215; Alexis Azevedo, *G. Rossini: sa vie et ses oeuvres* (Paris: Heugel et Cie., 1864), p. 295.
26. See the Introduction to $F^{21}4523–4710$ (Censorship of the Parisian Theaters), p. iv.
27. Jean Gourret, *Les Hommes qui ont fait l'Opéra,* p. 115.
28. Alphonse Royer, *Histoire de l'Opéra* (Paris: Bachelin-Delflorenne Editeur, 1875), p. 40; Bureau, *Le Théâtre et sa législation,* p. 123; Bossuet, *Histoire administrative,* p. 157. The director's contract was for a period of six years.

213

29. Gourret, p. 118.
30. *Robert le Diable,* Catalogue, p. 81. And Gourret, *Les Hommes,* pp. 120–3.
31. $F^{21}4633$, "Arrêté de M. le Comte Montalivet, Ministre de l'Intérieur, qui nomme une commission spécial, chargé de surveiller l'exécution des cahiers des charges de l'Académie Royale de Musique."
32. $F^{21}4633$ (folder 2), "Arrêté de M. le Comte de Montalivet," 28 fév. 1831.
33. *Nouvelle biographie générale,* sous la direction de M. le Dr. Hoeffer (Paris: Firmin Didot Frères, 1857) 9-10, p. 358.
34. *Biographie universelle ancienne et moderne,* sous la direction de M. Michaud (Paris: Chez Madame C. Desplaces, 1857), p. 696.
35. *Nouvelle biographie générale* 9-10, p. 290.
36. On *grandeur* in the ancien régime, see William Weber, "*La Musique Ancienne* in the Waning of the Ancien Régime," *The Journal of Modern History,* March 1984, pp. 58–88. This reference is from $F^{21}4633$, folder 2, "Réglement pour des théâtres," 25 avril 1807.
37. $AJ^{13}180$, "Cahier des charges de la direction," 28 février 1831.
38. $F^{21}4633$, Letter from the Comte de Montalivet, Ministre de l'Intérieur, to M. le Duc de Choiseul, 6 mai 1836.
39. This extended to even further details; see, for example, the exchange regarding the "Comité des contentieux de l'Opéra," in $F^{21}4633$, Registre 3, and those on the policies regarding the engagement of artists in Registre 5.
40. See $F^{21}4633$, »5, the undated report of the commission.
41. See $F^{21}4633$, folder 2, the undated report of the commission enumerating Véron's past infractions, beginning 9 Sept. 1832.
42. For example, "Castil-Blase," [sic], undoubtedly François Henri-Joseph Blaze, 1784–1857, music critic of the *Journal des débats* before Berlioz, as well as composer and arranger. He is referred to in $F^{21}4633$, Registre 3, report of the commission, 3 mars 1831.
43. See $AJ^{13}180$, Letter from the Académie Royale de Musique, Paris, 20 May 1831, from the "Secrétaire de la commission de l'Opéra," Cavé. And see *Robert le Diable,* Catalogue, p. 40.
44. Edgar Newman in John Merriman, ed., *1830 in France,* p. 39.
45. Emile Véron, *Mémoirs d'un bourgeois de Paris* (Paris: Librairie Nouvelle, 1856), p. 128; and Henri Girard, *Emile Deschamps dilettante* (Paris: Librairie Ancienne Honoré Champinion, 1921), p. 35. Ticket prices in this period ranged from 2 fr. 50 to 10 francs. A worker earned an average of 4–6 francs per day, according to Daniel Pistone in "L'Opéra de Paris au siècle romantique," *Revue internationale de musique française,* jan. 1981, p. 40. And see *Robert le Diable,* Catalogue, p. 41.

46. The Ministre du Commerce et des Travaux Publics was still the authority over the opera at this date. Gourret, p. 121.
47. René-Charles de Pixérécourt (1773–1849) is known today primarily as a leading writer of melodramas.
48. *Robert le Diable,* Catalogue, p. 17.
49. Véron, *Mémoires d'un bourgeois de Paris,* p. 289.
50. *Robert le Diable,* Catalogue, p. 50. The report is contained in the Archives Nationales $F^{21}968$.
51. *Robert le Diable,* Catalogue, pp. 11–12.
52. Catherine Join-Dieterle, "*Robert le Diable:* le premier opéra romantique," *Romantisme* 1980, p. 148.
53. See Anthony Esler, "Youth in Revolt: the French Generation of 1830," in *Modern European Social History,* ed. by Robert J. Bezucha (Lexington, Mass.: D. C. Heath, 1972).
54. Ibid.
55. Odile Krakovitch, *Hugo Censuré: la liberté au théâtre au XIXe siècle* (Paris: Calmann-Lévy, 1985), p. 28.
56. On myth and reality in Meyerbeer's relations with the Opéra, see John Robert's review of the article "Meyerbeer" in *The New Grove Dictionary,* in *19th Century Music,* Fall 1981.
57. *Robert le Diable,* Catalogue, pp. 15–17.
58. See Karin Pendle, "Eugène Scribe and French Opera in the Nineteenth Century" (thesis, Univ. of Illinois, 1970).
59. See the definition of the *Bibliothèque bleue* in note 27, Chapter One.
60. Not only did it help to define the new regime against the policies of its predecessor, it might well have made oblique or symbolic reference to the convent plays of the revolutionary period, and hence further reinforcing this political connection. See Marvin Carlson, *The Theater of the French Revolution* (Ithaca, N.Y.: Cornell University Press, 1966), p. 367.
61. $AJ^{13}201$, Report on *Robert le Diable,* 21 Nov. 1831, from the Commission de Surveillance to M. le Ministre du Commerce et des Travaux Publics.
62. Dieterle, p. 50.
63. Joseph d'Ortigue, *Le Balcon de l'Opéra* (Paris: Librairie D'Eugène Renduel, 1833), pp. 133–5; see Nicole Wild, "Un Demi-siècle de décors à l'Opéra de Paris: Salle Le Peletier 1822–1873," in *Regards sur l'Opéra.* Centre D'Art, Esthétique, et Littérature (Paris: Presses Universitaires de France, 1974), p. 19.
64. As discussed in *La Quotidienne,* 4 déc. 1831. Cited in Marie-Hélène Coudroy, *Les Créations de Robert le Diable et Les Huguenots de Meyerbeer à la critique* (Conservatoire Nationale Supérieur de Musique de Paris. Thèse de Musicologie, 1979), p. 88.

65. *Robert le Diable,* Catalogue, pp. 23, 17.

66. See the article on *Robert le Diable* and its origins as an *opéra-comique* by Hugh Macdonald in Peter Bloom, ed., *Music in Paris in the Eighteen Thirties* (Québec: Les Presses de l'Université Laval, 1985).

67. H. Lavoix, *Histoire de l'instrumentation* (Paris: Firmin-Didot, 1878), p. 389. And see William Runyan, "Orchestration in Five French Grand Operas," (Ph.D. dissertation, University of Rochester, The Eastman School of Music, 1983).

68. Jürgen Maehder, "*Robert le Diable.* Etude sur la genèse du grand opéra français," Program, *Robert le Diable,* Théâtre National de l'Opéra de Paris, juin–juillet 1985, p. 26.

69. Francis Claudon, "G. Meyerbeer et V. Hugo: dramaturgies comparées," in *Regards sur l'Opéra,* p. 107; and see Lionel Dauriac, *Meyerbeer* (Paris: 1913), pp. xii–xiii.

70. *La Liberté,* 16 mai 1898.

71. Karin Pendle goes into some detail concerning the relation of musical to visual and dramatic unit in Meyerbeer, employing the categories of "Dramatic tableau," "Scenic tableau," and "set number." See "Eugène Scribe and French Opera in the Nineteenth Century," pp. 726ff. As I shall show, this principle of coordination extends to other dimensions of the music as well. Also see Frese's discussion of how the music imparted a powerful sense of rhythm to the "timely romantic intrigue." Christhard Frese, *Dramaturgie der grossen Opern Giacomo Meyerbeers* (Berlin-Lichterfelde: Robert Linau, 1970).

72. *Robert le Diable,* Catalogue, p. 16.

73. *Le Constitutionnel,* 23 novembre 1831; *La France Musicale* 11 février 1838 and 28 janvier 1838.

74. Ibid., *Le Constitutionnel.*

75. *Robert le Diable,* Catalogue, p. 82, and *Le Globe,* 5 mars 1828.

76. See Henri Girard, *Emile Deschamp dilettante,* and Joseph d'Ortigue, *Le Balcon de l'Opéra,* p. 125. Joseph Louis d'Ortigue was an important contemporary writer on music and a critic, first for the *Mémorial Catholique,* in 1829, and soon after for *La Quotidienne.* He became chief editor of *Le Ménestrel* in 1863 and succeeded his good friend Berlioz as critic for the *Journal des débats* in 1864. For François-Joseph Fétis (Belgian critic, composer, and teacher), Meyerbeer's strength, like that of Gluck before him, lay in his effective new deployment of styles. See Peter Bloom, "Friends and Admirers: Meyerbeer and Fétis," *Revue Belge de Musicologie* Vol. XXXII–XXXIII (1978–79), p. 75.

77. *Le National,* 4 déc. 1831, as quoted in Coudroy, p. 83.

78. The former, as a colonel in the "1er régiment des husards," before the king's ascension, had assumed the task of "introducing the na-

tional colors in the countryside." But only five days after the premiere of *Robert le Diable* he was dispatched to Lyon to help put down the workers' insurrection. *Nouvelle biographie générale* Vol. 37–8, p. 835.

79. *Robert le Diable*, Catalogue, pp. 46, 21.

80. *Revue des deux mondes,* 29 nov. 1831, as quoted by Dieterle, p. 152, and *Le Courier des théâtres,* 23 nov. 1831.

81. From a letter of March 25, 1832, as quoted in J. Combarieu, *Histoire de la musique,* tome III, p. 50, and as cited in Coudroy, p. 53.

82. See Emile Véron, *Mémoires d'un bourgeois de Paris,* p. 179. For a literary incarnation of these beliefs and enthusiasms, see Honoré de Balzac, *La Comédie Humaine,* trans. by Katherine Wormeley, Vol. 28, *Gambara* (Boston: Roberts Brothers, 1896).

83. In 1837 two acts of *Robert* were performed at Fontainebleau for the marriage of the duc d'Orléans, thus making it back into a kind of royal *féerie.*

84. Moreover, in turning to history, the Opéra was once again in competition with the popular theaters that had sustained this interest since the Restoration. For example, on Nov. 15, 1831, the Théâtre des Nouveautés presented an opera in three acts entitled *Les Sybarites de Florence* based on the story of the Pazzi conspiracy against the Medici; typically, still, for the boulevard theaters, it dealt with the political tyranny of the sixteenth and seventeenth centuries.

85. For example, see the letter from the Académie Royale de Musique contained in the file of submissions in AJ^{13}200, to M. Matthieu, from Nancy.

86. Krakovitch, *Hugo Censuré,* p. 18.

87. Feuilleton du *Français,* 30 nov. 1868.

88. Gourret, p. 122. And see *Robert le Diable,* Catalogue, p. 21.

89. Paul Bastid, *Les Institutions de la monarchie parlementaire française 1814–1848* (Paris: Editions du Recueil Sirey, 1954), p. 124.

90. Ibid., p. 129, and Krakovitch, *Hugo Censuré,* pp. 62–3.

91. Ibid., Krakovitch, p. 28, and Bastid, *Les Institutions,* p. 381.

92. Krakovitch, *Hugo Censuré,* p. 60.

93. Ibid., p. 153, and Agulhon, *1848,* p. 7.

94. Waquet, *La Fête,* p. 113, and Béatrice Froger and Sylvaine Hans, "La Comédie-Française au XIX siècle: un répertoire littéraire et politique," *Revue d'histoire du théâtre* 1984 (3), p. 270.

95. He supposedly consulted the seventeenth-century historiographer, Paul Palliot, but for the costume of the Emperor Sigismund he might well have consulted Dürer's portrait.

96. A precedent for the use of horses on stage can be found in the staging of Spontini's *Olympie,* in 1819. See Camille Bellaigue, "Les

217

Epoques de la musique: le grand opéra français," *Revue des deux mondes* 1906, p. 616.

97. Charléty, *La Monarchie,* p. 105.
98. $AJ^{13}202$, Letter from the Commission of Surveillance to the minister, 13 fév. 1835.
99. See Christian Jouhaud, *Mazarinades: la Fronde des mots* (Paris: Aubier, 1985), pp. 8, 24.
100. *Le Constitutionnel* 25 février 1835, p. 1.
101. Ibid.
102. "Elle a indiqué à M. Véron des suppressions et divers changements dans les episodes de ses bals masqués, tels qu'un concert grotesque." $AJ^{13}182$, Letter, undated, from the commission to the minister.
103. For example, $F^{21}4633$ (undated report) states that on Sept. 9, 1832, "M. Véron est condamné à 1,000 fr. d'amende pour emploi de vieille décorations – arrêté du ministre approbatif de cette décision."
104. As documented in $AJ^{13}182$, Letter from the commission to the minister, undated.
105. Gourret, p. 123.
106. Ibid., p. 126. Although he was frustrated in the end, Véron's post at the Opéra was to provide a valuable entry into journalism and politics later.
107. As stated in $F^{21}4633$, folder 2, Decree from the Ministère de l'Inérieur, 31 août 1835.
108. $F^{21}4633$, folder 2, Cahier des charges for Duponchel, 15 août 1835, art. 62.
109. As enumerated in $F^{21}4633$. For example (folder 2), on Dec. 2, 1839, "M. Duponchel est condamné à 9,000 fr. d'amende pour avoir employé 39 costumes anciens dans *La Xacarella.*"
110. $AJ^{13}187$, Cahier des charges, Duponchel, 1835.
111. See Anthony Esler, "Youth in Revolt: the French Generation of 1830."
112. Gordon Wright, *France in Modern Times* (Chicago: Rand McNally Publishing, Inc., 1974), p. 117; and Roger Williams, *The World of Napoleon III,* p. 22.
113. On the changing meaning and use of visual imagery in this period, see Maurice Agulhon, *Marianne au Combat,* and Jack Spector, *Delacroix: The Death of Sardanapalus* (New York: Viking Press, 1974).
114. On the repertoire in this period, and the problems with it, see Charles de Boigne, *Petits mémoires de l'Opéra* (Paris: Librairie Nouvelle, 1857). And see Krakovitch, *Hugo Censuré,*. 86.
115. Ibid., Krakovitch, p. 84.

116. Ibid., pp. 81–3 and 100–4.
117. Rey M. Longyear, "Political and Social Criticism in French Opera 1827–1920," in Robert Weaver, ed., *Essays on the Music of J. S. Bach and Other Divers Subjects: A Tribute to Gerhard Herz* (Louisville, Ky.: Univ. of Louisville Press, 1981), p. 947.
118. Feuilleton du *Français*, 30 nov. 1868; and Gourret, p. 128.
119. Rémond, pp. 114–120.
120. Pierre Martino, *L'Epoch romantique en France 1815–1830* (Paris: Hatier, 1944), p. 118.
121. Longyear has advanced that the message is that "this will be the fate of Protestants, Liberals, and Catholic Moderates if the Legitimists and 'Chevaliers de la foi' regain power." Rey M. Longyear, "Political and Social Criticism in French Opera," p. 247.
122. See F²¹4633, folder 2, Undated report, citing the case of April 28, 1836, concerning Duponchel's infractions in the *mise en scène* for *Les Huguenots*.
123. See Herbert Lindenberger, *Historical Drama: the Relation of Literature and Reality* (Chicago: University of Chicago Press, 1975).
124. For a detailed discussion of this technique, see Lionel Dauriac, *Meyerbeer* (Paris: 1913).
125. *Le Moniteur*, quoted in Lionel de la Laurencie, *Le Goût musical en France* (Paris: 1905; Genève: Slatkine Reprints, 1970).
126. *Robert le Diable*, Catalogue, p. 24.
127. On Berlioz's perspective, see Hector Berlioz, *Memoirs*, ed. and trans. by David Cairns (London: Panther Books, 1970), p. 553; and H. Robert Cohen, "Berlioz on the Opéra (1829–1849): A Study in Music Criticism" (thesis, New York University, 1973), pp. 136–7; 147–48. The quote from Wagner is cited in Edgar Istel, "Act IV of *Les Huguenots*," *The Musical Quarterly* 1936, pp. 87–8.
128. Albert Boime, *Thomas Couture and the Eclectic Vision*, p. 14.
129. *Le Moniteur Universel*, 7 mars 1836, as cited in Coudroy, p. 205.
130. An awareness of the semiotic role of the *mise en scène* might well have been responsible for the treatment of the *mise* as "an integral and unalterable part of the composition," as H. Robert Cohen has put it in "Les livrets de mise en scène et la Bibliothèque de l'Association de la Régie Théâtrale," *Revue de Musicologie* 1978. But, as is evident, the reasons I see for this differ from those of Cohen, who proposes that the *régisseur* "permanently registered the *mise en scène* in view of exact reconstruction for revivals."
131. There has, for some time, been a question concerning who was responsible for the *mise:* the authors, the theater's director, or the *régisseur*. Historians in the later nineteenth century claimed that of the theater's three *régisseurs*, the second was in charge of the *mise,*

219

and called the *metteur en scène*. H. Robert Cohen, "Les livrets de mise en scène," p. 25.

132. Marvin Carlson, *The Theater of the French Revolution* (Ithaca, N.Y.: Cornell University Press, 1966), pp. 22–5.

133. Charléty, *La Monarchie*, p. 122.

134. Krakovitch, *Hugo Censuré*, pp. 81, 77–8, 86, 184.

135. Marie-Hélène Coudroy cites the *Revue de Paris* and the *Courrier Français*, among others, in *Les Créations de Robert le Diable et les Huguenots*, p. 130.

136. As cited by *Le Figaro*, 7 mai 1872.

137. Bastid, *Les Institutions*, p. 129. From 1840 to 1848 he led the opposition of the center Left.

138. The duchess was in hiding, supposedly ready to give the signal for a revolt. See Jean Lucas-Dubreton, *The Restoration and the July Monarchy* (New York: G. P. Putnam's Sons, 1929), p. 22.

139. For example, *La France*, 9 mars 1836 and *Le Charivari*, 2 mars 1836.

140. As Cohen notes, the *mises* were published not only in pamphlet form but in the major journals of the theatrical world. "Les livrets de mise en scène," p. 25.

141. *Les Huguenots*, Dossier d'Oeuvre. Bibliothèque de l'Opéra.

142. Agulhon, *1848*, p. 9.

143. Krakovitch, *Hugo Censuré*, pp., 123, 118. She cites the specific cases of *Benvenuto Cellini* and *Dom Sebastien* (pp. 158–9).

144. AJ^{13}180, Letter from the Préfet de police to M. le Ministre de l'Intérieur, 7 février 1843, signed G. Delessul.

145. AJ^{13}180, Letter of March 1843, from the Commission Spécial des Théâtres Royaux.

146. AJ^{13}187, Notice from the Préfet de police, 6 août 1845.

147. AJ^{13}187, *Arrête* from the Préfecture de police, mars 1845, "Concernant le tarif du prix des places dans les théâtres."

148. AJ^{13}180, Letter from the Préfet de police, 18 avril 1837, to the Ministre de l'Intérieur.

149. Gourret, p. 128.

150. Aguado died in 1841, and was replaced successively by the Marquis de Saint Mars and the Marquis d'Alegre. Gourret, pp. 128–30.

151. Ibid., p. 130.

152. *Wagner Writes from Paris: Stories, Essays, and Articles by the Young Composer*, ed. and trans. by Robert L. Jacobs and Geoffrey Skelton (New York: Harper and Row, 1960), p. 111.

153. F^{21}4633, Cahier des charges, Pillet, 1 août 1841.

154. Bastid, *Les Institutions*, p. 11.

155. F^{21}4633 (folder 2), "Rapport à M. le Ministre Secrétaire d'Etat au département de l'Intérieur," 5 août 1840.

156. Krakovitch, *Hugo Censuré*, p. 106.

157. $AJ^{13}183$, Letter to the minister from the commission, Nov. 1842.

158. $AJ^{13}183$, Letter to the minister from the commission reporting on the performance of 29 mars 1844.

159. $AJ^{13}183$, Report of the commission on the reading of the libretto for *David*, 22 août 1845. There are also numerous cases of concern with the representation of religious authority on the stage after *La Juive*. See the cases of *Le Drapier* and *La Reine de Chypre*, in $F^{21}969$, reports of 19 déc. 1839 and 21 déc. 1841.

160. $AJ^{13}180$, Letter from the commission to the minister, Jan. 1845. The list of "failures" included not only Berlioz's *Benvenuto Cellini* (1838) but also Niedermeyer and Deschamp's *Stradella* (1837), Auber and Scribe's *La Lac des fées* (1939), Marliani and Scribe's *La Zacarilla* (1839), Ruloz and Pillet's *La Vendetta* (1839), and many others.

161. Froger, "La Comédie-Française," p. 236. And see Nancy Nolte, "Government and Theater in Nineteenth-Century France: Administrative Organization for Control in the Comédie-Française Repertoire," (Ph.D. dissertation, University of Akron, 1984).

162. The Italian repertoire was already finding a place in the provincial theaters, since many could not come close to reproducing the effects of the Académie Royale, and this repertoire was very dependent on it.

163. Other works were revived as well, including Spontini's *Fernand Cortez*, Weber's *Der Freischütz* (with added recitatives by Berlioz), and Sacchini's *Oedipe à Colonne*.

164. Krakovitch, *Hugo Censuré*, pp. 88–9, 92.

165. See *L'Illustration*, 9 oct. 1847.

166. There was also a precedent for such a change of jurisdiction in the ancien régime, in 1749. See William Weber, "*La Musique ancienne* and the Waning of the Ancien Régime," p. 75.

167. See Charléty, *La Monarchie*, p. 63.

168. See Jouhaud, *Mazurinades*.

169. According to contemporary comments, he was very much the puppet of the singer, against whom public sentiment turned after her failure in *Robert Bruce*, in 1847.

170. $AJ^{13}180$, Cahier des charges, 31 juillet 1847, for Pillet, Duponchel, and Roqueplan. The latter, the son of an *instituteur*, had initially become a journalist, working for the Liberal political cause under Charles X; then, with Véron and Malitoune, he founded *La Charte*, in 1830, which became the official organ of Guizot's ministry. He subsequently became director of the Théâtre des Variétés. Roqueplan also used borrowed capital for his investment in the Opéra. Gourret, p. 132.

171. As T. J. Walsh explains, Adam's new theater was a result of his argument with the Opéra-Comique; see Walsh's *Second Empire Opera: The Théâtre Lyrique, Paris 1851–1870* (London: John Cader, 1981), p. 2.
172. I am here employing insights gained from Marvin Carlson's "The Semiotics of Opera Structures," paper delivered at the conference, "Théâtre, Opéra, Spectacle. Approaches Semiologiques," Royaumont, France, Sept. 1984.
173. T. J. Walsh, *Second Empire Opera: The Théâtre Lyrique*, p. 3.
174. See Jane F. Fulcher, "The Orphéon Societies: Music for the Workers in Second-Empire France," *International Review of the Aesthetics and Sociology of Music* Vol. X »1 (1979).
175. Le Vicomte de Pontécoulant, *La Musique chez le peuple ou l'Opéra National: son passé et son avenir sur le boulevard du Temple* (Paris: Chez Garnier Frères, 1847), p. 5.
176. On Fourier's theories of opera, see Jane F. Fulcher, "Music and the Communal Order: the Vision of Utopian Socialism in France," *Current Musicology*, Summer 1979.
177. See Jane Fulcher, "The Orphéon Societies," and for a discussion of *sociétés chantantes*, see Théodore Muret, *L'Histoire par le théâtre 1789–1851* (Paris: Amyot, 1865).
178. See *L'Atelier*, nov. 1847.
179. Louis Chevalier, *Classes laborieuses et classes dangereuses à Paris pendant la première moitié du XIXe siècle* (Paris: Plon, 1958), pp. 503–4.
180. See Jane Fulcher, "The Orphéon Societies." Also relevant is Nathan Therien's *Popular Song Entertainment as Social Experience and the Failure of Participatory Culture in France 1815–1914* (dissertation in progress, Harvard University).
181. *L'Atelier*, nov. 1847, p. 41.
182. Georges Duveau, *La Pensée ouvrière sur l'education pendant la Second République et le Second Empire* (Paris: Domat Montchrestien, 1948), p. 64.
183. The work might have been *Les Premiers pas, ou les deux génies*, a "musical prologue," presented on Nov. 15, 1847. Walsh, p. 3.
184. Krakovitch, *Hugo Censuré*, p. 35.
185. *L'Illustration*, 20 nov. 1847.

3 · RADICALIZATION, REPRESSION, AND OPERA: MEYERBEER'S *LE PROPHETE*

1. *Le Caricature*, 16 avril 1850.
2. Gottfried R. Marschall, "L'Opéra et son public de 1848 à 1852," *Revue internationale de musique francaise*, 1980/ 3.

222

3. René Rémond, *The Right Wing in France: From 1815 to de Gaulle* (Philadelphia: University of Pennsylvania Press, 1971), pp. 125–7.

4. See Maurice Agulhon, *Marianne au combat: l'imagerie et la symbolique républicaine de 1789 à 1880* (Paris: Flammarion, 1979). And see Maurice Agulhon, *1848 ou l'apprentissage de la république* (Paris: Editions du Seuil, 1973), p. 3.

5. On political imagery see Agulhon, *Marianne au combat,* pp. 95–7; 106–10, 116–119; and on commissions for visual art see Timothy J. Clark, *The Absolute Bourgeois: Artists and Politics in France 1848–1851* (London: Thames and Hudson Ltd., 1973).

6. See *Le National,* 16 janvier 1849, and *Le Constitutionnel,* 10 avril 1848.

7. Théodore Muret, *L'Histoire par le théâtre 1789–1851* (Paris: Amyot, 1865), p. 97; and see Agulhon, pp. 119, 75.

8. See Victor Hallays-Dabot, *Histoire de la censure théâtrale en France* (Genève: Slatkine Reprints, 1970, Réimpression de l'édition de Paris, 1862); and see James Billington, *Fire in the Minds of Men: Origins of the Revolutionary Faith* (New York: Basic Books, 1980), p. 237; Georges Bureau, *Le Théâtre et sa législation* (Paris: Paul Ollendorff, Editeur, 1898), p. 251.

9. Odile Krakovitch, *Hugo Censuré: la liberté au théâtre au XIXe siècle* (Paris: Calmann-Lévy, 1985), p. 208.

10. Ibid.; and see Muret, *L'Histoire par le théâtre,* p. 386.

11. Gottfried Marschall, "L'Opéra et son public de 1848 à 1852," p. 278.

12. Marschall, p. 378; and on the closing of the theater, see $AJ^{13}181$ (folder 2), Letter from the Ministère de l'Intérieur, Direction des Beaux-arts, Paris, 28 février 1848.

13. See the end of Chapter Two, and Jane F. Fulcher, "Music and the Communal Order: the Vision of Utopian Socialism in France," *Current Musicology,* Summer 1979. And see Agulhon, *1848,* p. 227.

14. Marschall, p. 381.

15. $AJ^{13}181$, Letter under "Projets": "Projet d'une nouvelle organisation pour l'Opéra," 60 rue de Richelieu (unsigned).

16. The concept of the *féerie* is discussed in Chapter One, and in Chapter Two in connection with *Robert le Diable.*

17. $AJ^{13}180$, Letter to "Citoyen Ministre," Paris, 3 juin 1848.

18. J.-J. Prod'homme, "La Musique et les musiciens en 1848," *Sonderdruck aus Sammelbände der Internationale Musikgesellschaft,* 14 Heft 1, Oct. 1912, p. 167; and Jacques Barzun, *Berlioz and the Romantic Century,* 2 vols. (Boston: Little, Brown, and Co., 1950), p. 264.

19. Jean Gourret, *Les Hommes qui ont fait l'Opéra 1669–1984* (Paris: Editions Albatros, 1984), pp. 131, 221.

20. J.-J. Prod'homme, "La Musique et les musiciens en 1848," p. 161.

21. Georges Duveau, *1848* (Paris: Gallimard, 1965), p. 105.
22. Duponchel was, however, outdone in his attire by the flamboyant Caussidière who, as always, sported two pistols and a saber, believing that "un préfet de police doit avoir de la tenue." Duveau, p. 108.
23. See *Le Constitutionnel,* 9 avril, 1848.
24. AJ^{13}218, Letter of 28 déc. 1836, under "Liste des entrées de droit et de faveur, l'Académie Royale de Musique pour l'année 1836." Ledru-Rollin was a deputy in 1841; in 1843 he was one of the founders of *La Réforme.* Although a minister in the provisional government, the June days were to send him into opposition, and in the legislative assembly he became leader of the "Montagne," the party of the so-called *petite bourgeoisie* with democratic tendencies. After the insurrection of June 13, 1849, he went into exile in England.
25. See *Le Constitutionnel,* 9 avril 1848.
26. *Le Constitutionnel,* 5 juillet 1869.
27. Agulhon, *1848,* p. 27.
28. Henri Lagrave, *Le Théâtre et le public à Paris de 1715 à 1750* (Paris: C. Klincksieck, 1972), pp. 213–16.
29. I am making reference here to an unpublished paper by Marvin Carlson, "The Semiotics of Opera Structures," p. 4, which he kindly put at my disposal. Two francs may have been just affordable for some workers, since, as Danièle Pistone has pointed out, workers in this period earned an average of 4–6 francs per day. See her "L'Opéra de Paris au siècle romantique," *Revue internationale de musique francaise,* jan. 1981, p. 40.
30. AJ^{13}181, Ville de Paris, 2e div., 2e bureau, 16 mars 1848.
31. AJ^{13}181, Letter from the Ministère des Travaux Publics, Ateliers Nationaux to M. le Directeur, Duponchel.
32. I am referring here to the chronology given by John Merriman in his book, *The Agony of the Republic: The Repression of the Left in Revolutionary France 1848–51* (New Haven: Yale University Press, 1978), pp. xxxi–xxxii. And see Agulhon, *1848,* p. 48.
33. *Le Constitutionnel,* 9 avril 1848. and Agulhon, *1848,* p. 42.
34. Marschall, p. 380, and Théodore Muret, *L'Histoire par le théâtre,* pp. 305–6.
35. See Prod'homme, "La Musique et les musiciens en 1848," p. 167.
36. See *Le Constitutionnel,* 9 avril 1848.
37. Ibid.
38. AJ^{13}182, Letter from the Ministère de l'Intérieur, 19 mai 1848.
39. AJ^{13}182, Letter from the Ministre des Travaux Publics, Ateliers Nationaux, 2 mars 1848.
40. Agulhon, *1848,* p. 52.

41. $AJ^{13}182$, Folder on Représentations nationale Gratuites, letter from the Mairie de la Ville de Batignolles-Monceaux, 20 mai 1848.
42. See William H. Sewell, Jr., *Work and Revolution in France. The Language of Labor from the Old Regime* (London: Cambridge University Press, 1980).
43. For several discussions of this issue, see *L'Atelier,* 1840.
44. See Françoise Parent-Lardeur, *Lire à Paris au temps de Balzac. Les cabinets de lecture à Paris 1815–1830* (Paris: Editions de l'Ecole des Hautes Etudes en Sciences Sociales, 1981). For numerous discussions of theater, also see *Le Travailleur* and *Mère Duchêne*.
45. *L'Atelier,* 26 mars 1848, p. 104.
46. Such performances may have been linked, moreover, with political *fêtes;* for a description and discussion of contemporary *fêtes,* see *Le Représentant du peuple,* 1848. See Maurice Agulhon, *La République au village* (Paris: Editions du Seuil, 1973), p. 265, and Pierre Brochon, *La Chanson sociale de Béranger à Brassens* (Paris: Les Editions Ouvrières, 1961), p. 60.
47. Brochon, pp. 34–5.
48. See Pierre-Joseph Proudhon, *Oeuvres complètes de P.-J. Proudhon,* Nouvelle Edition, publiée sous la direction de M. M. C. Boublé et H. Moyssett. Tome 15: *Du Principe de l'art et de sa destination sociale* (Paris: Marcel Rivière et companie, 1939).
49. See the catalogue, *Le Spectacle et la fête au temps de Balzac* (Paris: Maison de Balzac, 1978–79). For a penetrating theoretical discussion of workers' responses to the culture of other social groups see Pierre Bourdieu, *Distinction. A Social Critique of the Judgement of Taste* (Cambridge, Mass.: Harvard University Press, 1984). In this context, chapter one, "The Aristocracy of Culture," is particularly relevant.
50. Here, my view is thus opposed to that presented by Marschall, p. 380.
51. Agulhon, *1848,* p. 65.
52. T. J. Clark, *The Absolute Bourgeois: Artists and Politics in France 1848–51,* pp. 11–14; Theodore Zeldin, *France 1848–1945,* 2 vols. (Oxford: Clarendon Press, 1977), p. 484; Stewart Campbell, *The Second Empire Revisited: A Study in French Historiography* (New Brunswick, N.J.: Rutgers Univ. Press, 1978), p. 9; and John Merriman, *The Agony of the Republic.*
53. T. J. Clark, *The Absolute Bourgeois,* pp. 40–2; and see *Le National,* 22 fév. 1849.
54. Maurice Agulhon, *Marianne au combat,* p. 52.
55. Ibid.
56. Roger, Gustave-Hippolyte, 1815–1879, French tenor; Pauline Viar-

dot, 1821–1910, French mezzo-soprano. On the background to the work, see the letter from Pillet to Meyerbeer of 1843 contained in $AJ^{13}183$; also see Karin Pendle, "Eugène Scribe and the French Opera of the Nineteenth Century" (thesis, University of Illinois, 1970), p. 737. And for the contract for *Le Prophète,* as well as notes on its décor, see $AJ^{13}207$, contract dated 5 mars 1849, and "Notes des décors, *Le Prophète.*"

57. Agulhon, *1848,* pp. 90, 114–116, and Krakovitch, *Hugo Censuré,* pp. 208, 213.

58. John Merriman, *The Agony of the Republic,* p. xxxiv.

59. For the background, see "Dossier d'oeuvre," *Le Prophète,* Bibliothèque de l'Opéra. Rosen, in his introduction to the Garland edition of the score (1978), cites Berlioz's account of the premiere in the *Journal des débats,* 29 avril 1849.

60. Karin Pendle, "Eugène Scribe and French Opera in the Nineteenth Century," p. 744.

61. An excellent recent recording of *Le Prophète* is available on Columbia Records, # 34340, with Marilyn Horne, Renata Scotto, James McCracken, and Jerome Hines, conducted by Henry Lewis.

62. H. Robert Cohen, "On the Reconstruction of the Visual Element in Grand Opera: Unexplored Sources in Parisian Collections," *International Musicological Society Report,* Berkeley, 1977, p. 463.

63. Ibid.

64. Rosen advances, in his introduction to the score published by Garland (1978), that "The explosive combination of rape, religion, and political revolution . . . was given respectable distance by the historical costumes." But another perspective is possible, when one takes into account not only the issue of political credibility, as discussed in Chapters One and Two, but the observation that appeared in *La Populaire Royaliste,* in 1837: "La Galerie des costumes française est une peinture plus findèle de nos usages, de nos coutumes, et de nos moeurs que la collection de tous les mémoirs écrits sur l'histoire." Character and emotion is still thought of here as externalized, in both costume and gesture. Significantly, most contemporary books of illustrations of theatrical costumes not only display the characters in costume, but in their most characteristic poses and gestures.

65. Germain Bapst, *Essai sur l'histoire du théâtre* (Paris: Librairie Hachette et Cie., 1883), p. 580; and see *Le Constitutionnel,* 18 avril 1849.

66. Ibid.; and "Dossier d'oeuvre," *Le Prophète,* Bibliothèque de l'Opéra.

67. *Mise en scène, Le Prophète* by Pallianti, 1849, Bibliothèque de l'Opéra.

68. Agulhon, *1848,* p. 75.

226

69. Henri Blazes de Bury, *Musiciens du passé, du présent, et de l'avenir* (Paris: Calmann-Lévy, 1880), p. 130.

70. For a general theoretical background to these issues in theater, see Elizabeth Burns, *Theatricality: A Study of Convention in the Theater and in Social Life* (London: Longman, 1972), pp. 33 ff.

71. *L'Illustration*, 1849, p. 182, "Jean de Leyde, chef des Anabaptistes à Munster."

72. Agulhon, *1848*, pp. 91–3, 123.

73. *Le Moniteur Universel*, 25 avril 1849.

74. *Le National*, 18 avril 1849.

75. Agulhon, *1848*, p. 76.

76. Ibid., p. 137.

77. Nathan Therien, "Popular Song Entertainment as Social Experience and the Failure of Participatory Culture in France 1815–1914" (dissertation in progress, Harvard University); and see *Le Travailleur*, 1849.

78. Perhaps this is a reference to the election of representatives on May 13, in which the "*montagnards*" gained strength.

79. *Le Peuple*, 1849.

80. Ibid.

81. Agulhon, *La République au village*, p. 198.

82. I am here borrowing the insights of Roger Chartier, in his introduction to *Figures de la gueuserie*, Bibliothèque bleue (Paris: Montalba, 1982), p. 234.

83. Agulhon, *1848*, pp. 95–6.

84. Ibid., pp. 229, 88.

85. Marschall, p. 382.

86. Marschall, pp. 383–4. Thirty-seven performances of the opera were given in 1849, with forty more in 1850.

87. See Louis Chevalier, *Classes laborieuses et classes dangereuses à Paris pendant la première moitié du XIXe siècle* (Paris: Plon, 1958), and Nathan Therien, "Popular Song Entertainment." As Therien points out, officials knew and worried that the societies could easily be radicalized.

88. Duveau, *1848*, p. 121.

4. POLITICIZED ATTACKS ON GRAND OPERA AND THE GENESIS OF ALTERNATIVE MODELS

1. Alain Pléssis, *De la fête impériale au mur des fédérés 1852–1871* (Paris: Editions du Seuil, 1979), p. 22.

2. See René Rémond, *The Right Wing in France: From 1815 to de Gaulle* (Philadelphia: University of Pennsylvania Press, 1971), and Pléssis, *De la fête impériale*, p. 14.

3. For a good background, see Gordon Wright, *France in Modern Times* (Chicago: Rand McNally Publishing, Inc., 1974), p. 147; Maurice Agulhon, *Marianne au combat: l'imagerie et la symbolique républicaine de 1789 à 1880* (Paris: Flammarion, 1979); and René Rémond, *The Right Wing in France*. On the continuity of tradition in official culture, I am referring here to Arno Mayer's *The Persistence of the Old Regime: Europe to the Great War* (New York: Pantheon Books, 1981), p. 189.

4. Pléssis, *De la fête impériale*, pp. 19–21.

5. An example is the performance of *Guillaume Tell*, on August 15, 1864, for which the Opéra was accorded 8,000 francs; see $F^{21}1046$ on the funding of these performances. The other most frequently performed works on these occasions were *Robert le Diable* and *Les Huguenots*.

6. For the eighteenth century situation, see William Weber, "*La musique ancienne* in the Waning of the Ancien Régime," *The Journal of Modern History*, March 1984, p. 66.

7. On the character of the Opéra now, see Frederick Martins, "Musical Mirrors of the Second Empire," *Musical Quarterly*, 1930; and for the privileged audience, see $AJ^{13}162$, the file on free entries.

8. Ibid.

9. In addition, the surveillance of all theaters increased, subventioned and non-subventioned alike; Baron Haussmann razed the old boulevard theaters in order to help insure such control.

10. Jean Gourret, *Les Hommes qui ont fait l'Opéra 1669–1984* (Paris: Editions Albatros, 1984), p. 134. As Pléssis points out in *De la fête impériale* (p. 11), the emperor wanted to exercise a personal power in all senses of the word, and all large decisions remained dependent on him, including the modification of the role of each institution.

11. Gourret, *Les hommes*, p. 135. Crosnier replaced Roqueplan on November 11, 1855; on July 1, 1856, Crosnier was replaced by Alphonse Royer, who was himself replaced by Emile Perrin on December 20, 1862.

12. For example, see $AJ^{13}443$, Letter from the Ministère d'Etat, 16 mars 1861, to Royer. Also see $AJ^{13}443$, Arrêté, 1 juillet 1856, in which Royer is named the director, to be "soumis aux délibérations supérieurs" for such matters as "le budget, la réception des ouvrages, les règlements administratifs, les modifications au tarif des places, aux honoraires des auteurs, les admissions à la retraite, la répartition des fonds réservés par l'Empereur."

13. The function of this commission was replaced in 1860 by the Surintendance des théâtres impériaux. See Jean Gourret, *Les Hommes qui ont fait l'Opéra*, pp. 134–6.

14. Georges Bureau, *Le Théâtre et sa législation* (Paris: Paul Ollendorff,

Editeur, 1898), p. 217; it was formerly administered by a superinten-
dent, who was made part of the ministry of the Maison de
l'Empereur; this function belonged to count Caciochi, "premier
chambellan" of Napoleon III. An order addressed to him by the
emperor had to be obeyed without delay. Later, by a decree of
November 22, 1860, the Ministère d'Etat was given to Count Wa-
lewski, who thus took charge of the superior administration of the
Opéra, while the administration of the director was controlled by
the Liste civile. This complicated organization, however, became
burdensome for the Liste civile, and was ended by a decree of March
22, 1866, that made the director responsible and put the subvention
in the charge of the state. See Bureau, p. 217, and see Pierre Bossuet, *Histoire des théâtres nationaux* (Paris: Editions et publications
contemporains, n.d.), p. 157, and Emile Véron, *Paris en 1860: les
théâtres de Paris depuis 1806* (Paris: Librairie Nouvelle, 1860), p. 130.
Crosnier, a deputy of the "Corps législatif," was first charged with
its direction, under the superior authority of the Maison de l'Empereur; soon, however, he retired voluntarily and was replaced by
Alphonse Royer, in 1856. See $AJ^{13}443$, Decree of 30 juin 1854, from
the Ministre d'Etat et de la Maison de l'Empereur.

   Royer then directed the Opéra until it was entrusted to Perrin,
from 1862 to 1867. Perrin was originally a painter, and later, under
the Republic, a "Commissaire de la République à l'Opéra-
Comique"; when he took over the Opéra as a "private enterprise,"
he received a subvention of 820,000 francs, and another one from
the Liste civile of 100,000 francs; he was overseen by a "Commissaire Impérial." See Gourret, p. 137, and $AJ^{13}443$, Arrêté of 1866,
which names Perrin as Directeur-Entrepreneur, and specifies "Le
Directeur sera tenu de diriger l'Opéra avec splendeur qui convient à
ce premier théâtre Impérial, de le maintenir dans l'état de luxe qui
le distingue des autres théâtres."

15. By order of the government, May 16, 1853, performances were to
    begin at 7:30 p.m. and finish by midnight at the latest; this, of
    course, meant cuts in many of the grand works. See *Robert le Diable,*
    Théâtre National de l'Opéra de Paris, 2 juin–20 septembre 1985,
    Catalogue de l'Exposition par Martine Kahane.

16. For a general background, see Gustave Bertrand, *Les Nationalités
    musicales étudiés dans le drame lyrique* (Paris: Librairie Académique,
    1872), pp. 395 ff., and Guy de Charnacé, *Les Compositeurs français et
    les théâtres lyriques subventionnés,* p. 15.

17. See T. J. Walsh, *Second Empire Opera: the Théâtre Lyrique* (London:
    Calder, 1974). (Berlioz's opera *Les Troyens* was hence premiered at
    the Théâtre-Lyrique.)

18. Pierre Brochon, *La Chanson sociale de Béranger à Brassens* (Paris: Les Editions Ouvrières, 1961), p. 70. No meetings could be held without anthorization of the Préfet de police, and this included singing societies.

19. See Jean-Jacques Darmon, *Le Colportage de librairie en France sous le Second Empire* (Paris: Plon, 1972).

20. Emile Véron, *Paris en 1860*, p. 114.

21. See "*La Muette de Portici*. Edition populaire. Répertoire des Orphéons et des sociétés chorales. Collection des plus beaux choeurs pour voix d'hommes." It does not contain the "seditious" barcarolles but does include the innocuous "Cavatine de Sommeil," the "Choeur des Pêcheurs," the "Choeur du Marché," and the "Prière."

22. Ursula von Eckhardt-Bäker, *Frankreichs Musik zwischen Romantik und Moderne*, Band 2, *Studien zur Musikgeschichte des 19. Jahrhunderts* (Regensburg: Gustave Bosse, 1965), p. 162; and see William Weber, *Music and the Middle Class: The Social Structure of Concert Life in London, Paris, and Vienna* (London: Crooms Helm, 1975).

23. For the map of the theaters, see Maurice Crubellier, *Histoire culturelle de la France* (Paris: A. Colin, 1974), p. 204; and see André Lejeune and Stéphane Wolff, *Les Quinze salles de l'Opéra de Paris 1669–1955* (Paris: Librairie Théâtrale, 1955), p. 31, as well as Marvin Carlson, "The Semiotics of Opera Structures," Paper delivered at the conference 'Théâtre, Opéra, Spectacle. Approach semiologiques," Royaumont, France, Sept. 1984, p. 11.

24. Danièle Pistone, "L'Opéra de Paris au siècle romantique," *Revue internationale de musique française,* jan. 1981, p. 4. On the attempted assassination, see James Billington, *Fire in the Minds of Men: Origins of the Revolutionary Faith* (New York: Basic Books, 1980).

25. Irene Earles, "Napoleon III's Paris Opera and Les Halles: New Architectural Technology," paper read at the Western Society for French History annual meeting, Winnipeg, Manitoba, 1982.

26. See Neil van Zandten's discussion of Garnier in Arthur Drexler, ed., *The Architecture of the Ecole des Beaux-arts* (New York: The Museum of Modern Art; distributed by the MIT Press, Cambridge, Mass., 1977), p. 272 ff.

27. The "Neo-Baroque" style is identified as "eclectic classicism" by Bernard Knox, in "Visions of the Grand Prize," *New York Review of Books,* Sept. 27, 1984.

28. Van Zandten, pp. 272, 278–9; and Charles Garnier, *Le Théâtre* (Paris: Hachette, 1871).

29. Construction on the Opéra was begun on August 1, 1861; it took fourteen years to build.

30. See Gustave Bertrand, *Les Nationalités musicales étudiés dans le drame lyrique,* pp. 423 ff.

31. See the article from the *Journal Officiel* in the "Dossier d'oeuvre," *Le Prophète,* Bibliothèque de l'Opéra; for information on the revival of *Les Huguenots* in 1868, see $AJ^{13}506$, which includes a letter from Meyerbeer concerning the cuts made in 1853, and those to which he consents, as well as details of the new costumes.

32. For the revival of *Robert le Diable* in 1860, Cicéri's decors were "touched up" by Cambon and Thierry; in 1853, substantial portions of the second and fourth acts were cut. This included the scene where Robert is caught with the "rameau magique," which considerably lessens the dramatic force by making his crimes more ambiguous.

33. See *L'Indépendance,* Jan. 7, 1869.

34. November 30, 1868.

35. See the "Dossier d'oeuvre," *La Muette de Portici,* Bibliothèque de l'Opéra.

36. A large number of these may be found in the music division of the Bibliothèque nationale.

37. Quoted in Bronislaw Horowicz, *Le Théâtre de l'Opéra* (Paris: Editions d'Aujourd'hui, 1976), p. 15.

38. *Journal Officiel,* 5 juillet 1869.

39. See Jane F. Fulcher, "Meyerbeer and the Music of Society During the Monarchy of July," *The Musical Quarterly,* April 1981, p. 227; also see the *Revue et Gazette musicale,* 1865, p. 249.

40. Nils Sandblad, *Manet; Three Studies in Artistic Conception* (Lund: C. W. K. Gleerup, 1954), pp. 18–19.

41. For the exact identification of the figures, see Sandblad, *Manet; Three Studies in Artistic Conception.*

42. Roger L. Williams, *Gaslight and Shadow: The World of Napoleon III* (New York: Macmillan, 1957), p. 107.

43. As quoted in Alexander Faris, *Jacques Offenbach* (New York: Charles Scribner's Sons, 1980), p. 48.

44. Alexander Faris, *Jaques Offenbach,* p. 53; and Arthur Mitzman, "Roads, Vulgarity, Rebellion, and Pure Art: the Inner Space in Flaubert and French Culture," *Journal of Modern History,* Sept. 1979, pp. 509, 522.

45. Gustave Flaubert, *Madame Bovary* (Paris: Editions Garnier Frères, 1961), p. 208. On *Le Charivari* see the article by Gerald Turbow, "Art and Politics: Wagnerism in France," in David Large and William Weber, eds., *Wagnerism in European Culture and Politics* (Ithaca, N. Y.: Cornell University Press, 1984).

46. See Mitzman; Dominick LaCapra, *Madame Bovary on Trial* (Ithaca:

Cornell University Press, 1982); and Frederick Brown, *Theater and Revolution: The Culture of the French Stage* (New York: The Viking Press, 1980), p. 30. There were precedents for parody of the story, in the Revolution; see Marvin Carlson, *The Theater of the French Revolution* (Ithaca, N. Y.: Cornell University Press, 1966), pp. 256–7.

47. Faris, *Jacques Offenbach*, p. 64. "Charivari" may appear, in modern guise, in other instances as well, for example, in those numbers intended to be metaphors for the sexual act, such as Orpheus's discordant serenade to Eurydice and the duet of Eurydice and the fly.

48. Arthur Mitzman, in "Roads, Vulgarity, Rebellion, and Pure Art," sees a progression from parody to "pure art" in Flaubert, one that we might also see here, in the movement from Offenbach to Wagner.

49. Gerald D. Turbow, "Art and Politics: Wagnerism in France," pp. 137–8. Turbow cites cases of previous performances of Wagner in Paris: on November 24, 1850, the overture to *Tannhäuser* was performed at Segher's "Sainte-Cécile Concert." Though his music was not performed again in Paris until 1858, his writings were being discussed in the contemporary French press.

50. Ibid., pp. 140–2.

51. Pléssis, *De la fête impériale*, p. 15.

52. For example, in 1860 there were only twelve performances of *Robert*, eleven of *Les Huguenots*, and seven of *Le Prophète*.

53. As stated previously, Royer was director from 1856 to 1862. He came from a literary background, and was carefully watched by the Ministre d'Etat.

54. See Alphonse Royer, *Histoire de l'Opéra* (Paris: Bachelin-Delflorenne Editeur, 1875).

55. For background, see Elizabeth Bernard, "L'Evolution du public de l'Opéra de 1860 à 1880," in *Regards sur l'Opéra*. Centre d'Art, Esthétique, et Littérature (Paris: Presses Universitaires de France, 1976).

56. See AJ^{13}502, Letter to "Son excellence, le Ministre d'Etat," from Royer, inviting him to a Repétition générale of *Tannhäuser*, 23 fév. 1861; and see Gerald Turbow, p 149.

57. The "Feuille de Location des Loges et Slattes, 1er Représentation de *Tannhäuser*, 13 mars 1861" is contained in AJ^{13}502. Prominently included are ministers, bankers, journalists, artists, and imperial officials of all sorts.

58. Arthur Imbert de Saint-Amand, *Le Règne de Napoléon III* (Paris: Librairie Dentu, 1861), p. 86.

59. Ibid.

60. Ibid.

61. Alphonse Royer, *Histoire de l'Opéra*, pp. 202–3; and $AJ^{13}443$ – Letter from the Ministre d'Etat, 16 mars 1861, to Royer.
62. For a different interpretation of the situation, see Elizabeth Bernard, "L'Evolution du public de l'Opéra de 1860 à 1880," p. 35.
63. See Jane F. Fulcher, "Wagner, Comte, and Proudhon: The Aesthetics of Positivism in France," *Symposium* 1979, and Ursula von Eckhardt-Bäker, *Frankreichs Musik*, p. 75.
64. Eckhardt-Bäker, p. 111; and see Jules Fleury, or "Champfleury," *Grandes figures d'hier et d'aujord'hui: Balzac, Gérard de Nerval, Wagner, Courbet* (Paris: Poulet-Malassis et de Broise, 1861); Gerald Turbow notes (p. 152) that Théeodore de Banville also saw Wagner as a "democrat, a new man wanting to create for all the people."
65. Champfleury, *Chansons populaires des provinces de France* (Paris: Jules Tardieu, 1860). See Jane F. Fulcher, "The Chanson Populaire of the Second Empire: 'Music of the Peasants' in France," *Acta Musicologica*, Vol. LII (1981), Fasc. I.
66. Pierre-Joseph Proudhon, *Oeuvres complètes de P.-J. Proudhon*, Nouvelle Edition, publiée sous la direction de MM. C. Bouglé et H. Moyseet, Tome 15: *Du principe de l'art et de sa destination sociale* (Paris: Marcel Rivière et Companie, 1939).

It was in an attempt to claim the peasantry as the natural supporters and constituency of the Empire that the government turned to the collection of *chansons populaires* in France; and thus at the very moment when the "popular" art of the countryside was dying out, displaced by the forces of modernization, the government proclaimed that it had to be saved. In 1852, a compilation of traditional *chansons populaires* throughout France was requested: the collection, to be monitored by the minister of public instruction, Hippolyte Fortoul, was intended to preserve the purest and most spontaneous expression of the people of France.

Nowhere is the government's goal clearer than in the publication of the committee designated to organize the project, the *Bulletin du comité de la langue*. The section on philology was charged with the task, for the official concern was, above all, with a mode of popular expression that was appraently vanishing in France. The government, claiming to be supported by "la fidelité des sources poétiques du peuple," hence wanted to preserve popular models of beauty and naiveté. This simplicity and ingenuousness were, for the state, the essence of the expression of the people of France, of a constituency, a disposition, a language that ought to be preserved. And hence through codification of the *chanson,* as well as through the organization of musical life, the Empire hoped to promote that art which would further its specific political ends: it was to be an art that

233

would, above all, maintain the status quo, and allow each group to pursue its ends in harmony with the political goal. See Jane Fulcher, "The Chanson Populaire."

67. As quoted in Lionel de la Laurencie, *Le Goût musicale en France* (Genève: Slatkine Reprints, 1970), pp. 335–7. Also see a related argument in Baudelaire's article, "Richard Wagner and *Tannhäuser* in Paris," in Charles Baudelaire, *Selected Writings on Art and Artists*, trans. P. E. Charvet (Middlesex, Eng.: Penguin Books, 1972).

68. See Jane Fulcher, "Wagner as Democrat and Realist in France," *The Stanford French Review*, Spring 1981.

69. Sabina Ratner, "Richard Wagner and Camille Saint-Saëns," *The Opera Quarterly*, Autumn 1983, and Gerald Turbow, p. 140.

70. See Maxime Leroy, *Les Premiers amis français de Wagner* (Paris: Albin Michel, 1925).

71. Auguste de Gasperini, *De la Nouvelle Allemagne musicale: Richard Wagner* (Paris: Le Ménestrel, 1866), p. 9.

72. Nathan Therien, "Popular Song Entertainment as Social Experience and the Failure of Participatory Culture in France 1815–1914" (dissertation in progress, Harvard University). Turbow also notes (pp. 153–4) that one of the main factors affecting Wagner's reception after *Tannhäuser* in Paris was the performance of his music at the "Concerts populaires" of Pasdeloup, begun in October 1861 in the Cirque-Napoléon, which drew a new "mass" audience. See Turbow in Weber and Large, *Wagnerism*.

73. See *L'Orphéon*, 1863 and *La France Chorale*, 1869, which reported on *Rienzi* and *Le Prophète*, both revived that year. On March 10, 1863, it had discussed performances of the march from *Tannhäuser* and praised the work of Wagner. *L'Orphéon*, in 1863, ran a series of articles about the origins of opera in Italy and France. In 1860 it had chronicled Wagner's visit to Paris and reported on his concerts, including the performance of *Tannhäuser* in 1861. By 1863 commentators were noting the "dangerous symptoms in the *orphéons*," such as their "spirit of independence, lack of discipline, and willingness to take bad advice."

74. The Bibliothèque des Amis de l'Instruction, located in what is now the fourth arrondissement in Paris, contains the entire grand opera repertoire, as well as works of Wagner. Its musical holdings are listed in its *Catalogue générale*, of 1920, available at the Bibliothèque, which is still open to the public during specific hours. It includes works on the history and theory of music, from the mid and later nineteenth century, and particularly those works that emphasize the later eighteenth century on.

75. Georges Duveau, *La Penseé ouvrière sur l'éducation pendant la Second*

République et le Second Empire (Paris: Domat Montchrestien, 1948), p. 105.

76. *La Réforme théâtrale*, 5 avril 1865, p. 1.
77. Duveau, *La Pensée ouvrière*, p. 181. According to Duveau (p. 193) the quest of Proudhon and many workers was now for "la liberté de l'individu et de l'égalité sociale."
78. *Le Peuple*, 14 février 1869.
79. *La Réforme théâtrale*, 5 avril 1865, p. 1.
80. The four months after the opening of the "Palais Garnier" saw the presentations of *La Juive, La Favorite, Guillaume Tell, Hamlet,* and *Les Huguenots,* but within the next few years, with the awakening of a new French school, they were to lose appeal and favor, becoming more objects of nostalgia than artistic interest. This turn away from the grand repertoire was completed during the period of the growing influence of Wagner, in the 1880s and 1890s.

CONCLUSION

1. My concept of "interpretive frame" is closely related to the idea of an "interpretive ground," as discussed by Bernard Beckermann in *The Dynamics of Drama* (New York: Columbia University Press, 1970). It is also related to the kind of interaction that Stephen Orgel describes between monarch, work, and audience in *The Illusion of Power: Political Theater in the English Renaissance* (Berkeley: University of California Press, 1975).
2. This is certainly true of the Socialist government's plans for a new, more "popular" opera at the Place de la Bastille. Again, it communicates a spirit and vision, or a stance, as opposed to specific policy.
3. The most prominent among these is Maurice Agulhon, whose works have been cited throughout this study. In addition, jounalists today have increasingly noted the symbolic contestation that has been recurring with prominence in France, as in the case of the film *Danton,* and the plans for a statue of Captain Dreyfus. Political battles are still being fought in this realm, and they are taken just as seriously as in the nineteenth century.
4. Samuel Kinser, "Chronotypes and Catastrophes: the Cultural History of Mikhail Bakhtin," *The Journal of Modern History,* June 1984, pp. 304–5.
5. This is a position that, although with some nuance and modification, Theodore Zeldin assumes in *France 1848–1945* (Oxford: Clarendon Press, 1977).
6. These concepts are drawn from J. G. A. Pocock's *Politics, Language, and Time* (New York: Atheneum, 1971).

235

7. As stated earlier, this is the premise behind Herbert Lindenberger's *Historical Drama. The Relation of Literature and Reality* (Chicago: University of Chicago Press, 1975).

8. Michael Holquist and Katerina Clark, *Mikhail Bakhtin. A Biography* (Cambridge, Mass.: Harvard University Press, 1984), p. 20.

9. William Weber, for example, is currently studying the changing cultural and political meaning of Handel's oratorios, together with their changes in performance context in England.

10. For a more complete discussion of this issue in the context of broader tendencies in musicology today, see Robert Winter's review of Joseph Kerman's *Contemplating Music: Challenges to Musicology*, in *The New York Review of Books*, July 18, 1985, pp. 23–7.

11. Again, I have discussed this concept at length in my article "Current Perspectives on Culture and the Meaning of Cultural History in France Today," *The Stanford French Review*, Spring 1985, pp. 91–104.

APPENDIX – PLOT SYNOPSES

THE PLOT SYNOPSES that follow have been reprinted, with the permission of Garland Publishing, Inc., from its series *Early Romantic Opera* (New York, 1978), edited by Philip Gossett and Charles Rosen; they are all by Laura DeMarco.

SYNOPSIS – *LA MUETTE DE PORTICI*

Act I. At the palace of the Duke d'Arcos, Spanish viceroy at Naples, the people rejoice over the impending marriage of the duke's son, Alphonse, to the Spanish princess, Elvire. Alphonse, however, is filled with remorse for having seduced a beautiful but innocent Neapolitan girl, Fenella. Worse yet, as he confesses to his friend Lorezo, the poor girl is mute and, having rejected her because of his impending marriage to Elvire, he has heard nothing from her for a month. He fears she has been imprisoned by his father. Elvire is escorted by the chorus, and sings of her love for Alphonse. After dances from her native Spain are performed in her honor, she is informed that a young girl, purused by soldiers, seeks her protection. It is Fenella. The mute girl acts out the story of her seduction, of her imprisonment the past month, and of her escape. Elvire offers her protection and enters the chapel for her wedding. During the marriage ceremony, Fenella recognizes Alphonse. When Alphonse emerges from the chapel married to Elvire, Fenella indicates that he is the man who has betrayed her. Alphonse confesses his guilt, and Elvire is aghast. Amidst the confusion of the scene, Fenella rushes off and disappears.

237

Act II. At Portici, a seashore village between Naples and Mt. Vesuvius, fishermen prepare for their day's work. Their leader, Masaniello, arrives. He is disgusted by the tyrannical rule of the Spanish nobles, but advises that the time is not yet right to strike against them. Masaniello is Fenella's brother. So far, only his friend, Pietro, knows the story of Fenella's seduction, but Pietro tells Masaniello he still does not know who the girl is. Pietro and Masaniello swear vengeance against the Spanish nobility, which has not only oppressed the people but has taken advantage of their most innocent and defenseless subject. Just then Fenella appears. She expresses her despair, and indicates that she had even considered suicide, but first wanted her brother's pardon. When questioned, she refuses to disclose her seducer's identity, but explains that he is married and she, therefore, cannot redeem her shame. Outraged, Masaniello demands revenge. He summons the fishermen and rouses them to revolt against the Spanish.

Act III. The scene is the main square of Naples. Alphonse tries to convince Elvire of his love and repentance for having seduced Fenella. When he protests that should Elvire not forgive him, death will be all that remains, she relents and is finally reconciled to him. Alphonse orders the guards to find Fenella and bring her to Elvira. The people enter the square selling their wares and a tarantella is danced. Fenella enters, and the guards attempt to arrest her. However, Masaniello, who has arrived in the city, intervenes. When the guards try to arrest him too, he calls the people to help him. They produce concealed weapons and drive off the guards. Before Masaniello leads the rebels to further insurrection, he asks the people to pray that God guide them in carrying out their just cause. As the act ends, the people prepare to take the city.

Act IV. Masaniello, having led the people to victory, is in his hut at Portici, lamenting that success has bred license and destructiveness in the people and that his army consists of nothing but rabble. Fenella enters. She is terrified by the horror and death she has witnessed in the city; her brother calms her and sings her to sleep. Pietro and his companions arrive to request that Masaniello lead them once again to victory and revenge, but Masaniello says that now that they have achieved their goal of political control, they must avoid further bloodshed. All go to the back of the house. A knock is heard at the door. Fenella opens it, and Alphonse and Elvire enter seeking protection from the bloodthirsty rebels. At first Fenella refuses to help her rival, but she finally succumbs to Elvire's pleas for pity and vows to save them or die with them.

Masaniello enters and, not knowing Alphonse and Elvire, offers the strangers the hospitality of his home. Pietro returns with representatives of the people who have come to give Masaniello the keys of the city and ask that he be their ruler. Pietro recognizes Alphonse and wants to have him and Elvire killed on the spot. Fenella points out that Masaniello has already promised his protection, and his sense of honor compels him to uphold that promise. To the disgust of Pietro, Masaniello orders one of his men to conduct the Spanish couple to safety. The people enter hailing Masaniello. Against the chorus of praise, Pietro and his followers swear that Masaniello shall be next to fall.

Act V. In Naples in front of the viceroy's palace, Pietro proclaims the success of the revolt to the people and, aside to one of his followers, reveals that he has poisoned Masaniello for having become an even greater tyrant than those whom he had overthrown.

Another follower announces that Alphonse has assembled troops and is now marching against them. He further announces that as proof of God's anger against the rebellion, Mount Vesuvius is erupting. The people cry out that only Masaniello can save them, but Pietro and his followers reply that God has destroyed Masaniello's reason.

Masaniello emerges from the palace. The poison has taken its effect, for he is clearly mentally disturbed and unable to respond to the pleas of the people. Dazed, he repeats his barcarolle from the second act. When Fenella enters, however, his reason is momentarily restored, and he leads the rebels off to meet Alphonse's troops. As Fenella prays that her brother will return safely, Elvire rushes in declaring that Masaniello has just saved her from being killed by the rebels. Alphonse follows, stating that the rebels have killed Masaniello for having saved Elvire. But without his leadership, they quickly fell to Alphonse's forces. Overcome by despair over the loss of Masaniello, Fenella rushes to the top of Mt. Vesuvius and hurls herself into the burning lava.

SYNOPSIS – *ROBERT LE DIABLE*

The story takes place in the early eleventh century. Robert is the offspring of Berthe, Duchess of Normandy, and an emissary of hell who, in human form, had seduced her. So evil and dissolute has Robert's behavior been that his subjects drove him out of Normandy. Arriving in Sicily he met the Princess Isabelle, and the two fell in love. Carried away by his passion, Robert attempted to abduct her, but the knights of her father's court prevented him. They would have torn him to pieces had it not been for the intervention of a mysterious knight. The stranger bears the name of Bertram but unknown to Robert is really his satanic father. Since the rescue of Robert, Bertram has remained with him as his companion, hoping to take possession of his soul by luring him to eternal damnation.

Act I. In Sicily, Robert and Bertram join a group of knights in a drinking chorus; the knights do not know Robert, and are curious about him. One of the knights brings in Raimbaut to sing; he tells the tale of Robert le Diable, explaining Robert's entire history. Furious, Robert reveals himself and orders Raimbaut hanged. The terrified minstrel thereupon explains that he and his betrothed were sent from Normandy to deliver a sacred trust to him. Robert is excited by the description of Raimbaut's betrothed and orders her brought to him. When she arrives, Robert recognizes her as his foster sister, Alice, who is as good as Robert has been evil. He addresses the other knights to leave her untouched, and they grudgingly depart. Alone with Robert, Alice tells him that the extremely pious Berthe, on her deathbed, asked Alice to seek him out and to protect him from the evil constantly attempting to win control of him. Berthe had also requested Alice to deliver her will, to be read by Robert only when he has proved himself worthy. Robert, convinced he is not worthy, refuses to read it now. He then tells Alice of his love for Isabelle, the battle, and the mysterious knight who helped him. Alice encourages him to write a note to Isabelle, and agrees to deliver it. She asks only that Robert arrange for her marriage to Raimbaut by a holy man near the rocks of St. Irene. Bertram returns. Sensing the presence of evil, Alice recoils from him and departs.

Alice's presence and message have made Robert conscious of Bertram's evil influence upon him. Afraid of losing his son, Bertram assures Robert of his devotion. He suggests Robert chase away his sorrows by gambling with the knights, who now reappear. Thus seduced by Bertram's counsel, Robert gambles desperately and loses all his wealth – even his armor. The act ends with Robert distraught over his losses and threatening the knights.

Act II. At a hall in the palace Princess Isabelle is lamenting Robert's apparent abandonment. Worse, her father has pledged her hand to the Prince of Grenada. At that moment, Alice rushes in with Robert's letter. Encouraged by Isabelle's devotion, Alice leads in Robert, and he and Isabelle repledge their love. Robert learns of Isabelle's betrothal to the Prince of Grenada and of an impending tournament in which the Prince will participate. Robert expresses his hope to meet his rival in single combat at the tournament. Isabelle departs. Thanks to Bertram's evil plotting, however, Robert receives a message to do battle with the Prince of Grenada in a nearby wood. As a result of Robert's seeking his rival in the wood, he is unable to be at the tournament, over which Isabelle presides. After dances, the Prince of Grenada asks to be given his arms by Isabelle. As Robert has not arrived, she has no choice but to agree, as Bertram exults. The tournament begins, and Isabelle laments Robert's absence.

Act III. The scene represents the gloomy rocks of St. Irene. Raimbaut has come looking for Alice, but Bertram accosts him, offers him gold, and assures him that since he is now wealthy, he should enjoy himself rather than marry. Followed by Bertram's jeers, Raimbaut goes off. But Bertram is afraid that the influence of Alice's purity may undermine his control of Robert. He consults with the forces of evil to determine whether he may be permitted to carry out his design on Robert. The theater darkens, and demonic voices cry out from a cavern. Bertram enters the cavern. Alice appears, looking for Raimbaut. She hears the infernal chorus calling Robert's name and, horrified, faints. Bertram reappears, having learned that unless Robert freely yields to him by midnight the next day, a higher power will take him from Bertram forever. Bertram finds Alice as she begins to recover. Afraid that she has overheard (which she has), he threatens the girl as she desperately clings to a cross opposite the cavern, insisting she has witnessed nothing. Robert arrives, and Alice, threatened by Bertram with her own death and that of Raimbaut and her family, departs without speaking. Robert, overcome by shame from his disgrace at the tournament, has come to seek Bertram's advice. Arguing that Robert's rival has resorted to black magic, Bertram tells Robert that he can gain complete power and even immortality by plucking a branch that is always green from the tomb of St. Rosalie. Robert, although aware that committing such an act is a violation of heaven's laws, eventually yields to Bertram's plan. They agree to meet at the tomb.

The scene changes to the tomb of St. Rosalie. Bertram summons from their graves the spirits of nuns who, in life, were unfaithful to their vows. The ghostly nuns appear and their inanimate bodies are suddenly seized by passion. The Mother Superior, Hélène, leads him to the magic branch. As he plucks it, loud noises are heard, the earth trembles, thunder rolls, lightning flashes, phantoms appear in hideous shapes, and the entire cloister becomes a scene from hell. The act ends with an infernal chorus exulting over Robert's apparent damnation.

Act IV. Isabelle's attendants have come to her apartment to prepare her for bed. Isabelle exchanges a few words with Alice. Alice tells her she wishes to give Robert the letter from his mother, and hints of his danger. But Alice is interrupted by the arrival of the court, bringing bridal gifts from the Prince of Grenada, whom Isabelle is to marry the next day. Robert enters; using the power of the branch, he puts the entire household into a deathlike slumber and then enters Isabelle's bedroom. He attempts to carry Isabells off, but she appeals to his honor and finally through fervent prayers brings him back to virtue; he breaks the magic branch and destroys its hold over him. The knights awaken, crowd into Isabelle's room, and recognize Robert. Unable to escape, Robert breaks his sword. The knights seize him.

242

Act V. It is the cathedral of Palermo. After monks intone a chorus, the people offer prayers to God and enter the cathedral. Robert enters with Bertram. He has met the Prince of Grenada in combat but has lost. Once again he seeks Bertram's advice. Bertram offers to help him, but only on condition that Robert yield him his soul. Robert is about to agree, but suddenly the people can be heard repeating their prayer. Bertram, to counteract Robert's reaction to the celestial music, admits that Raimbaut has told the truth and discloses to him the mystery of his origin. Horrified to learn that Bertram is his demonic father, he is at the point of yielding once again, when suddenly Alice appears. She reveals that the Prince of Grenada, who is actually controlled by Bertram, could not enter the church, and that Isabelle awaits Robert at the alter. Robert wavers as the forces of good and evil, represented by Alice and Bertram, struggle within him. In desperation, Alice gives him his mother's will. He reads it, and Alice repeats the words: his mother prays for him in heaven. As Robert wavers, the clock strikes midnight. Since Robert has not yielded within the period permitted Bertram, Robert is saved. The earth opens, and Bertram plunges into a chasm. The scene shifts to the interior of the cathedral where Isabelle is waiting to guide Robert to the altar. Thus purity and virtue redeem Robert's soul through holy marriage to Isabelle.

SYNOPSIS – *LA JUIVE*

The Count de Brogni, Chief Magistrate of Rome, banished Eléazar and all other Jews from the sacred city. Before Eléazar left, the Neapolitans attacked and burned Rome in the magistrate's absence. De Brogni returned to find his home destroyed, his wife dead and infant daughter missing and presumed dead. Unknown to him, Eléazar rescued the little girl and, having seen his own children burned as infidels, decided to raise her as his daughter. De Brogni subsequently left his civic duties and sought solace by joining the Church, where he rose to the rank of Cardinal and attained great power in the service of Sigismund, emperor of the West.

Meanwhile, Eléazar settled as a jeweller and goldsmith in Constance, Switzerland, with de Brogni's daughter, whom he named Rachel and raised as a Jewess. Rachel has grown into a beautiful young woman and has caught the attention of Prince Léopold. Léopold has just succeeded in defeating the Hussites, but, to be near Rachel, he has disguised himself as a poor Jewish artist, taking the name Samuel, and has gone to work for Eléazar.

Act I. It is the year 1414, and the people of Constance are celebrating the victory of Prince Léopold over the Hussites. The Emperor has proclaimed a holiday, but Eléazar, unconcerned with a Christian feast day, continues to work. Ruggiero, the city provost, upon hearing the noise of work in Eléazar's shop, orders the goldsmith brought to him. Eléazar and Rachel are dragged out of the shop, and Ruggiero stirs the populace against the Jews for desecrating the feast day. Ruggiero orders Eléazar's execution, but is interrupted by the arrival of Cardinal de Brogni, who remembers Eléazar and orders him to be set free. When Eléazar rejects the cardinal's attempts to befriend him, de Brogni prays that divine enlightenment will come to the Jewish infidels.

Eléazar and Rachel return home where Léopold, disguised as Samuel, serenades her. She invites him to the Passover feast to be held that evening in her home. Léopold tries to turn her invitation aside, but is prevented from doing so when a crowd gathers to watch the Emperor and the soldiers who have defeated the Hussites march into the city. When Eléazar and Rachel climb the steps of the church to view the procession, Ruggiero sees another opportunity to set the crowd against them. Once again the mob curses them and threatens to throw them into Lake Constance. This time, however, they are saved by Léopold. Although he is still disguised, one of the soldiers knows that he is the prince and orders the mob held back. The crowd's attention is now diverted by the Emperor's triumphal entry. Rachel is astonished that Samuel has been able to save her and her father, but unaware of her lover's identity, she remains confused.

Act II. Eléazar, his family, Jews of the city, and Léopold are celebrating the Passover feast in Eléazar's home. Rachel notices that everyone is eating the traditional unleavened bread except Léopold; she wonders about his strange behavior. Suddenly a loud knock is heard at the door, and voices cry out in the name of the Emperor. Eléazar orders the ritual vessels put away, and everyone except

Léopold hides at the back of the house. Eléazar, fearing that the visit may mean trouble, asks him to remain.

Princess Eudoxie, the Emperor's niece and Léopold's wife, enters. The light in Eléazar's home is dim, and she does not recognize her husband. She has come to purchase from Eléazar a rare jewel that she wishes to present to Léopold at the victory celebration to be held upon his return the following day. Overhearing Eudoxie expressing her joy over his return, Léopold is filled with guilt and remorse for having betrayed her. When Eudoxie leaves, Rachel questions Léopold about his ability to stop the mob and his strange conduct during the Passover feast. Léopold agrees to meet her later that night to explain.

Rachel anxiously awaits Léopold, fearing the explanation he will offer her. Although Léopold, when he returns, does not tell Rachel his identity, he confesses that he is a Christian and begs her, despite the laws that would condemn them both to death, to run away with him. Rachel is about to leave with him when Eléazar enters. Infuriated that Léopold would betray him by running off with his daughter, Eléazar tells him that were Léopold not Jewish, he would kill him on the spot. Léopold, admitting he is a Christian, asks Eléazar to strike him, but Rachel pleas that her father forgive him are so strong that the old man relents. Eléazar tells Léopold to marry Rachel, but Léopold says he cannot and runs off.

Act III. The action shifts to the royal palace where Eudoxie is overjoyed at Léopold's return. When Léopold fled her home, however, Rachel followed him to the palace and asked to speak to Princess Eudoxie. Hoping to learn Léopold's secret, Rachel asks the princess whether she may spend one day as a servant in the royal household. Eudoxie does not understand the reason for Rachel's request but nevertheless grants it, and Rachel leaves.

Léopold enters and, overwhelmed with guilt, is about to explain everything to his wife when he is cut off by trumpets signaling the festivities in honor of victory. Eléazar appears with the jewel Eudoxie has purchased for her husband. As she prepares to decorate Léopold with the jewel, Rachel, recognizing her lover, "Samuel," steps forward to denounce him. Aware of the law that punishes with death liaisons between Christians and Jews, she admits that

Léopold has loved her. Eléazar asks whether Léopold's rank protects him from punishment, but de Brogni pronounces an anathema against all three . . . for having dared to break God's laws.

Act IV. Rachel, Eléazar, and Léopold have been condemned to death. Eudoxie, who still loves her husband, asks Rachel to retract her charge against Léopold. Rachel at first refuses, but finally agrees. Eudoxie leaves, and de Brogni enters. Rachel informs the cardinal that she wishes to make a confession before the tribunal and is led away. De Brogni wishes to save Rachel and her father and begs Eléazar to obtain a pardon by renouncing Judaism and embracing Christianity. But Eléazar refuses to be pardoned and resolves to die a Jew. He tells de Brogni, however, that his child did not die in Rome but was rescued by a Jew whose identity he alone knows. Despite the cardinal's pleas, Eléazar says he will carry the secret of the girl's whereabouts to his death.

Alone, Eléazar is torn by doubt, unable to decide whether his uncompromising hatred of Christianity warrants allowing Rachel to go to her death. He is about to relent when he hears the people savagely call out for death to the Jews. With new resolve, he swears that Rachel shall die, a reproach to their hatred and prejudice.

Act V. The people, gathered to witness the execution of the Jews, scream for their death. The crowd enters to an orchestral march. Ruggiero informs Eléazar that he and his daughter have been condemned to death, whereas Léopold's sentence has been commuted to banishment. Eléazar mutters that such a sentence is typical of Christian justice, but Rachel explains that it was her altered testimony that saved Léopold's life.

Rachel and Eléazar are taken to the scaffold from which they are to be hurled into a cauldron of burning oil. As de Brogni leads a prayer for them, Eléazar, unable to condemn Rachel to death, asks her whether she wishes, at the last moment, to abjure her faith and become a Christian. Rachel, however, proudly resolves to die as a Jew along with her father. As the executioners throw her into the burning cauldron, Eléazar turns to de Brogni and cries out to him that Rachel is his daughter. Before the eyes of the horrified cardinal, Eléazar mounts the scaffold to join Rachel in death.

Appendix

SYNOPSIS – *LES HUGUENOTS*

Act I. In Touraine the Count de Nevers, one of the leaders of the Catholic party, has invited his friends to a banquet. His guests – all young men of the Catholic nobility – are surprised to learn that de Nevers has invited a Huguenot noble, Raoul de Nangis. De Nevers explains that the King (Charles IX) wishes to establish a rapprochement between the Catholics and Protestants and asks his friends to receive Raoul kindly. Raoul arrives, and after the guests sing a chorus in praise of food and wine, de Nevers asks each of his guests to entertain the gathering with a tale of an amorous adventure. The young Huguenot tells of his meeting with an unknown and beautiful lady whom he had rescued from a band of riotous students near Amboise. Although he does not even know her name, he has fallen in love with her and is convinced that she loves him.

Raoul has been followed to the banquet by his servant, Marcel, an old soldier and ardent Huguenot. Shocked to see his master about to dine with leaders of the Catholic party, he intones the Lutheran hymn, "Ein feste Burg." The guests are rather amused by Marcel's warning, and so the old Huguenot rejoins with a far stronger Huguenot song that condemns all papists and all women for the ruination of men's souls.

De Nevers learns that a lady is waiting in the garden to speak to him. When de Nevers leaves to see her, his curious friends watch the meeting through an open window and assume the lady is de Nevers's latest mistress. Raoul is horrified, for the lady is none other than the unknown beauty of Amboise. Raoul and the guests leave the stage. As de Nevers returns, he mutters to himself that the lady was his fiancée, Valentine, who had begged to break off their engagement both at her own behest and at the request of Queen Marguerite de Valois, sister of the King. As a gentleman, de Nevers felt compelled to acquiesce to the queen's request and hence has broken the engagement. The guests return and tease de Nevers about his presumed mistress.

Urbain, a page, enters with a note for Raoul. The note invites Raoul to a secret rendezvous – on condition that he allow himself to be blindfolded and agrees not to ask any questions. Raoul, repelled to have discovered the apparent unworthiness of the

247

woman with whom he has fallen in love, is tempted by the prospect. Wondering what sort of amorous adventure is in store for him, he agrees to go. The letter is unsigned, but everyone—except Raoul—recognizes its seal as that of Queen Marguerite. Raoul is blindfolded and departs with Urbain and a group of masked men.

Act II. In the gardens of Chenonceaux, Queen Marguerite and her ladies amuse themselves as the page Urbain watches disconsolately. Marguerite receives Valentine, daughter of the Catholic leader, the Count de St. Bris. She knows that Valentine has loved Raoul ever since he rescued her and, like her brother the King, wishes to resolve the bloody differences between the Catholics and the Protestants. She believes she may be able to seal the peace by uniting the two great opposing parties—the Huguenot, de Nangis, and the Catholic, de St. Bris. Accordingly, she has Valentine rid herself of de Nevers in order to marry Raoul. Valentine tells Marguerite that although de Nevers has released her, her father, a fanatic Catholic, will never permit her to marry a Huguenot. Marguerite assures her she will settle the matter.

After the ladies-in-waiting bathe in the river, Raoul is led in, and Marguerite dismisses everyone. When Raoul removes his blindfold, he is overwhelmed by the queen's beauty and swears eternal devotion to her . . . When Urbain announces the arrival of Catholic and Huguenot nobles, she recalls her reason for summoning Raoul and proposes that he marry the daughter of St. Bris. Raoul, at last realizing that the lady with whom he has been speaking is the queen, agrees to the marriage. Before the assembled Catholic and Huguenot nobles, Marguerite explains her plan to end the Catholic and Huguenot differences through an alliance by marriage. The nobles swear their friendship. But when Valentine is led in, Raoul withdraws his promise to the queen and indignantly refuses Valentine's hand. Valentine is completely shaken, unable to understand why Raoul has publicly shamed and scorned her. The Catholics and Huguenots renew their threats and hatred.

Act III. The action has shifted to the Près-aux-clercs along the Seine in Paris. It is Sunday, and a boisterous crowd is celebrating the day of rest. In sharp contrast to the Huguenot battle song intoned by some soldiers is the Catholic litany heard in the chapel. De Nevers has renewed his engagement to Valentine, and they are about to be married. The presence of Catholic and Huguenot soldiers has made the crowd anxious and uneasy. Tension is heightened when Marcel enters to deliver a message to St. Bris but is unable to do so when the crowd assails the old Huguenot. Momentary relief is provided by the arrival of gypsy musicians.

With the wedding of Valentine and de Nevers completed, de Nevers, St. Bris, and another Catholic, Maurevert, come out of the chapel, where Valentine, upon fulfillment of a vow, has decided to remain alone in prayer until nightfall. The men are still outraged by Raoul's reprehensible behavior toward Valentine and seek revenge. They see their opportunity when Marcel at last manages to deliver to St. Bris a message from Raoul challenging him to a duel. After Marcel leaves, the three Catholics return to the vestibule of the chapel, where they plot to ambush Raoul as he duels with St. Bris. Valentine has overheard their conversation, however, and when Marcel reappears, she reveals the plot to him and warns him to bring an armed escort to cope with the soldiers whom St. Bris will have in ambush. Valentine confesses her love for Raoul to Marcel, but because she is veiled, he does not recognize her. Impressed by her sacrifice, though, he has begun to modify his condemnation of women and wishes to convey her warning to Raoul, but the participants in the duel are already arriving. They prepare for the encounter.

St. Bris's soldiers are about to fall on Raoul when Marcel calls Raoul's followers to intervene. A street fight between the two armed groups is averted by the arrival of Marguerite and her suite. Each side accuses the other. Marcel discloses that he learned of the plot against Raoul's life from a veiled woman inside the church. Just then Valentine reappears. St. Bris tears off the veil and recognizes his daughter. Raoul is struck dumb. Marguerite finally explains the whole story of how she had sent Valentine to de Nevers to break the engagement, and Raoul realizes the error of his assumption that she was de Nevers's mistress. De Nevers then arrives on a gaily decorated barge to fetch his bride. The festivities are marred, however, by the escalating tensions between Protestants and Catholics.

Act IV. Alone, Valentine's thoughts flit from Raoul, whose love she cannot forget, to her marriage without love to de Nevers, then to her father, who insisted upon the marriage, and finally to the cruel God, who permitted such unhappiness. Raoul arrives. He has resolved to die but wishes to see Valentine once more. Suddenly she hears her father approaching and hides Raoul. St. Bris and other Catholic nobles discuss their plans to massacre the Huguenots that very night, St. Bartholomew's Eve. Only de Nevers refuses to join the conspiracy, and Valentine tells her husband she loves him for his stand against the vile plot. De Nevers yields his sword to St. Bris and is led away, a prisoner. Monks bless the swords and daggers of the assassins, and all depart to await the signal that will begin the massacre – the tolling of the bells from the church of St. Germain l'Auxerrois.

Raoul has overheard the plot. His talk of love with Valentine and their hope of running off together are ended by St. Bris's signal. They run to the window and witness the beginning of the massacre, and Raoul rushes off to help his people as Valentine faints.

Act V. Raoul, covered with blood, bursts into the hotel de Nesle, where Huguenot leaders, unaware of the massacre, are celebrating the marriage of Marguerite de Valois and Henri de Navarre. Raoul announces that Coligny, the Huguenot leader, has been killed, tells of the massacre, and summons the Huguenots to battle to avenge those already slain.

The scene shifts to a Huguenot churchyard where Raoul and Marcel have taken refuge. Valentine rushes in. She wishes to save Raoul and begs him to adopt her faith. She explains de Nevers has died trying to protect Marcel, assassinated by his own people. She is therefore free to marry Raoul. At first Raoul begins to weaken but then, under the influence of Marcel, tells her he cannot marry her if it means sacrificing his religion. Valentine thereupon resolves to become a Huguenot and die with him. Marcel blesses their union to the background of the Huguenot prayer sung by women inside the church. Suddenly the prayer is interrupted by the arrival of soldiers, and the three realize all the Huguenots inside the church are being shot. Marcel is taken up in religious ecstasy and tells Raoul and Valentine that they too will be killed and will go to a glorious heaven. Marcel's vision is so ecstatic that Raoul and Valentine join in his rapture. At the climax of their fervor, Catholic soldiers storm the yard and order the three to recant or die. The three Huguenots manage to escape into the street.

The scene changes to a street near the quais. Raoul, who has been mortally wounded, is supported by Marcel and Valentine. St. Bris and his followers approach, demanding to know their identity. Raoul, with all the strength he has left, calls out "Huguenots." St. Bris orders his men to fire. Too late he recognizes his own daughter, who dies saying she will pray for him in heaven. Marguerite appears on her way to the palace. She tries to calm the angry soldiers, but they continue to call for death and extermination, declaring it God's will.

SYNOPSIS – *LE PROPHETE*

Act I. After peasants celebrate the fine weather in front of Oberthal's castle in Dordrecht, Holland, Fidès, mother of Jean of Leyden, arrives to escort the girl, Berthe, to Leyden to marry her son. Berthe, who is a vassal to the Count, cannot leave without his consent, and Fidès accompanies Berthe to make the request. The Anabaptists – Jonas, Mathisen, and Zacharie – enter. They are leaders of the Anabaptist revolt in nearby Westphalia and have come to incite further insurrection in Holland. Beginning with a stark but rousing religious chant, they turn the peasants against their tyrannical rulers. The peasants, however, lose their fervor when they see Count Oberthal and his retinue, and the Count's soldiers chase away the Anabaptists.

Berthe and Fidès, telling the Count of the first meeting of Berthe and Jean, beg him to permit Berthe to leave for her marriage, but the Count, struck by Berthe's beauty and innocence, refuses, claiming her for himself. Fidès calls the peasants for help, but once again they are cowed by the Count and retire helplessly as Oberthal seizes Berthe and Fidès. The Anabaptists reappear, and the peasants kneel before them in prayer.

Act II. As villagers in Leyden dance at Jean's inn, the three Anabaptists enter and are struck by Jean's resemblance to a portrait of

King David which hangs in the Cathedral of Münster in their native Westphalia. Informed that Jean is extremely pious, the Anabaptists question him. Jean asks their help in explaining a strange and frightening dream he has experienced in which he is crowned and hailed as the Messiah. The Anabaptists, planning to exploit Jean for their cause, insist that Jean's dream is a prophecy and urge him to join them, promising that he shall reign. But Jean, content with the simple life of an innkeeper, and concerned only with his future happiness with Berthe, shows no interest and dismisses them. Suddenly Berthe, who has escaped from the Count, rushes in, asking that Jean hide her. He does so, but when Oberthal enters threatening to kill Fidès if Jean refuses to hand over Berthe, Jean is forced to choose between his mother and his betrothed. He chooses his mother, and Fidès blesses Jean for sacrificing Berthe in order that her life be saved. The Anabaptists return to find Jean alone, burning for revenge. They promise Jean that when he reigns as the Prophet of God, he will be empowered to avenge oppression. He therefore agrees to play the part, even agreeing to abandon mother and country to give credence to the myth of his divine origin. Hence he departs with them, without a word to anyone.

Act III. The Anabaptists and the peasant army they have enlisted have set up camp in a forest near Münster. The nobles they have taken prisoner are led in, and the Anabaptists, taunting them mercilessly, put on view their bloodthirsty fanaticism. Some peasants skate on the nearby pond, others bring provisions. There is much dancing and revelry.

The scene changes to Zacharie's tent. After Zacharie and Mathisen make plans to attack Münster the following night, Jonas brings in Oberthal as prisoner, who, unrecognizable in the dark, claims he has come to join the Anabaptists. (In reality he has been on his way to Münster to help his father defend the city against the Anabaptists.) However, he is recognized when Jonas strikes a light and is condemned to death. Jean intervenes to spare the Count's life, for he has become disgusted with his association with the Anabaptists whom he now regards as butchers. Oberthal tells Jean that Berthe has once more escaped him and is somewhere in Münster. In order to save Berthe, Jean now resolves to take Münster and states that he will leave the Count's fate to her.

At the camp, the rebel soldiers have unsuccessfully attacked Münster without Jean. In their rage they have turned against him and are calling for his death. Jean then enters and the charismatic force of his personality and his religious appeal are enough to rally the rabble to his support. They decamp to attack Münster once again.

Act IV. Jean has led his army to victory, and it now occupies Münster, forcing the citizens to hail the Prophet. Fidès has come to the city, but believing Jean dead, is now reduced to beggary. She recognizes Berthe, who is disguised as a pilgrim, and informs Berthe that Jean has been killed by the Prophet – exactly the story spread by the Anabaptists to conceal Jean's identity. Berthe vows vengeance on the Prophet.

The scene changes to the interior of the cathedral. So great is the pomp and spectacle of the coronation ceremony that Jean almost persuades himself that he really is a prophet, but reality intrudes when Fidès recognizes him and calls out to him as her son. Jean is about to run to her when Mathisen threatens to kill Fidès, in order that the myth of the Prophet's divine origin be preserved. Jean has no choice but to deny her, and regaining his composure, offers to let the people kill him if he has deceived them. When he then asks Fidès whether or not he is her son, she realizes that to save his life she must pretend she has been mistaken. Jean's authority is magnified as the people believe he has miraculously restored reason to a mad beggar.

Act V. The last act opens in a vaulted cellar in the Palace of Münster. Zacharie, Jonas, and Mathisen have decided to betray Jean, for they know that the legitimate emperor of Germany is about to retake Münster and has offered to pardon the three if they turn the Prophet over to him. When they leave, soldiers bring in Fidès, once again imprisoned. Alone, she denounces Jean, but then, overcome by maternal love, prays that God forgive him. When an officer announces that the Prophet King will appear before her, she determines to restore Jean to his true faith. She first reviles and shames him and convinces him to abandon the fanatic Anabaptists and the sacrilegious path. He finally begs his mother's pardon and at last the two are reconciled. Berthe enters, telling Fidès that she has learned that the cellar is used to store powder. She intends to set it aflame and blow up the place to destroy the Prophet and his followers. Seeing Jean there, she is overjoyed to find him. The three rejoice at being reunited, but when Berthe learns Jean is the Prophet, she is horrified and, stabbing herself, dies. Jean resolves to sacrifice his own life in carrying out Berthe's plan.

A great feast for the Anabaptists is taking place in the banquet hall of the palace. As all praise him, Jean pretends to participate in the festivity. He then tells his officers that when they see the imperial army approach, they are to close the doors and run to save themselves. When Oberthal, leading the imperial army, rushes in, Jonas, Mathisen, and Zacharie and their followers appear to betray Jean. Suddenly, with all Jean's enemies present, the flames shoot up, and the powder magazine explodes. At the moment of the explosion Fidès enters to join her son in death. The people cry out in terror. Jean and Fidès unite in praise of God as the flames consume the palace in symbolic purification.

BIBLIOGRAPHY

BOOKS

Abbate, Carolyn. The Parisian Tannhäuser. Ph.D. dissertation, Princeton University, 1984.

Adamson, Walter L. *Hegemony and Revolution: A Study of Antonio Gramsci's Political and Cultural Theory.* Berkeley: University of California Press, 1980.

Agulhon, Maurice. *Marianne au combat: l'imagerie et la symbolique républicaine de 1789 à 1880.* Paris: Flammarion, 1979.

1848 ou l'apprentissage de la république. Paris: Editions du Seuil, 1973.

La République au village. Paris: Editions du Seuil, 1970.

Une Ville Ouvrière au temps du socialisme utopique 1815–1851. Paris: Mouton et Cie., 1970.

Albert, Maurice. *Les théâtres des boulevards (1789–1848).* Paris: Société française d'imprimerie et de librairie, 1902.

Allen, James S. *Popular French Romanticism.* Syracuse, N.Y.: Syracuse University Press, 1981.

Allévy, Marie-Antoinette. *Edition critique d'une mise en scène romantique: indications générales pour la mise en scène de Henri III et sa cour* (Drame historique en cinq actes, en prose, de M. A. Dumas) par Albertin, Directeur de la scène près de Théâtre-Français (1829). Paris: Librairie E. Droz, 1938.

Appia, Adolphe. *La Musique et la mise en scène.* Bern: Theater-kultur-Verlag, 1963.

Artz, Frederick B. *France Under the Bourbon Restoration.* New York: Russell and Russell, Inc., 1931.

Arvin, Neil C. *Eugène Scribe and the French Theater, 1815–1860.* Cambridge, Mass.: Harvard University Press, 1924.

Ault, Cecil. Design, Operation, and Organization of Stage Machinery at the Paris Opera 1770–1873 Ph.D. dissertation, University of Michigan, 1983.

Bibliography

Azevedo, Alexis. G. Rossini: sa vie et ses oeuvres. Paris: Heugel et Cie., 1864.

Bakhtine, Mikhail [V. N. Volochinov] Le Marxisme et la Philosophie du langage. Paris: Les Editions de Minuit, 1977.

Balzac, Honoré de. La Comédie Humaine. Trans. by Katherine P. Wormeley. Vol. 28: Gambara. Boston: Roberts Brothers, 1896.

Bapst, Germain. Essai sur l'histoire du théâtre. Paris: Librairie Hachette et Cie., 1883.

Barry, Jackson. Dramatic Structures: The Shaping of Experience. Berkeley: University of California Press, 1970.

Bartlet, Elizabeth C. Etienne Nicholas Méhul and Opera During the French Revolution, Consulate, and Empire: A Source, Archival, and Stylistic Study. Ph.D. dissertation, University of Chicago, 1982.

Barzun, Jacques. Berlioz and the Romantic Century. 2 vols. Boston: Little, Brown, and Co., 1950.

Bastid, Paul. Les Institutions de la monarchie parlémentaire française 1814–1848. Paris: Editions de Receuil Sirey, 1954.

Baudelaire, Charles. The Painter of Modern Life and Other Essays. Greenwich, Conn.: Phaidon Pub. Inc., 1969.

Selected Writings on Art and Artists. Trans. by P. E. Charvet. Middlesex, Eng.: Penguin Books, 1972.

Beach, Vincent W. Charles X of France: His Life and Times. Boulder, Colorado: Pruitt Publishing Co., 1971.

Beck, Thomas. French Legislators 1800–1834. Berkeley: University of California Press, 1974.

Becker, Heinz. Beiträge zur Geschichte der Oper. Regensburg: Bosse, 1969.

Beckermann, Bernard. The Dynamics of Drama. New York: Columbia University Press, 1970.

Beecher, Jonathon, and Bienvenu, Richard, editors. The Utopian Vision of Charles Fourier. Boston: Beacon Press, 1972.

Bellanger, Claude, ed. Histoire générale de la presse Française. 2 Vols. Paris: Presses Universitaires de France, 1969.

Berlioz, Hector. Memoirs. Trans. and ed. by David Cairns. London: Panther Books, 1970.

Bertier de Sauvigny, G. de. La Restauration. Paris: Flammarion, 1955.

Bertrand, Gustave. Les Nationalités musicales étudiées dans le drame lyrique. Paris: Librairie Académique, 1872.

Beulé, M. L'Opéra et le drame lyrique. Paris: Michel Lévy, 1872.

Billington, James. Fire in the Minds of Men: Origins of the Revolutionary Faith. New York: Basic Books, 1980.

Blaze de Bury, Henri Ange. Meyerbeer, sa vie, ses oeuvres, et son temps. Paris: Heugel, 1865.

Musiciens du passé, du présent, et de l'avenir. Paris: Calmann Lévy, 1880.

Bibliography

Bloom, Peter, ed. *Music in Paris in the Eighteen Thirties*. Quebec: Les Presses de l'Université Laval, 1984.

de Boigne, Charles. *Petits memoires de l'Opéra*. Paris: Librairie nouvelle, 1857.

Boime, Albert. *The Academy and French Painting in the 19th Century*. New York: Phaidon Publishers, Inc., 1971.

Thomas Couture and the Eclectic Vision. New Haven: Yale University Press, 1980.

Bollème, Genevieve. *La Bible bleue*. Paris: Flammarion, 1975.

Bondois, M.P. *L'Histoire de la Restauration*. Versailles: E. Aubert, 1889.

Bossuet, Pierre. *Histoire des théâtres nationaux*. Paris: Editions et publications contemporains, n.d.

Histoire administrative des rapports des théâtres et de l'état. Paris: Imprimerie Henri Jouve, 1909.

Boucher, Maurice. *Les idées politiques de Richard Wagner*. Paris: Aubier, 1947.

Brochon, Pierre. *Béranger et son temps*. Paris: Editions sociales, 1956.

Brochon, Pierre. *La Chanson sociale de Béranger a Brassens*. Paris: Les Editions Ouvrières, 1961.

Boulouis, J. *Essai sur la politique des subventions administratives*. Paris: Hachette, 1974.

Bourdieu, Pierre. *La Distinction*. Paris: Les Éditions de Minuit, 1979.

Questions de sociologie. Paris: Les Éditions de Minuit, 1980.

Briffault, Eugene. *L'Opéra*. Paris: Ladvocat, 1834.

Brooks, Peter. *The Melodramatic Imagination*. New Haven: Yale University Press, 1976.

Brown, Frederick. *Theater and Revolution: The Culture of the French Stage*. New York: The Viking Press, 1980.

Bulletin du comité de la langue, de l'histoire, et des arts de la France. Tome premier 1852–53. Paris: Impremeur Impériale, 1853.

Bureau, Georges. *Le Théâtre et sa legislation*. Paris: Paul Ollendorff, Editeur, 1898.

Burns, Elizabeth. *Theatricality: A Study of Convention in the Theater and in Social Life*. London: Longman, 1972.

Cabrol, Charles. *Richard Wagner*. Paris: Librairie Moderne, 1981.

Campbell, Stewart. *The Second Empire Revisited: A Study in French Historiography*. New Brunswick, N.J.: Rutgers University Press, 1978.

Carlson, Marvin. *The French Stage in the Nineteenth Century*. Metuchen, N.J.: The Scarecrow Press, 1972

The Theater of the French Revolution. Ithaca, N.Y.: Cornell University Press, 1966.

Cassagne, Albert. *La Théorie de l'art pour l'art en France chez les derniers romantiques et les premiers réalistes*. Paris: Dordon, 1959.

Bibliography

Castil-Blaze, Henri [Blaze, Francois Henri Joseph]. *Dictionaire de musique moderne*. Bruxelles: A l'Académie de Musique, 1828.

Théâtres lyriques de Paris. L'Académie Impériale de Musique. Tome Second. Paris: Castil-Blaze, 1855.

Célébration du centenaire de l'Orphéon de Neuchâtel (1852–1952). Neuchâtel, 1952.

de Certeau, Michel, Julia, Dominique, and Revel, Jacques. *Une politique de la langue: la révolution française et les patois*. Paris: Gallimard, 1975.

Charnace, Guy de. *Les Compositeurs Français et les théâtres subventionnes*. Paris: E. Dentu, 1870.

Charlety, Sebastien. *Histoire du Saint-Simonisme (1825–1864)*. Paris: Editions Gonthier, 1931.

La Monarchie de Juillet. Paris: Hachette, 1921.

Charlton, D. G. *Positivist Thought in France During the Second Empire 1852–1870*. Oxford, Eng.: The Clarendon Press, 1959.

Secular Religions in France 1815–1870. London: Oxford University Press, 1963.

Chartier, Roger, ed. *Figures de la gueuserie*. Bibliothèque bleue. Paris: Montalba, 1982.

Cheruel. *Dictionnaire historique des institutions et coutumes de la France*. 2 Vols. Paris: Hachette, 1865.

Chevalier, Louis. *Classes laborieuses et classes dangereuses à Paris pendant la première moitié du XIXe siècle*. Paris: Plon, 1958.

Chinn, Genevive. The Académie Impériale de Musique: A Study of its administration and repertory from 1852 to 1870. Doctoral dissertaion, Columbia University, 1969.

Clark, Timothy J. *The Absolute Bourgeois: Artists and Politics in France 1848–1851*. London: Thames and Hudson, Ltd., 1973.

The Image of the People: Gustave Courbet and the 1848 Revolution. London: Thames and Hudson, Ltd., 1973.

Coeuroy, André. *La Musique et le peuple en France*. Paris: Editions Stock, 1941.

Cohen, Howard Robert. Berlioz and the Opera (1829–1849): A study in Music Criticism. Thesis, New York University, 1973.

Les Graveurs musicales dans l'Illustration 1843–1899. Québec: Les Presses de l'Université Laval, 1983.

La Vie musicale en France au dix-neuvième siècle: études et documents. (Forthcoming)

Cent ans de mise en scène lyrique en France (c. 1830–1930). Catalogue descriptif des livrets de mise en scène, des libretti annotés et des partitions annotés dans la Bibliothèque de l'Association de la Régie Théâtrale. (Forthcoming)

L'Opéra de Paris à l'époque romantique. (Forthcoming)

258

Bibliography

Vingt-six livrets de mise en scène datant des créations Parisienne. New York: Pendragon, 1985.

and Gigou, Marie-Odile. *Cent de mise en scène lyrique en France.* New York: Pendragon, 1985.

Cole, David. *The Theatrical Event.* Middletown, Conn.: Wesleyan University Press, 1975.

Collins, Irene, ed. *Government and Society in France.* New York: St. Martin's Press, 1971.

Colloque d'histoire littéraire, Ecole Normale Supérieur de Saint-Cloud, 1966. *Romantisme et politique 1815–1851.* Paris: A. Colin, 1969.

Comte, Auguste. *A General View of Positivism.* Trans. by J. H. Bridges, 1848; reprint ed., Stanford, Calif.: Academic Reprints, 1953.

Cooper, Jeffrey. *The Rise of Instrumental Music and Concert Series in Paris 1828–71.* Ann Arbor, Mich.: U.M.I. Research Press, 1983.

Cooper, Martin. *Ideas and Music,* Philadelphia: Chitton Books, 1967.

Opéra Comique. London: Max Parish and Co. Limited, 1949.

Coudroy, Marie-Hélène. Les Créations de Robert le Diable et Les Huguenots de Meyerbeer à la Critique. Conservatoire Nationale Supérieur de Musique de Paris. Thèse de Musicologie, 1979.

Croston, William. *French Grand Opera: An Art and a Business.* New York: Kings Crown Press, 1948.

Crozet, Félix. *Revue de la musique dramatique en France.* Grenoble: Imprimerie de Prudhomme, 1866.

Crubellier, Maurice. *Histoire culturelle de la France, XIX–XXe siècles.* Paris: A. Colin, 1974.

Culler, Jonathan. *Flaubert: The Uses of Uncertainty.* Ithaca: Cornell University Press, 1974.

Curzon, Henri de. *L'Oeuvre de Richard Wagner à Paris et ses interprètes 1850–1914.* Maurice Senart et Cie., 1920.

Meyerbeer. Paris: H. Laurens, n.d.

Dahlhaus, Carl, ed. *Musikalische Hermeneutik.* Regensburg: Gustave Bosse Verlag, 1975.

Richard Wagner's Music Dramas. Cambridge: Cambridge University Press, 1971.

Danto, Arthur C. *The Transfiguration of the Commonplace.* Cambridge, Mass.: Harvard University Press, 1981.

Darmon, Jean-Jacques. *Le Colportage de librairie en France sous le Second Empire.* Paris: Plon, 1972.

Daumard, Adeline. *Les Bourgeois de Paris au XIXe siècle.* Paris: Flammarion, 1970.

Dauriac, Lionel. *La Dramaturgie de Meyerbeer.* Paris: Durlacher, 1911.

Meyerbeer. Paris, 1913.

La Psychologie dans l'opéra français (Auber, Rossini, Meyerbeer). Paris:

259

Bibliography

Ancienne Librairie Germer, Ballière et Cie., Félix Alcan Editeur, 1897.

Dent, Edward. *The Rise of Romantic Opera*. Ed. by Winton Dean. New York: Cambridge University Press, 1976.

Desarbres, Nérée. *Deux siècles à l'Opéra 1669–1869*. Paris: E. Dentu, Editeur, 1869.

Deshayes, A. *Idées générales sur l'Académie Royale de Musique et plus spécialement sur la dance*. Paris: Chez Mongir, 1822.

Descotes, Maurice. *Le Public de théâtre et son histoire*. Paris, 1964.

Desnoyers, Louis. *De l'Opéra en 1847: à propos de Robert Bruce: des directeurs passés, de la direction présente*. Paris: Imprimerie de E.-B. Delanchy, 1847.

Destranges, Etienne. *L'Oeuvre théâtrale de Meyerbeer*. Paris: Fishbacher, 1893.

Dollot, Rene. *Une Chronique de la Restauration: Stendhal correspondant des revues anglaises (1822–1829)*. Grenoble: Imprimerie Albier, 1943–44.

Donokowski, Conrad. *A Muse for the Masses: Ritual and Music in an Age of Democratic Revolution*. Chicago: University of Chicago Press, 1977.

Draper, F. W. M. *The Rise and Fall of the French Romantic Drama*. London: Constable and Co., Ltd., 1923.

Drexler, Arthur, ed. *The Architecture of the Ecole des Beaux-Arts*. New York: The Museum of Modern Art; distributed by the MIT Press, Cambridge, Mass., 1977.

Dubois, Jean. *Le Vocabulaire politique et sociale en France de 1869 à 1872*. Paris: Librairie Larousse, 1962.

Duveau, Georges. *La Pensée ouvrière sur l'éducation pendant la Second République et le Second Empire*. Paris: Domat Montchrestien, 1948. *1848*. Paris: Gallimard, 1965.

Duvignaud, Jean. *Les Ombres Collective; sociologie du théâtre*. Paris: Presses Universitaires de France, 1973.

Eckhardt-Bäker, Ursula von. *Frankreichs Musik zwischen Romantik und Moderne. Bande 2. Studien zur Musikgesschichte des 19. Jahrhunderts*. Regensburg: Gustave Bosse, 1965.

Eckhardt, Hans. *Die Musikanschauung der Französichen Romantik*. Kassel: Bärenreiter-verlag, 1935.

Egbert, Donald Drew. *Social Radicalism and the Arts*. New York: Alfred Knopf, 1970.

Eggli, Edmond, and Martino, Pierre. *Le Débat romantique en France*. Tome I: 1813–1816, par Edmond Eggli. Paris: Société d'édition "Les Belles Lettres," 1933.

Eggli, Eva. *Probleme der Musikalischen Wertästhetik im 19. Jahrhundert*. Winterthur: P. G. Keller, 1965.

260

Bibliography

Escudier, Leon. *Dictionnaire de Musique*. Paris: Michel Lévy, 1854.

Evans, David Owens. *Social Romanticism in France 1830–1848*. Oxford, Eng.: The Clarendon Press, 1951.

Evans, Raymond. *Les Romantiques français et la musique*. Paris: Librairie Ancienne Honoré Champion, 1934.

Faris, Alexander. *Jacques Offenbach*. New York: Charles Scribner's Sons, 1980.

Fétis, Edouard. *L'Art dans la société et dans l'état*. In *Memoires couronnés et autres mémoires*. Tome XXII. Bruxelles: Imprimeur de l'Académie Royale, 1972.

Fillonneau, Ernest. *Les Concerts de Paris: revue de la saison musicale de 1860*. Paris: Jules Tardieu, 1860.

Flaubert, Gustave. *Madame Bovary*. Paris: Editions Garnier Frères, 1961.

Fleury, Jules [Champfleury]. *Le Réalisme*. Textes choisie et présentés par Genviève et Jean Lecambre. Paris: Collection S. Hermann, 1973.

Richard Wagner. Paris: Librairie Nouvelle, 1860.

Grandes figures d'hier et d'aujord'hui: Balzac, Gérard de Nerval, Wagner, Courbet. Paris: Poulet-Malassis et de Broise, 1861.

Chansons populaires des provinces de France. Paris: Jules Tardieu, 1860.

Fox, Edward. *L'Autre France*. Paris: Flammarion, 1973.

Frese, Christhard. *Dramaturgie der grossen Opern Giacomo Meyerbeers*. Berlin-Lichterfelde: Robert Lienau, 1970.

Friguglietti, James, and Kennedy, Emmet, ed. *The Shaping of Modern France: Writings from French History Since 1715*. London: Collier-Macmillan Limited, 1969.

Fromich, Yane. *Musique et caricature en France au XIXe siècle*. Genève: Editions Minkhoff, 1973.

Fulcher, Jane. Musical Aesthetics and Social Philosophy in France 1848–1870. Ph.D. dissertation, Columbia University, 1977.

Fûret, François. *Penser la Révolution française*. Paris: Editions Gallimard, 1978.

Gail, J. F. *Réflections sur le goût musical en France*. Paris: Paulin, 1832.

Galimard, Auguste. *Examen du Salon de 1849*. Paris: Gide et J. Baudry, Editeurs, 1849.

Garnier, Charles. *Le Théâtre*. Paris: Hachette, 1871.

Le Nouvel Opéra de Paris. Ducher et Cie., 1876–80.

Gasperini, Auguste de. *De la Nouvelle Allemagne musicale: Richard Wagner*. Paris: Le Ménestrel, 1866.

Gautier, Theophile. *Ecrivains et artistes romantiques*. Paris: Librairie Plon, 1933.

Janin, Jules, et Philarete, Charles. *Les Beautés de l'Opéra*. Paris: Soulié, Editeur, 1845.

Gay, Peter. *Art and Act: On Causes in History: Manet, Gropius, Mondrian*. New York: Harper and Row, 1976.

Bibliography

Geertz, Clifford. *The Interpretation of Cultures*. New York: Basic Books, Inc., 1973.

Negara: the Theater State in 19th Century Bali. Princeton, N.J.: Princeton University Press, 1980.

George, A.J. *The Development of French Romanticism*. Syracuse, N.Y.: Syracuse University Press, 1955.

Gerard, Alice. *Le Second Empire. Innovation et réaction*. Paris: Presses Universitaires de France, 1973.

Gibson, Robert W. *Meyerbeer's Le Prophète: A Study in Operatic Style*. Dissertation, Northwestern University, 1972.

Girard, Henri. *Emile Deschamps dilettante*. Paris: Librairie Ancienne Honoré Champion, 1921.

Goncourt, Edmond. *Paris and the Arts 1851–1896: from the Goncourt Journal*. Ed. and trans. by George Becker and Edith Philios. Ithaca, N.Y.: Cornell University Press, 1971.

Grana, Cesar. *Bohemian Versus Bourgeios: French Society and the French Man of Letters in the Nineteenth Century*. New York: Basic Books, Inc., 1964.

Gross, Roger. *Understanding Playscripts*. Bowling Green, Ohio: Bowling Green University Press, 1974.

Gros, J.-M. *Le Mouvement littéraire socialiste depuis 1830*. Paris: Albin Michel, 1904.

Gourret, Jean. *Histoire de l'Opéra de Paris 1869–1971*. Paris: Les Publications Universitaires, 1977.

Les Hommes qui one fait l'Opéra 1669–1984. Paris: Editions Albatros, 1984.

Grove. *The New Grove Dictionary of Music and Musicians*. 20 Vols. Ed. by Stanley Sadie. S.v. "Meyerbeer," by Heinz Becker, "Opera, France," "Opera," and "Stage Design."

Guest, Ivor. *The Romantic Ballet in Paris*. Middletown, Conn.: Wesleyan University Press, 1966.

Guex, Jules. *Le Théâtre et la société française de 1815 à 1848*. Genève: Slatkine Reprints, 1973 (reimpression of l'Edition de Vevey, 1900).

Guichard, Leon. *La Musique et les lettres au temps du Wagnérisme*. Paris: Presses Universitaires de France, 1963.

Hallays-Dabot, Victor. *Histoire de la censure théâtrale en France*. Genève: Slatkine Reprints, 1970 (reimpression of l'Edition de Paris, 1862).

Hanslick, Eduard. *Die Moderne Oper*. Berlin: A. Hofmann, 1880.

Hemmings, F. W. J. *Culture and Society in France 1848–1896*. New York: Charles Scribner's Sons, 1971.

Hervey, Arthur. *French Music in the 19th Century*. London: Grant Richards, 1903.

Holtman, Robert B. *Napoleonic Propaganda*. Baton Rouge: Louisiana State University Press, 1950.

262

Bibliography

Holquist, Michael, and Katerina Clark. *Mikhail Bakhtin. A Biography.* Cambridge, Mass.: Harvard University Press, 1984.

Horowicz, Bronislaw. *Le Théâtre de l'Opéra.* Editions d'Aujourd'hui, Editions Pierre Horay, 1976.

Huet, Marie-Hélène. *Rehearsing the Revolution: The Staging of Marat's Death 1793–1797.* Trans. by Robert Hurley. Berkeley: University of California Press, 1982.

Huizinga, Johan. *The Waning of the Middle Ages.* Garden City, N.J.: Doubleday Anchor Books. 1954.

Hunt, H. J. *Le Socialisme et le romantisme en France.* Oxford, Eng.: Clarendon Press, 1935.

Imbert de Saint-Amand, Arthur Léon. *Le Règne de Napoléon III.* Paris: Librairie Dentu, 1861.

Iser, Wolfgang. *The Implied Reader.* Baltimore: Johns Hopkins Press, 1974.

Isherwood, Robert. *Music in the Service of the King: France in the Seventeenth Century.* Ithaca, N.Y.: Cornell University Press, 1973.

Jauss, Hans. *Pour une esthétique de la réception.* Traduit par Claude Maillard. Paris: Gallimard, 1975.

Jouhaud, Christian. *Mazarinades: la Fronde des Mots.* Paris: Aubier, 1985.

Jouvin, B. *D. F. E. Auber. Sa vie et ses oeuvres.* Paris: Heugel et Cie., 1864.

Jullien, Adolphe. *Paris dilettante au commencement du siècle.* Paris: Librairie de Firmin-Didot et Cie., 1884.

Kaes, Rene. *Images de la culture chez les ouvriers français.* Paris: Editions Cujas, n.d.

Kapp, Julius. *Meyerbeer.* Berlin: Schuster u. Loeffler, 1920.

Krakovitch, Odile. *Hugo Censuré: la liberté au théâtre au XIXe siècle.* Paris: Calmann-Levy, 1985.

LaCapra, Dominick. *Madame Bovary on Trial.* Ithaca, N.Y.: Cornell University Press, 1982.

Laforet, Claude [Bonnet-Roy, Flavien]. *La Vie musicale au temps romantique: salons, théâtres, et concerts.* New York: Da Capo Press, 1977 (first edition, Paris, 1929).

Large, David C., and Weber, William, eds. *Wagnerism in European Culture and Politics.* Ithaca, N.Y.: Cornell University Press, 1984.

Lang, Jack. *L'Etat et le théâtre.* Thèse pour le doctorat en droit, Université de Nancy. Paris: Librairie Générale de droit et de jurisprudence, 1968.

La Laurencie, Lionel de. *Le Goût musical en France.* Paris, 1905; Genève: Slatkine Reprints, 1970.

Lasalle, Albert de, et Raquet, Antoine. *La Musique à Paris.* Paris: Morizot, 1863.

263

Bibliography

Lasalle, Albert de. *Meyerbeer, sa vie et catalogue de ses oeuvres.* Paris, 1864.

Les Treize salles de l'Opéra. Paris: Librairie Sartouris, 1875.

Laudon, Robert. *Sources of the Wagnerian Synthesis: A Study of the Franco-German Tradition in 19th Century Opera.* Munich: Musikverlag Emil Katzbicher, 1979.

Lavignac, Albert. *Encyclopédie de la musique et dictionnaire du Conservatoire.* Premiere Partie. Paris: Librairie Delagrave, 1914.

Lagrave, H. *Le Théâtre et le public à Paris de 1715 à 1750.* Paris, 1972.

Lasserre, Pierre. *L'Esprit de la musique française de Rameau a l'invasion Wagnerienne.* Paris: Librairie Payot et Cie., 1917.

Lavoix, H. *Histoire de l'instrumentation.* Paris: Firmin-Didot, 1878.

Legouvé, Ernest. *Eugène Scribe.* Paris: Librairie Académique, 1874.

Soixante ans de souvenirs. Paris: J. Hetzel, 1886.

Leith, James A. *Media and Revolution: Moulding a New Citizenry in France During the Terror.* Canadian Broadcasting Corporation, Toronto, 1968.

The Idea of Art as Propaganda in France 1750–1799. Toronto: University of Toronto Press, 1965.

Lejeune, Andre, et Wolff, Stephane. *Les Quinze salles de l'Opéra de Paris 1669–1955.* Paris: Librairie Théâtrale, 1955.

Leroy, Maxime. *Les Premiers amis français de Wagner.* Paris: Albin Michel, 1925.

Levine, Neil. Architectural Reasoning in the Age of Positivism. The Neo-Grec Idea of Henri Labrouste's Bibliothèque Sainte-Geneviève. Thesis, Yale University, 1975.

L'homme, Jean. *La Grande bourgeoisie au pouvoir (1830–1880): essai sur l'histoire sociale de la France.* Paris: Presses Universitaires de France, 1960.

Lindenberger, Herbert. *Historical Drama. The Relation of Literature and Reality.* Chicago: University of Chicago Press, 1975.

Locke, Ralphe. Music in the Saint-Simonian Movement. Dissertaion, University of Chicago, 1981.

Loncke, Joycelynne. *Baudelaire et la musique.* Paris: Editions A.-G. Nizet, 1975.

Lossier, Jean-G. *Le Rôle sociale de l'art selon Proudhon.* Paris: Les Presses Moderns, 1937.

Lough, John. *Paris Theater Audiences in the Seventeenth and Eighteenth Centuries.* Oxford: Oxford University Press, 1957.

Lucas-Dubreton, Jean. *The Restoration and the July Monarchy.* New York: G.P. Putnam's Sons, 1929.

Manuel, Frank E. *The Prophets of Paris.* Cambridge, Mass.: Harvard University Press, 1962.

Maréchal, Henri. *Monographie universelle de l'Orphéon.* Paris: Delagrave, 1910.

264

Bibliography

Martino, Pierre. *L'Epoch romantique en France 1815–1830*. Paris: Boivin, 1944.

Marx, Karl. *The Revolutions of 1848*. Edited and introduced by David Fernbach. Penguin Books, 1973.

Matoré, Georges. *Le Vocabulaire et la société sous Louis-Philippe*. Genève: Droz, 1951.

Mayer, Arno. *The Persistence of the Old Regime: Europe to the Great War*. New York: Pantheon Books, 1981.

Merriman, John, ed. *Consciousness and Class Experience in Nineteenth-Century Europe*. New York: Holmes and Meier Pub., Inc., 1979.

1830 in France. New York: New Viewpoints, a division of Franklin Watts, 1975.

The Agony of the Republic: The Repression of the Left in Revolutionary France 1848–51. New Haven: Yale University Press, 1978.

Meyerbeer, Giacomo. *Briefwechsel und Tagebücher*. 3 Vols. Berlin: Verlag Walter de Gruyter & Co., 1970.

Journal. Bibliothèque de l'Opéra Réserve pièce 35 (9, 10).

Mirecourt, Eugene de. *Meyerbeer*. Paris, 1858.

Morazé, Charles. *The Triumph of the Middle Classes*. London: Weidenfeld and Nicolson, 1966.

Mosse, George. *The Nationalization of the Masses. Political Symbolism and Mass Movements in Germany from the Napoleonic Wars through the Third Reich*. New York: Howard Fertig, 1975.

Mouzin, Pierre. *Metz. Ecole de musique: succursale du Conservatoire Impériale* (1858).

Muret, Théodore. *L'Histoire par le théâtre 1789–1851*. Paris: Amyot, 1865.

Needham, H. H. *Le Développement de l'esthétique sociologique en France et en Angleterre au XIX siècle*. Paris: Librairie Ancienne Honoré Champion, 1926.

Niggli, A. *Giacomo Meyerbeer: Sein Leben und seine Werke*. Sammlung Musikakischen Vortraege »57 ed. Paul O. Waldusse.

Nochlin, Linda. *Realism*. Middlesex, Eng.: Penguin Books, 1971.

ed., *Realism and Tradition in Art 1848–1900*. Sources and Documents in the History of Art Series. Englewood Cliffs, N.J.: Prentice-Hall, Inc., 1966.

Nolte, Nancy. Government and Theater in Nineteenth-Century France: Administrative Organization for Control in the Comedie-Française Repertoire. Ph.D. Dissertation, University of Akron, 1984.

Noske, Frits. *French Song from Berlioz to Duparc: The Origin and Development of the Mélodie*. Trans by Rita Benton. New York: Dover Publications, 1970.

Nouty, Hassan. *Théâtre et pré-cinéma*. Paris: Editions A.-G. Nizet, 1978.

Nouvelle Biographie générale. Paris: Frimin Didot Frères, 1968.

265

Bibliography

Orgel, Stephen. *The Illusion of Power: Political Theater in the English Renaissance*. Berkeley: University of California Press, 1975.

d'Ortigue, Joseph. *De la Guerre des dilettanti ou de la révolution opérée par M. Rossini dans l'opéra française*. Paris: la Librairie de Ladvocat, 1829.

De l'Ecole musicale Italienne et de l'administration de l'Académie Royale de Musique a l'occasion de l'opéra de M. H. Berlioz. Paris: Imprimerie de Pollet, Soupe, et Grullois, 1839.

Le Balcon de l'Opéra. Paris: Librairie D'Eugène Renduel, 1833.

Ozouf, Mona. *L'Ecole de la France*. Paris: Gallimard, 1984.

La Fête révolutionnaire, 1789–1799. Paris: Gallimard, 1976.

Pallianti, L. *Petits archives des théâtres de Paris. Souvenirs de dix ans. Théâtre Impérial de l'Opéra*. Paris: Gosselin, 1865.

Parent-Lardeur, Françoise. *Lire à Paris. Les cabinets de lecture à Paris 1815–1830*. Paris: Editions de l'Ecole des Hautes Etudes en Sciences Sociales, 1981.

Paret, Peter. *The Berlin Secession: Modern Art and its Enemies in Imperial Germany*. Cambridge, Mass.: Harvard University Press, 1980.

Pendle, Karin. Eugène Scribe and French Opera in the Nineteenth Century. Thesis, University of Illinois, 1970.

Peyre, Henri. *What Is Romanticism?* Trans. Roda Roberts. University of Alabama Press, 1977.

Pinkney, David H. *The French Revolution of 1830*. Princeton, N.J.: Princeton University Press, 1972.

Napoleon III and the Rebuilding of Paris. Princeton, N.J.: Princeton University Press, 1958.

Pléssis, Alain, *De la fête impériale au mur des fédérés 1852–1871*. Paris: Editions du Seuil, 1979.

Pocock, J. G. A. *Politics, Language, and Time*. New York: Atheneum, 1971.

Pontécoulant (le vicomte de) et Ed. Fournier. *La Musique chez le peuple ou l'Opéra National: son passé et son avenir sur le boulevard du Temple*. Paris: Chez Garnier Frères, 1847.

Ponteil, Féliz. *Les Institutions de la France de 1814 à 1870*. Paris: Presses Universitaires de France, 1966.

Pougin, A. *Meyerbeer*. Paris: J. Tresse, 1864.

Price, Roger, ed. *Revolution and Reaction: 1848 and the Second French Republic*. London: Barnes and Noble, 1975.

Prod'homme, Jacques-Gabriel. *L'Opéra 1669–1925*. Paris: Librairie Delagrave, 1925.

Proudhon, Pierre-Joseph. *Les Confessions d'un révolutionnaire pour servir a l'histoire de la révolution de février*. Paris: Garnier Frères, 1850.

Selected Writings of P.-J. Proudhon. Ed. by Stewart Edwards. Trans. by

266

Bibliography

Elizabeth Fraser. Garden City, N.J.: Anchor Books; Doubleday and Co., Inc., 1969.

Oeuvres complètes de P.-J. Proudhon. Nouvelle Edition, publiée sous la direction de M.M. C. Bougle et H. Moysset. Tome 15: *Du principe de l'art et de sa destination sociale.* Paris: Marcel Rivière et companie, 1939.

Raynor, Henry. *Music and Society Since 1815.* New York: Schocken Books, 1976.

Récueil des costumes de tous les ouvrages dramatique représentés avec succès sur les grands théâtres de Paris. Paris: Vizentini, n.d.

Récueil pout la Commission Spécial des Théâtres Royaux (n.d.) [18?].

Rémond, René. *The Right Wing in France: From 1815 to de Gaulle.* Philadelphia: University of Pennsylvania Press, 1971.

Rochefoucauld, Sosthene de la. *Mémoires.* Paris: Michel Levy, n.d.

Rolland, Joachim. *Les Comédies politiques d'Eugène Scribe.* Paris: E. Sansat et Cie., 1912.

Rosselli, John. *The Opera Industry in Italy from Cimarosa to Verdi.* New York: Cambridge University Press, 1984.

Roqueplan, Nestor. *Les Coulisses de l'Opéra.* Paris: Librairie Nouvelle, 1855.

Rosenthal, Léon. *Du Romantisme au Réalisme: essai sur l'évolution de la peinture en France de 1830 à 1848.* Paris: Librairie Renouard, 1914.

Royer, Alphonse. *Histoire de l'Opéra.* Paris: Bachelin-Delflorenne Editeur, 1975.

Runyan, William. *Orchestration in Five French Grand Operas.* Ph.D. dissertation, University of Rochester, The Eastman School of Music, 1983.

Sandblad, Nils. *Manet; Three Studies in Artistic Conception.* Lund: C. W. K. Gleerup, 1954.

Schechner, Richard. *Essays in Performance Theory.* New York: Drama Book Specialists, 1977

Ritual, Play, and Performance. New York: Seabury Press, 1976.

Schrade, Leo. *Beethoven in France.* New Haven: Yale University Press, 1942.

Schuré, Edouard. *Le Drame musical.* 2 Vols. Tome II. *Richard Wagner.* Paris: Sandoz et Fishbacher, Editeurs, 1875.

Scudo, Paul. *Critique et littérature musicale.* Paris: Librairie de L. Hachette et Companie, 1856.

Séchan, Charles. *Souvenirs d'un homme du théâtre 1831–55.* Paris: Calmann Lévy, 1883.

Segalini, Sergio. *Meyerbeer.* Paris: Bebo, n.d.

Servières, Georges. *Richard Wagner jugé en France.* Paris: La Librairie Illustrée, 1887.

Bibliography

Sewell, William H. Jr. *Work and Revolution in France. The Language of Labor from the Old Regime to 1848.* London: Cambridge University Press, 1980.

Sloane, Joseph C. *French Painting Between the Past and the Present.* Princeton, N.J.: Princeton University Press, 1951.

Soubies, Albert. *Soixante-sept ans a l'Opéra en un page: au 'Siège de Corinthe' à 'Les Walküries' (1826–1893).* Paris: Librairie Fishbacher, 1893.

Soubies, Albert. *Histoire de l'Opéra-Comique 1860–1887.* Paris: Librairie Ernest Flammarion, 1893.

Spector, Jack. *Delacroix: The Death of Sardanapalus.* New York: Viking Press, 1974.

Stendhal, [Beyle, M.-H.]. *Vie de Rossini.* Préface de V. Del Litto. Lausanne: Editions Recontre, 1960.

Styan, J. L. *Elements of Drama.* Cambridge: Cambridge University Press, 1963.

Suleiman, Ezra N. *Politics. Power, and Bureaucracy in France: The Administrative Elite.* Princeton, N.J.: Princeton University Press, 1974.

Swart, Koenraad. *The Sense of Decadence in Nineteenth-Century France.* The Hague: Martinus Nijhoff, 1964.

Therien, Nathan. Popular Song Entertainment as Social Experience and the Failure of Participatory Culture in France 1815–1914. Dissertation in progress, Harvard University.

Thomson, Joan Lewis. Meyerbeer and his Contemporaries. Doctoral dissertation, Columbia University, 1972.

Thompson, J. M. *Louis Napoleon and the Second Empire.* New York: W. W. Norton and Co., Inc., 1967.

Tocqueville, Alexis de. *Souvenirs.* Paris: Gallimard, 1978.

Touraine, Alain. *Production de la société.* Paris: Editions du Seuil, 1973.

Toyon, Paul de. *La Musique en 1864: documents relatifs à l'art musical.* Paris: Arnauld de Vress, 1866.

Turner, Victor. *Dramas, Fields, and Metaphors: Symbolic Action in Human Society.* Ithaca, N.Y.: Cornell University Press, 1974.

From Ritual to Theater. New York: Performing Arts Journal Publications, 1982.

Van Tieghm, Philippe. *Le Romantisme française.* Paris: Presses Universitaires de France, 1944.

Véron, Dr. L. *Mémoirs d'un bourgeois de Paris.* Paris: Librairie Nouvelle, 1856.

(Député et membre du Conseil Général de la Seine). *Paris en 1860: les théâtres de Paris depuis 1806 jusqu'en 1860.* Paris: Librairie Nouvelle, 1860.

Wagner, Richard. *Prose Works.* Trans. by William Ellis. London: Kegan, Paul, Trench, Trubner and Co., 1892–99.

Bibliography

Wagner, Richard. *Wagner Writes from Paris: Stories, Essay, and Articles by the Young Composer.* Ed. and trans. by Robert L. Jacobs and Geoffrey Skelton. New York: Harper and Row, 1960.

Walsh, T. J. *Second Empire: The Théâtre Lyrique, Paris 1851–1870.* London: John Cader, 1981.

Weber, Johannes. *Meyerbeer. Notes et souvenirs d'un de ses sécrétaires.* Paris: Fishbacher, 1898.

Weber, William. *Music and the Middle Class: The Social Structure of Concert Life in London, Paris, and Vienna.* London: Crooms Helm, 1975.

Weinstock, Robert. *Donizetti and the World of Opera in Italy, Paris, and Vienna in the First Half of the Nineteenth Century.* New York: Pantheon Books, 1963.

Weisberg, Gabriel. *The Realist Tradition: French Painting and Drawing 1830–1900.* Cleveland: Cleveland Museum of Art, 1980.

Weiss, J.-J. *Le Théâtre et les moeurs.* Paris: Calmann-Lévy, 1889.

Williams, Roger. *Gaslight and Shadow: The World of Napoleon III.* New York: Macmillan, 1957.

Wright, Gordon. *France in Modern Times.* Chicago: Rand McNally Publishing, Inc., 1974.

Zeldin, Theodore, ed. *Conflicts in French Society.* London: George Allen and Unwin Ltd., 1970.

France 1848–1945. 2 Vols. Oxford: Clarendon Press, 1977.

JOURNALS CONSULTED (Nineteenth-Century France)

L'Ami du prolétaire

L'Atelier

Le Caricature

Le Charivari

Le Constitutionnel

La France Chorale (Moniteur des Orphéons et des sociétés instrumentales)

La France Musicale

La Gazette de France

Le Globe

L'Illustration

Le Journal des débats

Mère Duchêne

Le Moniteur Universelle

Le Nouveau journal de Paris

L'Orphéon

Le Peuple (1869)

La Phalange

Bibliography

La Quotidienne
La Réforme Théâtrale
Le Représentant du Peuple
Revue et Gazette Musicale de Paris
La Saison Musicale
Le Temps
Le Travailleur
La Voix du Peuple

ARTICLES

Alison, J. M. S. "The Political and Social Background of Naturalism." In *Courbet and the Naturalist Movement,* ed. by George Boas. Baltimore: Johns Hopkins Press, 1938.

Aulard, François V. A. "La querelle de *La Marseillaise* et du *Réveil du peuple.*" Etudes et leçons sur la Révolution française. 3e série. Paris: Félix Alcan, 1902.

Bailbé, Joseph-Marc. "Les Représentations Parisiennes du *Prophète* de Meyerbeer." *Revue internationale du musique française,* »3 (1980).

Baker, Keith. "French Political Thought at the Accession of Louis XVI." *The Journal f Modern History* 1978, pp. 279–303.

Becker, Heinz. "Die historische Bedeutung der Grand Opera." In Walter Salmen, ed. *Beiträge zur Geschichte der Musikanschauung im 19. Jahrhundert.* Regensburg: Bosse, 1965.

"Der Marcel von Meyerbeer." *Jahrbuch des Staatlichen Institut für Musikforschung-Preussischer Kulturbesite* 1978/80, pp. 79–100.

Bellaigue, Camille. "Les Epoques de la musique: le grand Opéra français." *Revue des deux mondes,* 1906.

Bernard, Elizabeth. "L'Evolution du public de l'Opéra de 1860 à 1880." In *Regards sur l'Opera:* Centre d'Art, Esthétique, et Littérature. Paris: Presses Universitaires de France, 1976.

Besnier, Patrick. "Berlioz et Meyerbeer." *Revue de musicologie* LXIII (1977), pp. 35–40.

Bloom, Peter. "Friends and Admirers: Meyerbeer and Fétis." *Revue Belge de Musicologie* 1978/79.

Bourgault-Ducoudray, L. A. "Meyerbeer, souvenirs d'autrefois." *La Revue musicale* IV (1904), pp. 452–5.

Chartier, Roger. "Livres bleus et lectures populaires." In *Histoire de l'Edition Française.* Paris: Promodis, 1984. Tome II *Le Livre triomphant 1660–1830.*

Claudon, Francis. "G. Meyerbeer et V. Hugo: dramaturgies comparées." In *Regards sur l'Opera* (see above).

270

Bibliography

Cobban, Alfred. "The 'Middle Class' in France, 1815–1848." *French Historical Studies* V (Spring 1967): 39–52.

Cohen, H. Robert. "Les Gravures musicales dans *l'Illustration*." *Revue de Musicologie* Tome LXII (1976).

"Les livrets de mise en scène et la Bibliothèque de l'association de la Régie Théâtrale." *Revue de Musicologie* 1978.

"On the Reconstruction of the Visual Element of French Grand Opera: Unexplored Sources in Parisian Collections." *International Musicological Society Report,* Berkeley, 1977.

Combarieu, J. "Bibliographie des oeuvres de G. Meyerbeer; quelques lettres inédites." *Revue musicale* IV (1904), pp. 433–52.

Cooper, Martin. "Opera in France." In *The New Oxford History of Music* Vol. VII. London: Oxford University Press, 1973.

Curzon, Henri de. "L'Opéra en 1843: mémoire du Directeur Léon Pillet." *Revue de Musicologie* 1921.

Debofle, Pierre. "Théâtre et société à Paris sous la Restauration." *Bulletin de la Société de l'histoire de Paris et de l'Ile-de-France* 1974–75.

Dean, Winton. "Meyerbeer's Italian Operas." In *Music and Bibliography. Essays in Honor of Alec Hyatt King.* Oliver Neighbor, ed., New York: K. G. Saur, 1980.

"Opera Under the French Revolution." *Proceedings of the Royal Musical Association* 1967–68.

Döhrung, Sieghart. "Die Autographen der vier Hauptopern Meyerbeers: Ein erster Quellenbericht." *Archiv für Musikwissenschaft* 39 (1982), pp. 32–63.

Eckart-Bäker, Ursula. "Der Einfluss des Positivismus auf die französische Musikkritik im 19. Jahrhundert." In Heinz Becker, ed., *Beiträge zur Geschichte der Musikkritik.* Regensburg: Bosse, 1965.

Darnton, Robert. "Revolution sans Revolutionaries." *The New York Review of Books* Jan 31, 1985, pp. 21–3.

Esler, Anthony. "Youth in Revolt: The French Generation of 1830." In *Modern European Social History,* ed. by Robert Bezucha. Lexington, Mass.: D. C. Heath, 1972.

Fischer, David J. "The Origins of the French Popular Theater." *Journal of Contemporary History* 12 (1977).

Fétis, F.-J. "Robert le Diable." *Revue Musicale,* 1831.

"Le Prophète." *Revue et Gazette Musicale,* 22 avril 1849.

Foucault, Michel. "The Subject and Power." *Critical Inquiry,* Summer 1982.

Froger, Béatrice, et Sylvaine, Hans. "La Comédie-Française au XIX siècle: un repertoire littéraire et politique." *Revue d'histoire du théâtre* 13 (1983): 260–75.

Fulcher, Jane. "Current Perspective on Culture and the Meaning of Cul-

Bibliography

tural History in France Today." *The Stanford French Review*, Spring 1985.

"The Chanson Populaire of the Second Empire: 'Music of the Peasants' in France." *Acta Musicologica* Vol LII (1981), Fasc. I.

"French Grand Opera and the Quest for a National Image: An Approach to the Study of State-Sponsored Art." *Current Musicology* »35.

"Melody and Morality: Rousseau's Influence on French Music Criticism." *International Review of the Aesthetics and Sociology of Music* Vol. II (1980).

"Meyerbeer and the Music of Society During the Monarchy of July." *The Musical Quarterly* April 1981.

"Music and the Communal Order: the Vision of Utopian Socialism in France." *Current Musicology*, Summer 1979.

"The Orphéon Societies: Music for the Workers in Second-Empire France." *International Review of the Aesthetics and Sociology of Music* Vol. X »1 (1979).

"Utopie Philosophique et la critique musicale à tendence conservatrice en France." *Revue Internationale de musique française*, juin 1984.

"Wagner, Comte, and Proudhon: the Aesthetics of Positivism in France." *Symposium*, Summer 1979.

"Wagner as Democrat and Realist in France." *Stanford French Review*, Spring 1981.

Fûret, François. "Naissance d'un paradigme: Tocqueville et le voyage en Amerique (1825–1831). *Annales. Economies, sociétés, civilisations*, mars–avril 1984, pp. 225–39.

Gay, Peter. "On the Bourgeoisie: a Psychological Interpretation." In John Merriman, ed. *Consciousness and Class Experience in Nineteenth-Century Europe*. New York: Homes and Meier Pub., Inc., 1979.

Geertz, Clifford. "Art as a Cultural System." *Modern Language Notes* 91 (1976).

"Centers, Kings, and Charisma: Reflections on the Symbolics of Power." In *Culture and Its Creators: Essays in Honor of Edward Shils*, ed. by Joseph Ben-David and Terry N. Clark. Chicago: University of Chicago Press, 1977.

Grandville, Fréderic. "Le Conservatoire et la République de 1848." *Revue internationale de musique française*, no. 3 (1980).

Isherwood, Robert. "Entertainment in the Parisian Fairs in the Eighteenth Century." *The Journal of Modern History*, March 1981.

Istel, Edgar. "Act IV of *Les Huguenots*." *The Musical Quarterly* 1936.

Join-Diéterle, Catherine. "La Monarchie, source d'inspiration de l'Opéra a l'époque romantique. *Revue d'histoire du théâtre* 4 (1983): 430–41.

"*Robert le Diable:* le premier opéra romantique." *Romantisme* 1980, pp. 147–66.

Bibliography

Jullien, Adolphe. "*Robert le Diable*. Le Mystère. L'Opéra-comique avant l'Opéra." *Revue et gazette musicale de Paris »*48, 49, 50, 1879.

Kinser, Samuel. "Chronotypes and Catastrophes: the Cultural History of Mikhail Bakhtin." *Journal of Modern History*, June 1984, pp. 301–310.

Klapish-Zuper et Ph. Braunstein. "Les Rituels Publics." *Annales. Economies, sociétés, civilisations*, 1983, pp. 110–24.

Lang, Paul Henry. "French Opera and the Spirit of the Revolution." In *Studies in 18th Century Culture* Vol. II *Irrationalism in the 18th Century*, ed. by Harold E. Pagliaro. Cleveland: Case Western Reserve Press, 1972.

Lechavalier, Jules. "Questions politiques de l'intéret de l'art et des artistes." *Revue de progrès sociale*, 1834.

Legouvé, E. "Scribe." *Le Menestrel* 1874, pp. 108–9.

Lespinard, Bernadette. "Les Masses chantantes de la Deuxième Republique." *Revue internationale de musique française*, no. 3 (1980).

Longyear, Rey M. "La Muette de Portici." *Music Review* 19 (1958).

"Political and Social Criticism in French Opera 1827–1920." In Robert Weaver, ed., *Essays on the Music of J. S. Bach and Other Divers Subjects: A Tribute to Gerhard Herz*. Louisville, Ky.: University of Louisville Press, 1981.

Maehder, Jürgen. "*Robert le Diable*. Etude sur la genèse du grand opéra français." Program, *Robert le Diable*. Théâtre National de l'Opéra de Paris, juin–juillet 1985, 22–7.

Marschall, Gottfried R. "L'Opéra et son public de 1848 à 1852." *Revue internationale de musique française*, no. 3 (1980).

Martens, Frederick. "Musical Mirrors of the Second Empire." *Musical Quarterly*, 1930.

Mitzman, Arthur. "Roads, Vulgarity, Rebellion, and Pure Art: the Inner Space in Flaubert and French Culture." *Journal of Modern History* Sept. 1979, pp. 504–24.

Montrose, Louis A. "Shaping Fantasies: Figurations of Gender and Power in Elizabethan Culture." *Representations*, Spring 1983.

Oliver, Richard A. "Romanticism and Opera." *Symposium*, Fall–Winter 1969.

Pendle, Karin. "Eugène Scribe and French Opera in the Nineteenth Century." *Musical Quarterly*, 57 (1971).

Pistone, Daniele. "Le Cadre politico-sociaux et la vie musicale." *Revue internationale de musique française*, no. 3 (1980).

"L'Opéra de Paris au siècle romantique." *Revue internationale de musique française*, jan. 1981

Prod'homme, J.-J. "La Musique et les musiciens en 1848." *Sonderdruck aus Sammelbände der Internationale Musikgesellschaft* 14 Heft 1, Oct. 1912.

Bibliography

Prodhomme, J.-G. "La première de *Robert le Diable* il y a cent ans." *Le Ménestrel*, Nov. 1931.

Reddy, William. "The Textile Trade and the Language of the Crowd at Rouen 1752–1871." *Past and Present* »74.

Riggins, Stephen H. Insitutional Change in Nineteenth Century French Music. Ph.D. dissertation, University of Toronto, 1980.

Robert, Frédéric. "*La Marseillaise* pendant la Deuxième République." *Revue internationale de musique française*, no. 3 (1980).

Roberts, John. Review of the article, "Meyerbeer" in *The New Grove Dictionary*. In *19th Century Music*, Fall 1981.

Rosen, Charles. "What Did the Romantics Mean? *New York Review of Books*, Nov. 1, 1972.

—— and Henri Zerner. "The Unhappy Medium." *New York Review of Books*, May 27, 1982.

Schorske, Carl E. "The Quest for the Grail: Wagner and Morris." In *The Critical Spirit: Essays in Honor of Herbert Marcuse*, ed. K. Wolff and B. Moore. Boston: Beacon Press, 1967.

Scudo, Paul. "De l'influence du mouvement romantique sur l'art musicale et du rôle qu'a voulu jouer M. H. Berlioz." *La Revue Indépendante* 1846.

Simon, W. "The Two Cultures in 19th Century France: Victor Cousin and Auguste Comte." *Journal of the History of Ideas*, 1965.

Spitzer, Alan B. "The Good Napoleon III." *French Historical Studies*, Spring 1962.

Starn, Randolph, and Partridge, Loren. "Representing War in the Renaissance: the Shield of Paolo Uccello." *Represenations*, Winter 1984, pp. 33–65.

Stupy, Hippolyte. "La Liberté au théâtre." *La Philosophie positive*, 1867.

Tiersot, Julien. "La Chanson populaire." In *Encyclopédie de la musique et dictionnaire du Conservatoire. Deuxième partie*. Tome V s.v.

Touraine, Alain. (Interview with) "Nous sommes tous des libéraux." *L'Express*, 22–28 juin 1984, pp. 79–90.

Turner, Victor. "Social Dramas and Stories About Them." *Critical Inquiry*, Vol. 7 »1 (1980).

Vauthier, Gabriel. "Le Jury de lecture et l'Opéra sous la Restauration." *La Revue Musicale*, 1910.

Vaudin, J.-F. "Les Arts démocratiques." *La Saison Musicale*, 1866.

Vernillot, France. "L'Orientation de l'opinion publique a travers la chanson de 1848 à 1852." *Revue internationale de musique française*, no. 3 (1980).

Weber, William. "Artisans in the Concert Life of Mid-Nineteenth-Century London and Paris." *Journal of Contemporary History*, 1978.

274

Bibliography

"La musique ancienne in the Waning of the Ancien Régime." *Journal of Modern History*, March 1984, pp. 55–88.

Wild, Nicole. "Un demi-siècle de décors a l'Opéra de Paris: salle le Peletier 1822–1873." In *Regards sur l'Opera* (see above).

Winter, Robert. "A Musicological Offering" (review of Joseph Kerman's *Contemplating Music: Challenges to Musicology*), *The New York Review of Books,* July 18, 1985, 23–7.

Zola, Emile. "The Realists in the Salon of 1866." In Eugen Weber, ed., *Paths to the Present: Aspects of European Thought from Romanticism to Existentialism*. New York: Harper and Row, 1960.

EXHIBITION CATALOGUES

Juillet 1830. Musée Carnavalet, 8 juillet–2 novembre 1980.

The Second Empire and Philadelphia. Philadelphia Museum of Art Bulletin. September 1978.

The Realist Tradition: French Painting and Drawing 1830–1900. Cleveland: Cleveland Museum of Art, 1980.

Robert le Diable. Théâtre National de l'Opéra de Paris, 2 juin–20 septembre 1985. Catalogue de l'Exposition par Martine Kahane.

Le Spectacle et la fête au temps de Balzac. Paris, Maison de Balzac, 1978–79.

UNPUBLISHED PAPERS

Baker, Keith. "Politics and Public Opinion in 18th Century France." Paper delivered at Indiana University, Nov. 19, 1984.

Carlson, Marvin. "The Semiotics of Opera Structures." Paper delivered at the conference "Théâtre, Opéra, Spectacle. Approaches semiologiques." Royaumont, France, Sept. 1984.

Earles, Irene. "Napoleon III's Paris Opera and Les Halles: New Architectural Technology." Paper read at the annual meeting of The Western Society for French History, Winnipeg, Manitoba, Oct. 1982. (It has since been published, in a revised version, in *Proceedings of the Western Society for French History*.)

Revel, Jacques. "The Forms of Expertise: Intellectuals and Popular Culture." Paper presented at the conference "Popular Culture in Europe and America," Cornell University, April 1982.

Therian, Nathan. "The Orphéons and the Failure of Amateurism." Paper read at the annual meeting of The American Historical Association, Washington, D.C., Dec. 1980.

Bibliography

ARCHIVAL SERIES CONSULTED

AJ^{13} – The Archives of the Opéra. See the complete inventory, *Archives du Théâtre Nationale de l'Opéra. $AJ^{13}1$ à 1466. Inventaire.* Par Brigitte Labot-Poussin, Conservateur. Paris: Archives Nationales: diffusé par la Documentation Française, 1977.

F^7 – Police archives. See especially »6692, reports on the theatrical disturbances in the provinces.

F^{18} and F^{21} – Censorship of Parisian theaters. On the organization of theatrical surveillance, see the introduction to the *Inventaire* of $F^{21}4523-4710$. For the reports of the Commission of Surveillance for the Opéra, see $F^{21}4633$, "Commission des théâtres royaux. Procès verbal."

BIBLIOTHÈQUE DE L'OPÉRA

Much valuable, uncatalogued information is contained in the various "Dossiers d'oeuvres" and "Dossiers d'artistes"; see especially those for *Robert le Diable, Les Huguenots,* and *Le Prophète,* as well as for *Meyerbeer.* The library also has an extensive holding of iconographic sources, from which the majority of illustrations for this study have been drawn.

SCORES

For musical examples of the operas discussed, see the facsimile edition, *Early Romantic Opera,* edited by Philip Gossett and Charles Rosen, and published by Garland Publishers, Inc., 1978.

INDEX

Index

Index

279

Index